Songs in Their Heads  W9-BSA-387

WITHDRAWN

12/07

Songs in Their Heads

Music and Its Meaning in Children's Lives

Patricia Shehan Campbell

New York   Oxford   •   Oxford University Press   1998

Oxford University Press

Oxford   New York
Athens   Auckland   Bangkok   Bogota   Bombay
Buenos Aires   Calcutta   Cape Town   Dar es Salaam   Delhi   Florence
Hong Kong   Istanbul   Karachi   Kuala Lumpur   Madras   Madrid   Melbourne
Mexico City   Nairobi   Paris   Singapore   Taipei   Tokyo   Toronto   Warsaw

and associated companies in
Berlin   Ibadan

Copyright © 1998 by Oxford University Press, Inc.

Published by Oxford University Press, Inc.
198 Madison Avenue, New York, New York 10016

Oxford is a registered trademark of Oxford University Press

Library of Congress Cataloging-in-Publication Data
Campbell, Patricia Shehan.
Songs in their heads : music and its meaning
in children's lives / Patricia Shehan Campbell.
p.   cm.
Includes bibliographical references (p.) and index.
ISBN-13 978-0-19-511101-9 (pbk.)
1. Music—Instruction and study.   2. School music—Instruction and study.
3. Musical ability in children.   I. Title.
MT1.C228 1998
372.87—dc21   97-14663
MN

          7 8 9

Printed in the United States of America
on acid-free paper

To Andrew, Kelly, Shannon, and Jimmy

Foreword

I found this a fascinating book. It is about the musical culture of children. It contributes to the understanding of music education, but perhaps more properly, of musical education in the sense that it goes well beyond the concerns of formal schooling and into issues of the way in which music is transmitted, how learning takes place within the fundamental concepts and values of culture. Most important, it is an "anthropology of children's music." Following in the footsteps of John Blacking—who arguably first made the case that children are not simply musical embryos waiting to become musical adults but have a musical culture of their own, with its own musical and social rules, and with functions such as integration of person and expression of ethnicity—Patricia Campbell paints a picture of the musical culture of American children.

Using the methods of musical ethnography developed by ethnomusicologists, the first two sections of *Songs in Their Heads* present the author as participant-observer: first as the careful describer of children's uses of music as they play, and then as the initiator of conversations in which children reveal their ideas about music. These children, American but from a great variety of ethnic, cultural, and economic backgrounds, turn out to be amazingly sophisticated and thoughtful in their understanding of music as sound and as culture. Presented in a lively and colorful way, they are the heroes of this book.

Alternating with the pure though engagingly written observations, Campbell comments and reflects on what she observes, referring frequently to a large body of literature from education, systematic musicology, anthropology, and particularly ethnomusicology, making comparisons with African, Asian, Australian, and other cultures, thus providing a world context for her American findings. Throughout, there is emphasis on the ways in which the diversity of cultures and subcultures from which the children come informs the ideas and musical activities in which they engage.

A work primarily in the discipline of music education, *Songs in Their Heads* provides important insights to ethnomusicologists, one of whose fundamental assumptions is that in order to understand the character of a musical culture, one must understand its subcultures—such as that of children—and must also comprehend the way it is transmitted. In the book's third section Campbell returns to the immediate concerns of the music educator and draws together the need to observe and interpret with the imperative for action, providing the building blocks of a philosophy designed to develop musical education. Music, long thought to be exclusively a domain of pure aesthetics and entertainment, is increasingly seen as a force that not only reflects and expresses culture but also one that drives society, and is treated here as a fundamental domain of culture that, in John Blacking's words, "may be profoundly necessary for human survival."

Bruno Nettl

Preface

The idea behind *Songs in Their Heads* was percolating in my mind for a long while before I began to give it shape here on paper, spurred and stirred by my interactions with colleagues, students, and of course, children. In my ongoing observations of and discussions with education majors soon to be teachers, I had become uneasily aware of the times when we follow the recipes for teaching without considering the ingredients of our classes and individual students, when we prescribe antidotes for children's education without full knowledge of their conditions and symptoms. In music methods classes, in seminars on field observations, and throughout the student teaching experience itself, we discovered together that we may be most effective as teachers when we consider children less as blank slates for us to fill than as thoughtful minds—musical minds, already taking shape through the process of enculturation. We also learned together to view the children we teach less as some homogenized conglomerate whole than as musically inventive and expressive individuals. I thank my students for the occasions during which we developed these insights.

I am much indebted to the children whose ideas and musical behaviors transpired over many months and even years and now fill these pages. They were eager and trusting of my best intentions and willing to share with me their thoughts and sentiments, much of it personal and some of it profound. Wide-eyed and innocent, some of them poured out sizable segments of their lives to me. I have concealed their identities but well recognize that there could be no text— nothing to talk about—without their music, words, and deeds. To the teachers and parents who unlocked the gateways for me to observe and talk with their children, particularly Patricia Casey, Diana Edgar, Gary Harding, the Kehoes and the Kerns, Mary Lansing, Jeanne Moore, Gary Roberts, Peter Runland, and Sue Williamson, I extend my appreciation.

While I am first and foremost a teacher, I willingly admit my attraction to the world of ethnomusicology for some twenty years. It is not only the music which these music-and-culture scholars have turned up that invigorates me but also the field methods which they have employed; that these ethnomusicological methods are now being applied to music education research will no doubt prove enlightening in the future. I am grateful for the research models, writings, and/or words of good counsel that Terry Miller, Bruno Nettl, Dan Neuman, Lorraine Sakata, and Chris Waterman have given to me. Their words through e-mail, over a meal, at a seminar, or while passing in the hallways inspired and guided me in taking aspects of "ethno" to "ed" settings. I must extend special thanks to Barbara Reeder Lundquist, who for thirty years has used the ethnomusicological method in so many myriad ways to "push the envelope" on music in the schools, meeting head-on the challenges of musically educating young people; and to Rita Klinger, my colleague and collaborator on multiple projects involving children and their music. While they are not to "blame" for this project, it is in broad and all-encompassing ways that I acknowledge their efforts and accomplishments and their ongoing influences on my own ways of thinking and doing.

I sought to write a book that might venture out from some of the standard studies so often cited in publications of this sort, in order to produce a nonthreatening and largely nontechnical volume that ponders key points on children, music, and education. I intentionally avoided some of the density of text and the jargon that comes with citation-laden literature and chose to abandon the incessant mentions of dissertation studies and journal articles typical of scholarly tomes so as to bring to light in a more straightforward manner the musical nature of children. The challenge has been to capture the essence of children on music and as they are musically engaged in an "up-front" and unhackneyed manner (Parts I and II), while also paying tribute to key writings that address music, education, and culture pertinent to children at different points of maturation—in their families, schools, and communities at large (Part III). My aim was to describe music and its meaning in children's lives, to argue its critical importance to them, and to suggest a model for further probing by those whose interest is children and their music.

Do these field-based observations and interviews constitute "research"? If "research" is critical inquiry aimed at the discovery and interpretation of new knowledge, then the designation is a fitting one. This new knowledge is derived partly from the words and actions of children reported here, but it also springs forth from the wealth of experiences in my own life as a teacher—experiences that go unreported here but that nonetheless color my view. Importantly, will these pages serve to describe what children musically think and do in the everyday events of their lives? For that is the intent, with my own efforts tipping the balance in favor of what I, feeling unbounded by designs and procedures, have been able to learn about children's musical selves in the recent and more distant past. In cutting across the fields from music and education to anthropology, ethnomusicology, and folklore, I hoped to tease out a number of perspectives on children's musical culture(s) so as to stimulate thoughtful teachers (and more than a few parents) in their efforts to enrich children's lives through music, and to learn something more of ethnographic techniques that apply to my research in the fields of children. While the book may not have turned the corner to the light entertainment of bedtime reading, I do hope that the voices of children will project from these pages their simply-put yet profound ideas concerning the realities of their musical lives.

Most of the spinning out of this project happened at St. John's College, Cambridge University. There, on the top floor of the new red-brick-and-glass library, I spent many misty mornings overlooking the Cam River, peacefully transcribing, reading, and thinking. For the comfort and quiet of these accommodations, I am thankful to the members of St. John's College and to Andrew MacIntosh, president. As ever, I am grateful to Charlie for giving up more than a few hours of our cycling and hiking time while I hung with this project. He gave the good weight and great energy that kept the project alive, well, and evolving.

Contents

Songs in Their Heads

One of the people, an older woman, came forward.

"Welcome," she said. "Haere mai." She took the young woman's arm and led her forward to meet the others. "I see you found your way here, then. We've been expecting you. Did you get any help on the way?"

"Yes," said the young woman. "Yes, I did. They all gave me their music."

"Oh, how nice!" said the older woman. "And what did you do with it?"

"I don't know," said the young woman. "It went into me. It filled my head. It changed me."

"No," said the older woman. "It didn't change you. What did you do as you came to us?"

"I sang a song."

"Was it the music you had heard?"

"Yes. No."

"It was your song," said the older woman. "The song only you can sing. That's what music has done for you. It has helped you find yourself."

—from John Drummond, *Music for Life*

Introduction:
Musical Children

Every morning, when I wake up, I have songs in my head.
Nathan, age 7

I hadn't expected Nathan's comment, and it stopped me cold. It was freely volunteered as I walked through the gate to the schoolyard at Vista Elementary School, and I found myself in conversation with him. What songs? Where had they come from? How did they sound, and what were the words? What did they mean to him? Was music so integrated within the life of this child that he could be asleep with, and awakening to, these songs? I was from that moment on intrigued with the notion of children like Nathan in every schoolyard with *songs in their heads,* in possession of music and ideas about music that I had naively assumed could only happen through formal training—in school, in private lessons, under the direction of experts. Were these the songs of the musically gifted? Or do all children carry within them musical gifts—songs, musical "urges," and thoughts about music—at the edge of their consciousness?

I began to wonder whether music may be more central to children's lives that it may seem, at least from the perspective of adults—"outsiders" to their culture. Perhaps the issue was not so narrowly the content of songs they knew (although that could be of interest) but whether music—live or mediated—was of much importance and use to them. Despite my many years of teaching music to children, I had precious little information on music's place in their lives. It had been a long while since I had my own inside track on childhood, and the nature of children's thoughts and values; my own childhood was now a blur in the distant past. If I

3

was to expect to communicate with them, to reach them where they musically are, then I needed to listen to and watch them in an open and receptive, yet focused and uncluttered way.

Coincidentally, I stood at the periphery of that same Vista Elementary School's yard a year later, fulfilling my time as a teacher assigned to playground duty, and found myself listening to the children. As they ran past me, calling and shouting to one another, I heard distinctive pitches, then phrases and full melodies. I saw patterns in their movements, alone and together, that were both rhythmic and regular. Were these the natural musical behaviors of children? Or some combination of their musical enculturation (music in the home and mass-mediated music) and schooling? What melodies and rhythms were prominent? Just how were children using music in their play? It occurred to me then that while I poured experiences into them in their weekly music classes, I had seldom observed children in their own undirected play for evidence of their music—natural or acquired, songs or song segments, even rhythms without pitches—but their music, nonetheless.

A theme was emerging, and with this project I took aim—at children for who they musically are, and at teachers and parents responsible for who their children musically can become. Through a combination of what I'd hoped would be nonreactive, unobtrusive observations and interviews with children in rather free-flowing conversations, I decided that I would direct my efforts toward knowing children, their music, and the meaning of their musical behaviors, thoughts, and interests. It was a rational decision to cut to the quick, to consult with children as the primary sources of what I needed to know. I would go from and return to my own perspective as teacher and parent, and figure ways of fitting what insights children might offer on their musical lives into thoughts about their education and schooling. The mission set and the course laid out, the mysteries of musical children began to unravel themselves to me.

The Serious Business of Musical Play

Clearly, music *happens* to children. Some of it may be hidden, untapped, and yet spinning within them. Yet much of it is "visible" and surely audible. It shows itself in the songs they sing and in the rhythms and pitched inflections of their play—on swings and slides; in the toy cars, wagons, and bicycles they ride; through the stories they enact with stuffed bears, dolls, and the imaginary drivers of their tiny race cars; and in the jumprope chants, hand-clapping rhymes, ball games and stick games, and ring and line games they play. Children think aloud through music. They socialize, vent emotions, and entertain themselves through music. Their bodies stretch, bend, step, hop, and skip in rhythmic ways, while their melodic voices rise and fall, turn fast and then slow, loud and then soft. Their music can be "seen" and heard in their playful behaviors, some of it a realization of the songs in their heads. It is almost as if children exude music.

John Blacking (1973) posited that music is not an optional relish for life but a phenomenon that lies at the foundation of society. He maintained that music-making is "an inherited biological predisposition which is unique to the human species" (p. 7), a trait that emerges early and often in the lives of children and adults alike. Yet if the music children think and do is one of the key features of their childhoods, it frequently goes unrecognized by adults, overlooked by the very people who most want the fuller development of children as thinkers, "feelers," and doers—now and in their maturity. Children's engagement in music frequently is paid minimal attention by teachers and parents, even when it may be the rich repository of children's intimate thoughts and sentiments. They have opinions about music, perspectives about where and when they listen and "do" music, and for what reasons. They have decided what music is, what it is not, and how much of it to allow into their lives. Music may be the treasure children prize for their own personal pleasure, and a tool for their use in understanding the world in which they live. Music may be their own expansive and expressive thinking at work, a means through which to develop thoughtful reflections of their experiences. But we have seldom taken time to tap either the musical thoughts or the natural musical behaviors of children or to seek systematically the function of music in their daily lives.

If music is a childhood constant, then it must be meaningful to them. This book is about music and its meaning in children's lives. It explores their musical interests and needs, based on their expressed thoughts and actual "musicking" behaviors.[1] It is a blending of songs they sing, rhythms they make, and roles music plays for them. It is a search for how music is personally and socially meaningful to them, and what values they place on particular musical styles, songs, and functions. Its "stories" are intended to present children as individuals, each with a unique set of personal experiences, who reflect on their relationship to music and their musical choices, and who also behave musically—in musical collectives of children—while at play. This volume provides glances into the musical lives of children—children of various ages and stages, classes and cultures—and it may also give a more complete picture of children and music in our society. Importantly, it upholds the position articulated by Christopher Small (1977) that "music is too important to be left (only) to the musicians," as music is already in the possession of children prior to schooling or specialized training.

Charles Seeger long advocated the use of folk music in the classroom—"music that people have in them already" (in Dunaway, 1980, p. 168), for this music summarizes the beliefs and values of individuals, their communities and cultures.[2] The music children have within them, as well as their thoughts about music, are starting points for understanding their values, their knowledge, and their needs. Their voices, as much as the voices of experts, should help to determine something of an educational plan for them, for this is how a musical education can be in touch with their lives and experiences. Through our astute observations of music

that happens to children, we are better situated for considering instructional interventions and enrichments for them.

A Cross-Disciplinary Interest

The images of musical children presented within these pages builds upon the work
of ethnomusicologists, folklorists, sociologists, and educators that have come before. Some have centered their study on an analysis of the musical content of
children's songs, while several key studies have sought out the social and cultural
significance of music in children's lives, and the manner in which they acquire,
create, preserve, and transmit music. In his classic study of children's play songs,
Constantin Brailoiu (1954) examined their rhythms for the parallel components in
Europe and parts of Africa and Asia. He noted quarter- and eighth-note durations
that, while extremely simple in principle, were combined by resourceful children
in almost unlimited variation. John Blacking's detailed analysis of children's songs
among the Venda of South Africa (1967) is a much-acclaimed examination on the
subject of musical children, with its review of musical (and social and cultural)
patterns and their relationships to the music of adults. Nearly a generation later,
Bruno Nettl (1983) issued a call for the scholarly study of children's music as a
means of understanding the central repertory and style of a society (p. 332). He
noted the significance of children's songs as a musical subset for gaining a wider
view of a particular culture as well as understanding something of certain universal properties in children's music—including short forms, restricted scales, and
repetitive rhythms (1990). As ethnomusicologists consider the premise that a society may be musically divided according to age and maturation, repertoires and
musical behaviors of children open for examination.

Indeed, the occasional convergence of ethnomusicological and educational interests have enlightened and have begun to shape a more comprehensive understanding of children, music, and society at large. Educators have just begun to
apply aspects of the ethnomusicological (and ethnographic) method to children's
songs and musical play, in an attempt to discern the complexity of both children's
performance practice and the contemporary musical .environment in which they
are enculturated. Pragmatically, implications for educational practice often follow
collection and analysis, with suggestions for the development of curriculum that
honors children's demonstrated musicking. Studies of musical play have been directed toward children in American urban schools and playgrounds (Campbell,
1991a; Harwood, 1987; Merrill-Mirsky, 1988; Riddell, 1990), British-Canadian
children (Osborn, 1988), Jamaican children (Hopkin, 1984), Portuguese children
(Prim, 1995–96), Ghanian children (Addo, 1996), Australian inner-city school-
children (Marsh, 1994, 1995), and children in an aboriginal Australian Pitjantjara
settlement (Kartomi, 1991).

One classic descriptive study of children's musical explorations was the Pillsbury Project (1978). Initiated by Gladys E. Moorhead, an educator, and composer Donald Pond in 1937, young children at the Pillsbury Foundation School in Santa Barbara, California, were introduced to an environment enriched by an array of percussion instruments (including Indonesian *saron* [xylophones], Chinese and Japanese theater drums, and various gongs and bells) and tracked for their interest and interactions with them. The children learned as they engaged in creative play, sometimes with their teacher but often through their free explorations. Their musical ideas were recorded, transcribed, analyzed, and reported. The children's expressive output varied widely and was sometimes particularly complex. In a review of the school some thirty years after its closure, Donald Pond retrospectively remarked that children appeared to have a predeliction for building sound-shapes, for improvising alone and together, and for using polyphonic rather than harmonic structures in their expressions (1981).

The efforts of folklorists to study the traditional songs and singing games of children has been increasingly apparent since the late nineteenth century. Lady Alice Gomme's work on traditional children's games (published in multiple volumes from 1894 through 1898) preserves rhymes and rituals in England, Scotland, and Ireland that were already historical relics, "survivals of primitive custom" (p. vii). Her American contemporary, William Wells Newell, contributed his *Games and Songs of American Children* in 1883, with an expanded edition published in 1903. Both Gomme and Newell are credited with providing the foundation and impetus for the extensive interest in the literary content of children's lore through the next century. Roger D. Abrahams (1969), Simon Bronner (1988), and Brian Sutton-Smith (1976) have examined the games, rhymes, songs, chants, and other playful interactions of children; their literature is now so strong that they are sometimes distinguished as specialists in "childlore." Peter and Iona Opie (1985) richly and in intricate detail accounted for the singing games of children, tracing some to medieval carols and courtship dances and to variants in the far corners of the English-speaking world. These accounts of childlore and "childsong" have been important in initiating one strand of the present search.[3]

The Lomaxes—John Avery Sr., his son, Alan, and his daughter, Bess Lomax Hawes—worked "in the seams" between the fields of folklore and ethnomusicology to document folk song in various regions and contexts throughout the United States. From cowboy songs (1910) to ballads (1934, with its twenty-second printing in 1968), these songs were sung by adults to children and, as well, by children to children. Ruth Crawford Seeger's seminal book *American Folk Songs for Children* (1948) was a result of her transcriptions of songs from the Lomax recordings that she deemed appropriate for use with young children. In collaboration with Georgia Sea Island singer Bessie Jones, Hawes prepared a volume that would document the musical lore of African American children living on the islands off the southeastern American coast (1972). While some choose to study the literary content of children's songs, the Lomax-Seeger-Hawes efforts were directed toward understanding the musical reflections of children as an important segment of American society.

In 1994, my colleagues and I took a slightly different tack on a collection of children's songs with the publication of *Roots and Branches*. Rather than recording children at play, we tapped the memories of sixteen adults by inviting them to remember songs from their childhoods; these were recorded, transcribed, and described by singers from as many cultures (Campbell, McCullough-Brabson, and Tucker). For us, their contextual descriptions were as important as the tunes themselves. It was startling to observe how their remembered games and animated gestures seemed to magically shed years from their lives as they became—while they sang—like the children they once had been.

The issue for many folklorists and educators has been to determine the musical and textual properties of children's songs, and certainly one component of this text is to build upon and extend this knowledge. Yet these pages are more centrally devoted to the critical need for a fuller knowledge of children's sense-making of their musical worlds, and of their personal worlds through music. At the brink of the millenium, the questions flow. What do children musically do, on their own and unassisted by adults? Are they engaged in musical play in ways typical of a generation or two ago? Do they "make up" their own music in active ways, or do they seek out the mediated music of tapes and videos to stimulate or lull them? How do children acquire music, and what parts of this repertoire and activity do they value enough to retain? Is music meaningful to them? From the very young to the prepubescent, and regardless of the socioeconomic levels and lifestyles of their families, children's musical impulses may be more similar than different, with more to unite than divide them. But this is mere musing at the moment, and the impetus for seeking, gathering, and telling the tales of the children who are willing to share them.

The work of Charles Keil and his colleagues Susan D. Crafts and Daniel Cavicchi (Crafts, Cavicchi, and Keil, 1993) in their Music in Daily Life Project was an important springboard to this volume. Their intent in the presentation of forty interviews, including six children, was to reflect upon the idiosyncratic musical worlds in which people live. They applied the art of semistructured and unstructured interviews as means of understanding "the unique configuration of ways to be 'into' those musics that emerges from each interview" (p. 211). They sought to understand how people use and enjoy music, and how music is persuasive and powerful to them. From a sociological perspective and a bona fide interest in the human need for and use of music, they presented a picture of music in the daily life of (mostly) adults. Their project continues, even as this one followed one of its tangents.

Another launch to this volume was the set of ethnographic tales told by members of an ethnographic seminar conducted by Bruno Nettl in *Community of Music*

(Livingston et. al., 1993). They presented in rich contextual description the lives of musicians working in Champaign-Urbana, Illinois. Using record stores, jazz clubs, country-western bars, practice rooms, and sidewalk cafes as their settings, they probed musicians and their audiences to determine what repertoire and practices were alive and well in that midwestern community. Through a variety of ethnographic techniques, they gained insights into the roles that music played for people in these contexts. As I read these tales, I found myself wondering why groups of children have not been much studied in similar ways for their own musical "works," practices, and thoughts. In their array of neighborhood gatherings and school assemblages, they, too, constitute a community worthy of careful examination for the music they make.

The Contextual Study of Children and Their Music

An understanding of children's musical worlds to which this work orients itself requires knowledge of music, children, and research method. While there is a body of research on children's perception and cognition of music and their musical skills, knowledge, and attitudes, much of it is antiseptic, dry, and disconnected from children-as-real-people. It is often devoid of context and without the flavor of children in their "real-life" dimensions of talking about and "doing" music. Further, this literature is associated with stages of child development that are inevitable, rather than allowing consideration of the unpredictable waywardness of the everyday child. In these conversations and cases of musical play, aspects of the ethnographic method are alive and well, particularly in the contextual descriptions of children and their music, the application of strategies in nonparticipant observation, and interviews that bordered on those utilized in phenomenological research. The lived experiences of individual children were sought, such that I was able to go to children with questions about musical uses and meanings but could also abandon these issues at will when their streams of consciousness led us elsewhere (Stewart and Mickunas, 1990). In the spirit of (and through techniques espoused by) Howard Becker (1986), Clifford Geertz (1973, 1983), and John van Maanen (1990), the aim of this project was to give voice to the children on their musicking and musical thinking. I suspected that individual children and groups of children would reveal to me much about themselves but that they would also provoke thinking about the nature of musical children as a whole.

I sought "slices of life" through techniques that would allow me to identify and discuss important musical values and meanings in the world of children. From semistructured and open-ended, "free-flow" interviews and mostly nonparticipant observations, I produced fieldnotes, audio- and videotaped records and their transcriptions, and musical notations.[4] These data form the substance of the cases and conversations that follow, the results of sixteen months (more or less) spent listening to the children. Yet some of my comments and reflections spin also from my many years as a teacher of music to children, from thousands of hours I have gladly spent listening and watching them, talking to them, making music with them. Other reflections are linked to some of the literature that exists at the interface of music, education, anthropology, ethnomusicology, and folklore and are a result of my attempts to corroborate my own experiences with those of others who have put their research and ideas into print. The text that unfolded within and at the periphery of the collected data offers an amalgam of impressions, a bit of theory, my own brand of teacher's intuition and instinct, personal convictions based on my experiences with children, and conclusions based on examination of these parts; it is a cross between the product of ethnographic research and straightforward reporting that emanates from observations of children in the "field" of classrooms, and at large in the world beyond. I was "condemned," as Clifford Geertz called it (1973: p. 13), to a dialogue between the foreign culture (children) and my own adult culture. Any broad profile or summary extrapolated by the reader from these pages is undoubtedly bound to be more than the sum of data gathered for this project, and I take full responsibility for shifting out of a more scholarly mode (when I do) in an attempt to provide a realistic, if even a homespun, sense of musical children. In these pages instead is a weaving of the children described, the literature cited, and the equally influential realities of well over twenty years of my experiences as a teacher of music to children.

I would be remiss were I not to note three books of recent vintage which, while not relevant to the subject of children and music, were nonetheless vivid models of contextual description of music in culture, and of musical communities. Henry Kingsbury's *Music, Talent, and Performance: A Conservatory Cultural System* (1988) is his dissertation of detailed observations of a major East Coast conservatory, in which he profiled students and their teachers in lessons, in ensemble settings, and at practice. Ruth Finnegan wrote *The Hidden Musicians: Music Making in an English Town* (1989), providing glances at the various ways in which people in the town of Milton Keynes, England, were engaged as musicians—in choirs, rock groups, symphonies, jazz bands, chamber music ensembles, and school groups, among others. Bruno Nettl's *Heartland Excursions: Ethnomusicological Reflections on Schools of Music* (1995) is a view of the society of musicians encompassed within a school of music at one of the major state universities in the midwestern American "heartland." These works were in mind as I pursued my conversations and gathered my fieldnotes, and they gave further direction to my pursuit of music as it is contextualized in children's lives. Their authors freshly define and extend the meaning of culture and led me to the realization of children as one large age-culture, but also as separate school and playgroup cultures. Along with Charles Keil's somewhat phenomenological approach to individuals as "idiocultures" (1994) and the premise advanced by Bruno Nettl and his seminarians (Livingston et al. 1993), that there are musical ethnographies to be fashioned from a host of contexts, these writings gave weight and direction to the current project.

In Pursuit of a Trilogy

The following trilogy presented here argues for recognizing the quality of children's natural musical selves in their somewhat unadulterated (although not unabridged) forms, as a means of developing a more meaningful musical (and general) education for them.

"In Music: Children at Musical Play" comprises brief ethnographic descriptions of music children make while engaged in play or in social interaction with one another. Their vocalizations and rhythmic movements and the manner in which they infuse songs and musical fragments into their play are documented. Musical notations fill out and amplify these cases. The settings I have selected for description include those in school (the schoolyard, a preschool play yard, a school cafeteria, and the music room itself), and several locales beyond school (a school bus and a well-stocked, premier, and popular toy store). I have sought out children's interactions with musical or, minimally, "sound," objects—and have listened and watched carefully for the musical nuances of their vocalizations, gestures, and full-body movements. From mostly nonparticipant, "fly-on-the-wall" observations, I attempted to write narrative tales of children who use music unknowingly or intentionally, but mostly beyond the direct influence of teachers or other adults.[5] As in the case of the conversations, my commentaries are intended to highlight particular expressions and actions that demonstrate the musical nature of children who play and think aloud in musical ways and to consider how these observations compare to what we profess to already know about their musical behaviors.

"On Music: Conversations with Children" divulges the substance of my dialogues with children from ages four through twelve and offers their views of music and its meaning to them, in their own words. It probes the music they know, listen to, sing, and play regularly, and also that which they discard. Again, notated examples of some of their own musical expressions offer further description of their music and musical thinking. Sometimes explicitly and in concrete times, and other times in inventive and imaginative fashion, the musical thoughts and preferences of children are conveyed in dialogue form, much as they had occurred in the classrooms, cafeterias, hallways, schoolyards (and clothes closets!) of our conversational meetings. Seldom did I adhere rigidly to pat questions or concerns during these meetings; rather, I attempted to allow the spontaneity and freshness of children's own flow of ideas and to preserve them here. While there were global issues I hoped to raise with the children, I had decided at the outset to press gently—and to release—if a child did not appear interested or comfortable.[6] My brief commentaries follow each dialogue, as I ponder aloud some of their striking thoughts that confirm, challenge, or add to the knowledge on children's musical selves.

Part III, "For Children: Prospects for Their Musical Education," summarizes some of the distinctive features of children's music, musical practices, and thoughts about music. Their own natural musical behaviors, and those developed through their interactions with family members, other children and adults within their neighborhood community, and the media, are discussed as initial, midway, and resultant products of who they musically are. These reflections lead to further musings as to how formal instruction can be made more relevant when emanating from our knowledge of children's musically enculturated skills and knowledge. While the first two sections allow the voices of the children themselves to be heard, the third part recommends some ways of applying the views of musical children to our teaching and child-rearing practices. It is the practical part of the text, yet it does not offer lessons per se. Rather, it calls further attention to children's needs and interests in music and muses about some of the pathways adults—teachers and parents—can take in nurturing them. The intent of the trilogy is woven through the three sections, with its crux embedded in this final section: the development of an awareness of children as incipient musicians all, awaiting the intervention and stimulation of strong instructional programs.

Listen to the children, I kept telling myself, so as to learn who they musically are. That was my goal as I launched this project, and my advice to those eager to know children's musical reckonings and reasonings. For teachers, and parents, too, who make music with children, hoping to develop their musicking abilities, the dialogues and descriptions that follow portray children's musical selves, from the songs in their heads to the music they make out loud. They direct pathways toward the realization of children's individual and collective musical potentials. Embedded within the words of children are the seeds for more appropriate instruction relevant to their needs, just as wrapped within their behaviors are the telling signs of what they can musically do. From these revelations of songs, rhythms, and musical reflections can come not only a deeper perspective of the musical nature of children but also the basis for their more effective musical education.

1
In Music:
Children at
Musical Play

Narrative Tales

In the nooks and crannies of home, school, and neighborhood, and even within the times and places reserved for musical study, there is a steady current of children's own music-in-the-making that underlies the various activities in which they engage. Sometimes they are unaware of this musicking, as it flows almost in a stream-of-consciousness way from their voices and bodies. Yet it is also made by children with the full intent of preserving a song, rhythm, or game buoyed by music. This music may even be their concentrated efforts to make up music that expresses their thoughts in musical ways.

Ethnomusicologists have examined music-in-the-making in cultures both foreign and familiar, abroad and at home. In the early life of the discipline, much of the research occurred elsewhere, often in exotic settings almost anywhere but at home. Scholars once flew off for India, Java, the Congo, the Pacific, and the Native American lands to seek out the meaning of music in culture and as culture. Then, with the growth of urban populations and the rise of the subdiscipline of urban anthropology (along with the dissipation of funding for research in isolated rural fields abroad), it became fashionable by the early 1970s to "do ethnomusicology" at home in the cities and suburbs of North America (Nettl, 1992). A flood of works began to pour forth on blues, gospel, jazz, polka, mariachi, country, and rock music in American contexts. Western European art music is the "last bastion" style now undergoing examination by ethnomusicologists (Nettl, 1995); techniques once reserved for the music of the Chopi or the minority peoples of China are now being applied to the study of the musical cultures of urban American cultures

(Nettl, 1978), small cities (Finnegan, 1989), conservatories (Kingsbury, 1988), and schools of music (Nettl, 1995).

Yet there is still another "bastion" to be challenged, and to be understood through field research. The musical culture (or cultures) of children have been largely overlooked and under-researched by ethnomusicologists and has rarely been studied ethnographically by educators. The former may view children as naive subjects for their research, as their typical thrust is to know the central music of a culture as it is typically perceived, conceived, and performed by adults. Research in education, on the other hand, has been largely devoted to the study of children in formal instructional settings, where experimental and behavioral procedures so characteristic of educational research in the past are applied to determine the effects of one or another treatment on knowledge and skill acquisition and on attitudes toward music and its instruction. This research is grounded in the supposition that children learn music at school, and while it does not deny children's musical development and learning outside of school, it has all too seldom sought out issues or raised questions beyond the classroom. The possibilities for the ethnographic, even ethnomusicological, examination of groups of children as their own individual musical cultures loom large. The challenge beckons, and it is tantalizing.

Thus, I began my probing of children's informal musicking. As I watched and listened to children gathering in various settings, I asked a basic research question: "What (musically) is going on here?" It seemed that Bronislaw Malinowski's advice (1922), recently professed by Nettl (1995) as an approach to ethnographic research, was well worth heeding: to note "the imponderabilia of everyday life." Thus, as I became aware of how children dressed, what children ate, how a room was decorated, and who interacted with them, I made notes. As children spoke, sang, gestured, danced, and became rhythmic in their vocalizations and their movement, I "wrote it down." I decided that maybe the little things *were* worth looking at and could inform me later as I sat back to ponder the "imponderables."

The six settings of children at musical play, all located within a large American metropolis, represent just over half of the eleven settings I had systematically observed over a period of about one year (in one case, over several years.) Some settings were abandoned early on because of my inability to gain further access to them for a sufficient number of repeated observations. One was set aside because of insights already gained through observations of other settings, and two more were abandoned because of the sparsity of musical "moments."[1] The communities from which these descriptions are drawn are both urban and suburban and represent various strata of lower- and middle-income classes (and a few that are undeniably affluent). The girls and boys in these settings range in age from preschool to prepubescence and hail from a variety of social and ethnic-cultural backgrounds. Just a few of the same children with whom I conversed in Part II appear among the children described in these group settings, but for the most part they are not the children featured in these observations. In fact, most children described in these cases make their only appearance here in this section, and not beyond it.

My approach to these cases of children at musical play shows signs of classic ethnography, yet none of them arise from the characteristic three-way union of observations with interviews and "material culture," that is, a review of written documents. My intention was not to produce "ethnographie à clef."[2] Rather, the descriptions emerge almost exclusively from my nonparticipant, nonreactive observations and may be seen as akin to the field experience observations that educators make in evaluating teaching and learning in school classrooms. I fully intended to act as an anthropological "fly on the wall" and to attempt to know something of their musical and social worlds from what I could see and hear— but without becoming a participant in their musical play. The teacher in me sometimes yearned to join in with the children, but, true to the traditional field experiences of education majors (and also due to my promise to teachers and caretakers to be unobtrusive), I remained on the periphery. In all but one case (where I only "field-noted" children's behaviors and remarks), I audio- and/or videotaped children for later recall and analysis. Not all of my taping served me well, however, so I abandoned several blurred and hazy (if not undecipherable) dialogues on tape and often resorted to my jottings and field notes to guide my writing and reflection. In all instances, I re-visited the same setting (and for the most part, the same group of children) four or more times. Children were generally aware of my presence and were sometimes curious enough to question me about my purpose. Some inquired as to what I was writing and why I was writing and examined my tape and video recorders; several even peered over my shoulder to read what I had noted in my book. Whatever I experienced, including children's verbal remarks to me, I made note of for my own contemplation later. I jotted down my observations and typically "wrote up" my field notes and impressions within a few days' time. I took notes from the tapes and listened to or viewed certain segments repeatedly to aid me in notating music or analyzing what had transpired.

I have chosen to write these observations as narrative tales, basing the text on careful analysis of field notes but attempting to use standard literary conventions to keep the interest of the reader. Of the types of ethnography which John van Maanen (1988) described, my narrative tales may come closest to the realist sort: "author-proclaimed descriptions" and "explanations for certain specific, bounded, observed cultural practices" (p. 45).[3] The field notes were the building blocks, however; these tales are not fictionalized essays but real children in real settings, making real music. Would that I could emulate John McPhee's approach to writing nonfiction (Howarth, 1976); I might then have shaped my observations in his style of "the literature of fact," turning my observations into the literary genre he has fashioned.[4] But lest we would become lost in a too-dense collage of poetic descriptions, I tapered the extent to which elaborate modifiers and word-heavy images were fit into the text. From lavish texts that might sideswipe important facets, I have in multiple revisions come to a more controlled (though perhaps not so very literary) set of descriptions.

Each narrative tale is infused with my occasional asides and remarks, my personal reflections of children's use of music, notes on the content of their songs, chants, and rhythmic movements, and the process by which they preserved and transmitted these "pieces." Norman K. Denzin's image of crafting a bricolage is a fitting one (1978), as in the end I hoped that the various notes, transcriptions, and comments might offer a portrait of children's musicking at a particular time and place. I attempted to restrict my comments to the children observed and rarely refer to what children do or believe at large within these tales; at this stage, I think it valuable to locate any of my statements of belief in particular events and persons observed.[5] Frequently, I remind myself that I am seeking understanding of children through these tales, as a dialectic of experience and interpretation. This is the stance of James Clifford (1988), and I have attempted to make it mine.

The Tales

The Horace Mann Schoolyard

I initially wondered whether the steady drizzle would prevent the children from taking their noontime recess in the schoolyard but learned later of the school policy that stipulated that indoor play was reserved only for times of fierce cold or stormy weather. I could hear them over a block away, an even, high-pitched package of continuous sound. By the time I pulled into a parking space in front of the Horace Mann School, I could see the children running, skipping rope, climbing the slide and the monkey bars, and huddling in colorful groups at the periphery of the playground. The soccer field was soggy and thus empty, so the blacktop of the schoolyard proper was crowded with bodies that bobbed and bounced.

As I approached the gate to the fenced yard, two small boys, probably in second or third grade, greeted me. "Hey! Are you a substitute or something?" "No, I'm just here because I'd like to learn about some of the things you and your friends do at recess." "Go for it," one of them said, thumbs pointing upward, and then they walked away. At this first visit, I found myself besieged by questions relevant to my role and purpose. I explained simply about my interest in the music they made as they played, and I saw the children chatter, curious about the tape and video recorders slung over my shoulder, and my rather fancy leather-bound notebook. "What are *we*? Your guinea pigs?!" one of the older girls asked. Her friend elbowed her. "Hey, if she wants to look, let her look. Maybe we'll be famous," she said as she eyed my tape recorder. (By the third visit of five observation sessions, the children had come to take me for granted, a part of the schoolyard "furniture." I realized that even when I moved from one location to another, I had passed into obscurity as they became centered again on their own activities.)

The Horace Mann School

Horace Mann School is located in a working-class neighborhood within the limits of a large metropolitan city. The 400 children enrolled there are largely Euro-

American. There are 48 children of Asian descent, mostly of Japanese and some of Chinese and Vietnamese backgrounds, and 35 African American children. Over three-quarters of the children's families are intact, with both father and mother present in the home. In the greatest number of cases, both parents work, often in professional and managerial positions. There are few bilingual families, and most children are at least third-generation Americans.

The school's neighborhood comprises postwar bungalows and ranch homes, many framed by neatly manicured lawns and flower-and-rock gardens. A few high-rent apartment complexes form the neighborhood's southern boundary, with views of the lake and mountains. There are several small shopping centers in the vicinity, each with a grocery, pharmacy, video store, and assorted specialty shops. Within walking distance of Horace Mann School are six churches and one synagogue, all of which attract a fair share of worshipers on weekends.

The children at Horace Mann dress casually but carefully. Boys wear collared shirts and full-length pants, usually black or blue cotton or jeans. Several of the younger girls wear dresses, but by third grade, most are in cotton or corduroy pants with odd or matching shirts or sweaters. Many of the younger girls display rather elaborate bows or clips in their hair. Tennis shoes are de rigueur footware for all children, and hightops are especially popular with the older boys. There is no official dress code in the school, yet an unofficial one is noticeably in play.

While the brown-brick school building itself was built in the late 1940s, the schoolyard itself appears far newer. The leather swing seats in the playground are bright red and blue, and there is a sprawling cedar and steel complex of platforms, large tubes for tunneling, climbing ladders, and a spiraling covered slide that occupies nearly one-quarter of the yard. There is various play paraphernalia in use at any given time: basketballs, volleyballs, baseballs and bats, tennis balls (but no rackets) in sight, a badminton set, plastic jump ropes, and a somewhat flimsy set of plastic horseshoes. One hopscotch and two four-square designs are painted on the blacktop, and two basketball hoops are attached to the outside wall of the gymnasium. It seemed that no stones were left unturned in an attempt to provide for the recreational needs of children.

At Play

In my grand sweep of children's play behaviors at the Horace Mann schoolyard, I heard and saw a tremendous variety of sounds, movements, styles, and interactions. Some children made use of school equipment, particularly jump ropes and basketballs, and the swings and play complex were always occupied. On days when the ground was dry enough, groups of older children (chiefly grades four, five, and six) occupied the field to play loosely organized games of soccer or baseball. Yet many children played without "props," in games of tag and make-believe—enactments of stories they knew from books, TV, and videotapes. Some strolled in groups of two and three, telling jokes, and talking excitedly about what they did the night before or planned for the evening to come. Freestyle movement was also common, from running, which, while prohibited, was nonetheless very much in evidence, to skipping and hopping that had no apparent link to games.

Children tended to play in same-age and same-gender groups, and often in same-class groups as well. Girls from one fourth grade, for example, formed two small groups and one duo but did not mix with the girls from the other fourth grade, who formed their own play groups. Likewise, third-grade girls jumped rope in two groups, defined by the class to which they belonged. Boys on the blacktop engaged in more aggressive play than girls and often made bodily contact with each other, sometimes pretending to fight and occasionally fighting "for real." Girls' play involved formal games with ordered sequences, turn-taking, and a greater use of words as compared to boys' penchants for shouting and noise-making. Both boys and girls exhibited continuous motor activity, but while boys typically used their whole bodies, the movement of girls often showed an isolation of one or two body parts, such as clapping and stamping.

The play activities during the noon hour were heavily laden with singsong taunts, calls and cries with definitive pitches, and a wide array of rhythms conveyed through clapping, patting, stepping, and tapping. The supposed childhood "ur-song" was occasionally—though not regularly—evoked. This entailed the singing of a descending minor third (sol-mi), to which a rising fourth was sometimes added. This pattern was frequently given to name-calling or the giving of directions or to signal the end of a game like hide-and-go-seek.

Ma - ya come here ____   You   are   a   tat - tle tale   All - ey All - ey in - free

Other pitch patterns featured intervals of the second, fifth, and octave. Their occasions varied, including the call of one seven-year-old girl to her friend,

Cher - yl, I   got some-thing for   you.

the chant of a rhyme learned in class by two second-grade girls,

I'd rath-er have fin-gers than toes, oh yeah!   I'd rath-er have eyes than a nose, you bet!

and the heartful singing of one six-year-old girl as she pumped on a swing.

A - live, I'm a - live!   I'm   free   can't you see?

These melodic chants appeared to be spontaneously generated but were likely to have been influenced by earlier musical experiences.

Two third-grade girls jumped out a hopscotch pattern on the painted blacktop, singing familiar songs as they jumped. I heard segments of a TV theme, a few commercial jingles, a verse of "Oats, Peas, Beans, and Barley" (an Anglo-American singing game), and many repetitions of "Sansa Krama" (a singing game from Ghana). Children were playing with the music they knew from their various experiences in and out of school, sometimes preserving intact and sometimes altering in small ways the text or musical content of these melodies.

At the monkey bars, two fifth-grade girls were perched at the top, talking. Below them, one girl was jumping, her arms raised to reach them. She was chanting:

Her friends soon joined in, adding to her rhythm:

Together, these two phrases formed a hocketed, holistic pattern.

On one occasion, four eight-year-old boys spent close to ten minutes in the rapping of a rhythmic rhyme. As one leader spoke several phrases, the other three boys produced a rhythmic ostinato with their voices as a background "track" to the words.

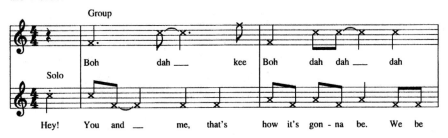

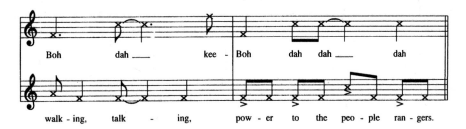

Each boy took his turn at rapping the phrases, and each led the chant before assuming the part of the rhythmic background. As they rapped and sounded their background ostinato, the boys thrust themselves into some of the characteristic moves of the MTV rappers they might have seen.

On the swings, two third-grade boys were laughing and shouting "go, go, go." They were pumping their legs with great energy, each contesting for the highest arc, the most quickly. Next to them, two third-grade girls were swinging at the same high speed, screaming "teach-er" repeatedly, a raised pitch on the first sylla-ble, and the second descending a minor third. (There were no teachers present, so the meaning of that call was unclear to me.) Four sixth-grade girls were standing near the swings, laughing and talking in an animated fashion, their hands and arms flying, their torsos twisting. One moved her feet sideways in a pattern that ended in a hop, and was soon followed in mirror image by the others: ♪♪♪♩ ♪♪♪♩ ‖.

Singing Games

Several jump-rope chants and songs, counting-out rhymes, hand-clapping songs, and singing games comprised the formal, more complete displays of musical play. Peter and Iona Opie, both renowned for their thorough examinations of children's lore since the mid-1950s, claimed that singing games (some apparent since antiq-uity) were in their "final flowering" prior to their abandonment by children to TV and other technological attractions; they wondered aloud whether the singing game tradition would still be alive in the next century (1985, p. 29). In the Horace Mann schoolyard, there was little evidence of its fading from prominence.

The principal participants in ring (circle) games and in hand-clapping and jumprope activities were first-, second-, and third-grade girls between the ages of six and nine. By the fourth grade, girls played more rarely, perhaps just often enough to remind them of the repertoire they had learned at a younger age. Jump-rope and hand-clapping activities, accompanied by rhythmic chants, seemed to peak in popularity in third grade, although there were jump-rope groups of girls from grades two through five in the Horace Mann schoolyard. Counting-out rhymes preceded games and operated as a means of determining teams or "sides." Examples of these genres are found below, in "Miss, Miss" (jump rope), "Blue Bells" (jump rope), "Eeny Meeny" (counting-out), "Hey, Little Walter" (ring game), "My Sailor" (hand-clapping), "Little Sally Walker" (ring game), and "Jump In" (ring game/impersonation).

Along with "Blue Bells," "Miss, Miss" is a jump-rope rhyme that requires no pitch-matching to perform. Both were chanted rhythmically, loudly, with accents and occasional rises and falls of the speaking voice. The third-grade children who presented this version of "Miss Miss" kept a very strong beat with their plastic-covered rope and articulated with precision the accents and the rests between the words of the chant.

Miss, uh, Miss, uh.   Pret-ty lit-tle miss, uh.   When she mis-ses,   she   mis-ses like this.

Two third-grade girls jumped rope, facing each other and holding hands, as their classmates chanted the words to "Blue Bells." The "yes, no, maybe so" could have been a remnant from another chant, but here it served more as a bridge between the first ("Blue Bells") and second ("Ice Cream Soda") sections. In the last two phrases, several of the chanting classmates added a "stamp-clap" motion as closure.

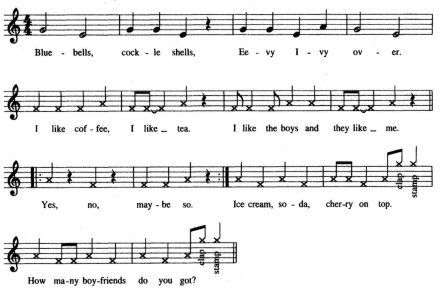

Blue - bells,   cock - le shells,   Ee - vy   I - vy   ov - er.

I   like   cof - fee,   I   like _ tea.   I   like the boys and   they like _ me.

Yes,   no,   may - be   so.   Ice cream, so - da,   cher-ry on   top.

How ma-ny boy-friends   do   you   got?

A group of nine girls and five boys from a fourth-grade class gathered in a tight circle one afternoon to choose sides for playing "Dungeon," a type of game that combines hide-and-seek and tag (tagged players are sent as prisoners to a "dungeon," hence the name). In choosing teams, players placed their right feet in the circle, and a designated counter tapped pulsively from one foot to the next while singing "Eeny Meeny." This clapping chant knows many variants, with this minor tetratonic melody a resemblance of one encountered by Carol Merrill-Mirsky in Los Angeles (1988, p. 139).

Ee - ny mee - ny min - ey moe.   Catch   a ghos - tie by   the toe.

If   he hol - lers let   him go.   Ee - ny mee - ny min - ey moe!

Two second-grade girls sang "My Sailor" while alternating between patting each other's vertically positioned hands on beats one and three and clapping their own hands on two and four. They saluted on "sea" and "see." In subsequent verses, they substituted "neck," "chest," "belly," "knee," and "shin" for "see," tapping and slapping these various body parts. "My Sailor" is a popular melody that has been clapped or bounced with a ball in many English-speaking countries for at least sixty years (Opie and Opie, 1985, p. 468).

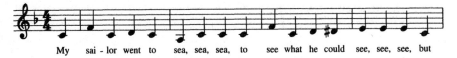

My sai - lor went to sea, sea, sea, to see what he could see, see, see, but

all that he could see, see, see, was the bot-tom of the deep blue sea, sea, sea.

A group of second-grade girls formed a ring to perform "Little Sally Walker." This historic verse and its game is classified by the Opies (1985, p. 167) as a "wedding ring," in which one player is invited to crouch down in the middle of the circle until she chooses a new center-person on the word "best." (In the original wedding games played by girls and boys, the boy chosen by the girl was to become her husband—or, at least, her kissing partner.) The version on the Horace Mann playground has been fairly well-known to African American girls for at least thirty years; another version collected in Los Angeles by Cecilia Riddell is strikingly similar (1990, pp. 301–4). Its many variants are found in the British Isles, and in the Caribbean as well (Opie and Opie, 1985, pp. 169–70).

Lit-tle Sal-ly Walk-er, sit-ting in a sau-cer. Rise, Sal-ly rise. Wipe your weep-ing eyes. Put your

hands on __ your hips and let your back bone-slip. You got - ta shake it to the east, you got - ta

shake it to the west, you got - ta shake it to the ver - y one that you love the best.

"Jump In" was performed by nine children (seven girls and two boys) from a first-grade class. They stood in a ring and moved freestyle (stepping from one foot to the other, or swaying, or nodding) as they sang the minor third interval and chanted. With each repetition, a new child became the focus of the chant, claiming what she or he wanted to "be" (singer, dancer, teacher, spaceman) at the appropriate time. The other children gave a response to this "call," then watched while the lead child impersonated or danced the roles she or he claimed during "until the day I die." This was followed in imitation by the group in the final phrase.[6]

In another ring, there were eight children from a second-grade class who were tiptoeing and spinning as they sang. They sang "Hey, Little Walter" in a "spooky" timbre, quietly and almost in a whisper. The song was a parody of "Wade in the Water," a well-known African American spiritual, its verse followed by a whispered chant that mixed triplets with pulses and their eighth-note subdivisions. Each phrase had a distinctive movement to it, with children tiptoeing into, then out of, then back into the circle (with individual spins in place at the close of each phrase), and the last phrase a "free-fall-out" wiggling, spinning, and wild gesturing of the hands. At the chanted rhythm, children joined hands in the circle and moved clockwise on tiptoes, looking dramatically this way and that for "little Walter."

Skillful Musicians

In these more formal means of children's musical play—these games and activities—there are several noteworthy structural features. The melodic ranges of children's own songs tend to fall within their speaking range, often from about G or A to just over an octave above (b). The few melodies that I had heard before in larger ranges were condensed by the young singers, modified by range and sometimes tonality, too. Pitch was invariably established by the leader of the game or activity, or by the loudest (or louder) child. Songs and chants of this nature are more frequently arranged in strophic form, with each verse sung to the same melody; several showed this trait ("My Sailor," "Jump In"). All these songs fell into simple duple 2/4 or 4/4 meter.

In every instance (including musical interactions observed but not described here), the songs and chants were accompanied by rhythmic movement. The rope kept the pulse in jump-rope songs, which was embellished by the players who created accents and occasionally jumped twice as fast as the pulse. In "My Sailor," the girls clapped hands steadily to match the song's pulse. Likewise, the counting-out rhyme ("Eeny Meeny") featured pulse-keeping by way of the counter's tapping of each child's foot while singing. In several of the activities, the hands and feet were often involved in clapping or stepping movements that matched the song's pulse or perhaps some of the melodic rhythms.

In just five hours, on five separate visits, I had experienced a rich musical spectrum at the Horace Mann schoolyard, from musical utterances, calls, cries, and shouts to the highly stylized singing games. Whether consciously created and practiced according to the "rules" of a song's tradition, or arising from the sheer need to express or communicate, more than an earful of children's musical moments could be had for the listening. Beyond knowing a shared repertoire, it was obvious that they were enjoying the playfulness of performing together; there were smiles, laughs, "arms around," and bouncelike, buoyant expressions.

In my fourth session, a fifth-grade girl came to me as I was sitting on one of the steps to the school, changing a battery in my tape recorder. She had been sent by her classmates to invite me to join them in learning one of their new hand-clapping patterns, a series of quick pats, snaps, claps, and slaps to an old rock-and-roll song called "Rockin' Robin." "We thought you'd been working pretty hard, running your tape recorder and writing fast notes and all, and that you might learn more about our music if you did it." In my subsequent struggle to learn the song and its movement, one matter became vividly clear: that schoolyard music, while seemingly whimsical, can require skillful listeners, singers, and players to do it *right*.

The Lakeshore Zebras

Because children's musical interests and abilities are already clearly evident by the time of their entrance to kindergarten (Moog, 1976; Scott-Kassner, 1992), I was curious as to what music—and how music—fits into their daily lives prior to schooling. I was drawn like a sleuth, a true bloodhound, to the pack of wee ones who wandered the rooms and playgrounds of the Lakeshore Child Development

Center. This was no cut-and-dried investigator's assignment which I had imposed upon myself, however, and to which I would need to drag myself reluctantly to complete. Through two years as a volunteer music teacher at the preschool, I had become enamored of the educational program, the teachers, and the youngsters. Yet beyond the realm of our music sessions, I had not had occasions for carefully noticing the music which children embrace and use by themselves, beyond their teachers' intervention. I came away from eight mornings of observations one June with new eyes and ears, as I learned from the Lakeshore Zebras—a group of three- and four-year-olds—just how incessant and integrated music was within their playful lives.

The Lakeshore Mission

Lakeshore Child Development Center (LCDC, or "the center") is located in a gentrified section of the city, in a neighborhood of homes that hang on bluffs overlooking the city and its waterfront. The community was recently rated as one of the most affluent in the country, with household incomes averaging $130,000 per year. All but three of the children enrolled at LCDC live within a two-mile radius of the preschool, well within the perimeter of this prosperous community. Their parents can well afford the monthly fee of $750 for full-time toddlers, $700 for the older, out-of-diapers crowd.

Nineteen years ago, the center was founded by the current director and two of her colleagues, all graduates of the early childhood education program at the nearby university. They recognized the need for an "educationally substantive" preschool and child-care facility in the area, so they established themselves in an office space at the end of a rather posh set of specialty shops. They grew from just one to four interconnected offices which they converted into three "pods" of children, and a combined office, kitchen, and storage area. There are grassy play yards on two sides of the building, each with climbing equipment, picnic tables, scooters, and tricycles. In the larger of the two yards, there are also two swings, a sandbox, a small vegetable garden, and several mature trees to which a wooden ladder had been nailed.

The pods were named at their inception for animals of the zoo, and membership in them is determined by age. The Pandas comprise eight children between twenty-four and thirty-six months, the Zebras are eight children who turned three by the first of September, and the Lions are the ten four- and five-year-old prekindergarten children who will enter public or private school the following year. The children are engaged in activities and eat lunch, play, and nap in their separate pod areas, but the playgrounds are the "commons" onto which children from all pods can converge.

The LCDC staff claims as their mission the provision of "high quality educational and recreational experiences in a safe and supportive environment." The parents' handbook explains that the center's program "allows for children to learn and grow at their own unique pace" by undertaking activities that are appropriate to children's interests and individual levels of development. These activities are concrete and community-based, with many opportunities to develop conceptual knowledge through hands-on experiences in school and on field trips. The wide and varied activities offered at LCDC span the gamut of the academic and pre-academic knowledge domains in the arts and the sciences, with special attention given to the development of "language skills, number concepts, large and fine muscle coordination, and cooperative play in music and art activities."

Paula, the director of the center, explained that she, her three certified early childhood education teachers, and an afternoon teacher's aide are intent on offering experiences that emanate from a developmental perspective. She asserted that they gear their program according to "typical textbook stages" of children's developmental knowledge and skills, but she quickly added that they "make a point to seek out each child's strengths and needs" and are sensitive to where he or she individually lands on a developmental continuum. Paula remarked that during weekly staff meetings, she and her teachers meet to design experiences relevant to the needs of individual children and to determine how they might coordinate activities within and across pods according to particular themes. In units such as "alone/together," family and community, animals of the rain forest, or "spring things," the teachers spin ideas for integrating music, painting, storytelling, movement, and creative dramatics to reinforce centerwide themes they have selected. Thus, even though the toddling Pandas might be channeled toward the discrimination of colors and shapes while the prekindergarten Lions focused on prereading and -writing skills, the broader themes allow for a sense of unity across the pods for the sake of sharing resources and experiences (visitors, videotapes, and field excursions) that enrich and stimulate children at their individual levels of learning. Weekly movement classes by a trained dance educator and my own weekly music sessions are also prepared with the center's developmental and thematic considerations in mind.

Musical Times with the Zebras

The eight Zebras are at home in their bright green room with one door opening to the center hall and another to the play yard. Katie, Sarah, Robbie, Lana, Eric, Tyler, Clara, and Molly are the Zebras, and by June they are all in their late threes and early fours. After nearly a year as Zebras, they will graduate to the Lions group at the end of the summer. There are large prancing zebras painted across two of the walls of their room, a sink in one corner, a long table with seven chairs just a few feet from the sink, two play corners (one with dress-up clothes and the other set up with Legos, erector-set parts, a train set, and some puppets), cupboards and shelves lining another wall, and a large space for movement and free play in the center of the room. I located myself in various places in the room and outdoors as they played in one spot or another, taking my tape and video recorders with me as I went. Their teacher, Tanya, carried on with her program of activities as if I was not there, all through the eight mornings I spent with them.

On my first visit, Eric wanted to know what instruments I had brought for them to play. He was soon joined by Tyler and Clara, who sat down expectantly in front of me awaiting a sing-and-play session to begin. Eric started to sing "Oranges and Lemons," one of our recent favorites, and soon Tyler, Clara, and Sarah chimed in. When I explained that I was here to watch and listen to them play, the children retreated for awhile (although they returned sporadically to tell me a story, ask for my help, tattle and blame one of their little friends for some mishap, or share their projects).

Most of the activity during the month of June was happening outside in the play yards. I turned my attention to the four girls at a picnic table who were painting lacy paper doilies. "I'm going to wear a dress of these doilies at a party," piped Katie. "I'll be dancing" (she vocalized on *loo* and *la* a melody in triple meter that resembled an eighteenth-century minuet) "and my lacy pink and yellow dress will flutter in the wind. You know, a beautiful princess." Her friends seemed to know exactly the image she was conjuring up for them, for they nodded in agreement as they blotted their doilies with tissues that spread and smeared the paints in various images.

"Let's go to the pet store," suggested Clara to Sarah. The two of them trotted in through the open door to the dress-up corner of the Zebras' room. As Clara pulled on a large flowery hat and Sarah wrapped herself in a multicolored scarf with fringes, they talked together.

Sarah: "OK. I'd like a dog for my little girl."

Clara: "You'll have to take Meeko instead." She handed Clara a stuffed raccoon.

Sarah: "Can you paint with all the colors of the wind?" She intoned the words much like the melody to the popular ballad from *Pocahontas*. "That's not Flit, you know."

Clara: "No! Meeko's my friend, on the riverbend. He's just at the end, Meeko, my friend." Sarah danced the raccoon in the air as she rhythmically chanted her spontaneous rhyme. Tanya later verified that it *was* spontaneous, possibly prompted by the focus she had recently given in their "circle time" to rhymes and rhyming words.

Robbie had dumped a large basket of colored blocks out on the floor. With a cowboy hat and oversized boots on, he clomped across the floor telling no one in particular that "I'm going to catch a mouse in here." He held the basket out, calling "here, mousie" in a sustained sol-mi pattern. He soon abandoned the mouse-catching for a wheel-rolling activity, to which he chanted

Wheel-y, dee-dle-dee Dee-dle doo-dle Wheel-y wee wee dee dee

In the garden one morning, Tanya was picking green beans, and Lana, Eric, Tyler, and Molly were with her. Tanya sang a triadic melody to "Where are you, bean?" that set off a series of the children's recitative-like comments. As Lana groped for a bean to pick, she repeatedly chanted:

I   want   a   bean.

Eric's voice rang out a full octave:

Where are you hid - ing, bean?

Tyler followed with another large melodic leap:

Where are you? Are you in there?

Molly and Lana formed a small chorus with Tyler, repeating this leaping tune. One melodic phrase led to the next, each one utilizing the triad of pitches that Tanya had initiated in her opening phrase.

An old blue and white painted wooden wagon proved quite popular with the children. Katie sat enjoying a ride in it one day as Molly pushed her over the bumpy ground, vocalizing up and down a minor third on *ah*. There were no words to her arhythmic tones, just a songful expression of sheer pleasure. Robbie ran up to them with a stick he was holding diagonally across his chest like a guitar, and as he pretended to strum, he sang:

Yah yah   yah yah   yah   yah   Yah yah   yah yah   yah   yah

Katie and Molly turned sharply away, and as they did so, they both took up Robbie's melody.

Late one sunny morning, Clara, Sarah, and Lana were playing in the sandbox. They had all taken off their shoes and were hovering over small plastic pots that they had filled with sand. At Sarah's request, Tanya sat a pail of water at the side of the sandbox, and the three girls were quietly scooping up water with their shovels and dribbling it into their pots of sand. The cool water and the grainy wet sand aroused their musical utterances. As Clara patted the sand with her shovel,

she chanted the word "crunch" in a syncopated pattern. She took a breath, and
then added words and pitches:

First you get a sho - vel, then you get a pa - il. Crun-chy, crun-chy cr-u-u-u-nch.

Sarah was digging her hands into her pot of sand and water, using Clara's rhythm
for her spontaneous song.

Feel - ie, feel - ie, san - dy. San - dy san - dy fee!

Robbie took the same rhythm as he hammered a stick into the sand with his
shovel. The scene was idyllic, the little girls looking like those from a pastel-
colored beach scene in an impressionistic painting. I hoped that the mood would
hold for awhile, but in the next instant Molly had jumped with both feet into the
pail. Clara, Sarah, and Lana all called for Tanya, their voices rising and then
falling in complaint. As Tanya diverted the children's attention by complimenting
them on their "neat and tasty-looking" sandpies, Molly stood firmly in place, happily expressing herself in song:

I love to stay in the wa - ter. The cold - er the bet - ter it

is. _____ it's hap - py here, hap - py wa - ter here.

Inside the Zebra pod one chilly day, Katie, Eric, and Tyler were building a
small city of Lego blocks. Eric had constructed a gas station, he claimed, and was
in the process of building a high chimney atop it. On *doo,* he alternated from do
to sol in a straightforward, steady-beat pattern. He had set the pitches for the
children's chant that followed. When Tyler attempted to add another block to Eric's chimney, four inches of it came tumbling down. Katie gasped, wagged her
finger in Tyler's face, and then chided him:

If you drop it, pick it up.

Katie's chant became like a mantra as Eric soon added his own voice and wagging
finger to it, the two of them singing to Tyler, who by then was rebuilding the
chimney. Nearly an hour later, while the children sat around the table eating their

lunches, Molly dropped a pickle out of her sandwich. Tyler sang the very same mantra melody that had been sung to him, adding a "tag" ending to it.

If   you   drop   it,   pick   it   up   with   your mouth!

In between mouthfuls of yogurt, cheese, ravioli, and cookies, a litany of silly "tags" were sounded by various children: "with your spoon," "with a stone," "with your nose," "with a shovel," "with a banana." They were singing and laughing, and quite unaware of their amazing ability to imitate Tyler's (Katie's) melody so accurately. I found myself in awe of these young children, of their skillful listening and capacity to reproduce music, of their spontaneous addition of partial phrases to a "root phrase," and of their retention of a melody for earlier play until now.

Long on Music

Musical spontaneity ran rampant among the eight Zebras at the Lakeshore Child Development Center where, unchecked and unhampered (and not redirected) by adults, children frequently interspersed music throughout their playful activities and social interactions. They vocalized their own invented rhymes, chants, and tunes, and their rhythms were as visible in their movement as they were audible. Their melodies consisted of seconds (as in the sandbox songs of Clara and Sarah), thirds and broken triads (as in the "bean" songs), and leaps of a fifth (as in Katie's signal tune of dropping and picking up). In straightforward pulses and subdivisions (notated as quarters and eighths), and occasionally through triplets and syncopations, their voices rose and fell with the words they used to communicate to their friends, to think aloud, and sometimes to express their feelings to no one in particular.

There were unusual musical moments throughout the children's meanderings, with the meters of Molly's water song among the most noteworthy. That she would move her melody midstream out of a lilting 6/8 feeling is indicative of a change in her manner of thought and expression, from a melodious reflection to a declamatory statement—perhaps not unlike the turn a soprano may take out of an aria to a recitative. But the metric shift of the melody to a definitive sense of $3+2+2$ is of further interest as a stunning example of the manner in which text presides over melody in children's musicking. Metric shifts in music may be perceived by musicians as an advanced concept to be developed late in a student's pedagogical sequence and as a phenomenon that can only be accomplished by sophisticated musicians who perform complex works by Igor Stravinsky, Olivier Messian, and Gyorgi Ligeti. Yet here was a preschool child who had demonstrated the concept with ease and nonchalance, and with considerable feeling. It is striking that later, once out of her childhood, Molly may encounter metric shifts in the music her studio teacher or ensemble conductor assigns her. She is then as likely as anyone else to struggle with it intellectually, never remembering that she had once expressed it so naturally. If, through training, the musical sensitivity of children like Molly could be captured and reinforced, their natural musicianship might then be retained and used as the basis of greater musical knowledge and skills.

I pondered Paula's assertion of "typical textbook stages" of children's development and could not help but wonder whether a certain few textbooks (and plenty of actual instruction) might require the sort of revision that could reflect the considerable perception and performance abilities which the LCDC Zebras had demonstrated. These youngsters were exuding music in more ways than I could have fathomed, and much of it seemed to be their own creative expressions— inspired and nurtured as they were by the musical experiences they have already known in their short lives. It seemed clear to me that they were "long on music," in that many of their daily doings were wrapped up into the musical expressions they could demonstrate. I knew that as a result of what I had observed, I would need to find ways of bringing children's musical utterances and complete songs into my future music sessions with them. I vowed that somehow, I would find ways to blend *their* music with *my* music.

The Rundale School Cafeteria

As teachers daily gravitate to the faculty lounge for their lunchtime salads and sandwiches, they deposit their classes of children at the gateway to the Rundale School Cafeteria. Even a first-timer like me had no difficulty locating the cafeteria, following her nose to the source of the scents of charcoaled cheeseburgers, fried potatoes, cucumber salad, and banana pudding; indeed, by late morning, the aromas permeate the halls. At the cafeteria's gateway, the scents seemed more institutional, made less pleasant by the spilled milk from a previous lunch that had gone undetected and had soured far off in one corner or another.

An initial peek over the turnstiles brought the cafeteria's bright yellow, blue, green, red, and orange tables into focus, each connected to matching benches that ran the table's length on the two sides. Against a closely cropped brown carpet, they appeared like the paints on an artist's neutral palette. There were basketball hoops hanging at two ends of the room, and a raised stage lined the far side and was framed by two doors, each crowned with a red-lit Exit sign. A microphone stand was placed center-stage, its wires plugged in and ready for use.

The children filed through the turnstile entrance, passing a table where a stocky woman sat with a cash box. Beyond her, three women in the kitchen were working in assembly-line fashion to fill Styrofoam and plastic containers with the daily specials; they were talking and laughing as they worked. The children paid their lunch fee: $1.35 for a lunch pack of hot and cold food, or twenty cents for white or chocolate milk. The line moved quickly as the children offered their prepaid lunch tickets or small change to the cash box woman. They picked up their purchases and headed for a table designated for their class. They seated themselves, most already wearing their sweaters and jackets, many of which were made of rain-repellant material and had hoods.

Rundale is a suburban school in a bedroom community for upwardly mobile professionals who commute to two larger cities north and south of it or who regularly fly out to their appointments from the nearby international airport. There are older homes at the hub of the old town center of Rundale, but spanking new subdivisions of homes and condominiums stand on land given up by farmers as recently as a decade ago. The school is like most of the suburb: contemporary, colorful, and still growing.

I spent four lunch hours in the Rundale School cafeteria (literally an hour each time), watching three shifts of children arrive, eat, and depart for their lunchtime recess in the playground. My location was a table nearest to the door that was reserved for slower eaters; when the bell signaled the start of the lunch group's outdoor recess, those few children who were still finishing their meal joined me at this table. I held no discussions with children but recorded on paper and occasionally on audiotape those musical behaviors I could manage to see and hear. Since I chose not to "rove" much, I undoubtedly caught only a small fraction of the musical sounds and interactions there may have been.

Music at the Meal

For each shift, there were two classes of each grade level who filled about twelve tables. They made their way, walking at various tempi, skipping, trotting, galloping, hopping, "clomping" loudly, or walking on tiptoe. They sat side by side, shoulder to shoulder, twelve children to each table. Many of the children wiggled throughout their meal, several in a regular rhythmic manner. Some of the little ones whose legs were too short to reach the floor swung them back and forth in the space beneath the table. They bobbed their heads rhythmically or manipulated lunch boxes, cardboard lunch packs, foil tins, or milk cartons across their table space in recurring patterns. There was no music piped into the cafeteria, but evidently some internalized music may have been driving them to emit sounds, movements, and gestures that were as regular as the clock's ticking (though not in the same tempo).

A glance down one table of first-grade children offered a snapshot of the polyrhythmic texture of their movement. One little girl was pulsively rotating her sandwich on its Saran wrap in half-circles in front of her. The next girl was tapping at top speed the base of two carrots on the table. Next to her, a boy was bouncing the bottom of his milk carton on the table in a syncopated pattern: ♪ ♩ ♪ ♩ 𝄾. Still another boy was waving his cookie, a wafer that he had bitten in the vague shape of a truck, drawing a slow figure-eight in front of

him and his friend. One girl was loudly sucking her lollipop in a rhythmic ♪ ♩ ♪ ♩ pattern, thrusting her head upward before each lick. Several
others at the table were nodding or shaking their heads, stretching their arms repeatedly, or twisting in their seats. Another boy was playing out a pantomime of
strumming on a guitar. Quite remarkably, a few children were producing regular
rhythmic gestures with their arms or head even as their feet swung independently
of these gestures, their various body parts creating polyrhythmic textures of sound
and movement.

Although most of the children's interactions contributed to the undiscernible
din of sounds (made louder yet "dinnier" by the barnlike acoustics of the space),
the gist of some nearby conversations was notable. Two third-grade girls compared
the sizes of their apples, while two boys commented on the *Toy Story* illustration
on the cover of one of their lunch boxes. Two fourth-grade girls were gesturing
wildly while they described to each other some of the swimming strokes they
knew. Several fifth-grade boys recalled play by play the events of a recently tele-
vised boxing match, punching and jabbing the air as they went. One boy was
enacting a particular strategy: "And then he did this. . . ."

In response to the demonstration, three of his friends began to push at each other,
bringing a monitor swiftly to the scene to separate them.

More rhythmic segments were evident to me than vocalizations, perhaps because of the "live" nature of the space (and my choice to stay situated in one
place throughout the periods of observation). Yet pitched segments did resound,
from minute melodic fragments to whole melodies. One older girl called to her
friend, "Yoo hoo," singing it loudly as a descending minor-third interval. A third-
or fourth-grade boy was singing repetitively on *da:*

Two small girls were piecing together a hand-clapping song, singing in between
their bites of food:

One second-grade girl alternated between sol and mi as she sang:

Three girls were singing bits and pieces of favorite songs: "Doo Wah Diddy Diddy," "Step Back, Sally," "Colors of the Wind" (from *Pocahontas*), "Can't You Feel the Love Tonight" (from *The Lion King*), and themes from *Mr. Rogers* ("It's Such a Good Feeling"), *Jeopardy, Friends,* and *Lamb Chops Play Along.*

The rhythms of two older boys were particularly notable for their complexity and interlocking patterns. Finished with their lunches, they were waiting for the sound of the bell to usher them out to the playground. One sat straddled sideways across the bench and used it as the "drum" for an ostinato pattern he tapped with two plastic forks:

Meanwhile, his friend was devising a longer pattern that he pounded with his fists and hands on the table. He played the accented beats with his fists and then opened to the palm of his hands.

Together, they played this rhythm for several minutes, while several children at their table bobbed their heads as an expression of interest and approval. A monitor was ambling her way toward them just as the bell signaled their recess; she stopped, perhaps to think about whether to proceed with an admonition or to let them go. While she was still considering her next move, the boys were already racing out the door.

Monitors of Sound

The volume of the children's voices increased as they settled into their meals, as they were energized by the starch, sugar, and protein they were consuming. By midway through the period, the children were very animated. Some were turning from one side to the other, gesturing with their hands in elaborate ways, shouting to their neighbors seated down the table or at other tables scattered through the room. Some of the gestures were playful, while others were clearly teasing and even hostile or rude. Since the teachers were at lunch in the faculty room, it was the monitors who were charged with keeping some sense of order in the Rundale School cafeteria. As one monitor remarked, "We are their surrogate teachers and parents for 20 percent of their day." She added, somewhat begrudgingly, "We ought to be paid like them," referring to the teachers.

There were three women who served as monitors during the lunch periods. All were in their later thirties or early forties. All were mothers, but none had children at Rundale. They wore slacks and sweaters, covered by light blue denim aprons. They greeted the children, helped a few of the younger ones open their milk cartons, guided them to filling one seat after the next at the tables, and circulated through the small maze of lunching children at their tables to "keep the peace." Two of the monitors also served time at playground duty, while the head monitor was there to supervise a small cadre of fifth- and sixth-grade children who helped with cleanup at the close of the lunch hour.

Occasionally, the head monitor stepped up to the on-stage microphone. She sternly reminded children of the extent of sound she was willing to accept. "May I have your attention." The talking quickly faded, and sounds of the ventilator, a dishwasher in the kitchen, and some distant cries from the school playground could be heard. She continued: "I hear too many loud sounds, even shrieks from cute little girls. I want you to lower your voices. I want indoor—not outdoor— voices. No shouting, no singing, no playing the tables like drums. If you can't keep these rules now, you'll sit and think about them during your recess." As the children were dismissed to the playground by the buzzing of the bell soon after- ward, I was struck by two overlapping thoughts: (1) the complementary activities of eating and making music—one social event quite naturally stimulates the other, and in many communities and contexts the combination is not only acceptable but encouraged, and (2) the extent to which these musical behaviors were seen to be disruptive by those in charge, and thus needful of restriction. The Rundale School children were criticized for their participatory, albeit scattered and somewhat inci- dental, musical behaviors in the cafeteria, while in many cultures people typically sing, play, and dance before, during, or following their meals.[7] I could not help but wonder whether children's behaviors could somehow be harnessed and viewed in a more favorable light, such that their musicking could be accepted as a positive feature in their daily lunch experience.

On another day, the head monitor again focused on children's singing and drumming in her advisory words from the stage. Several groups of children were called down for the music she perceived as chaotic and disruptive. "You guys are way too loud. It's not too hard to lower your voices. You're not to be talking from table to table, or singing." She pointed to a group of fifth-grade girls. "That group of girls over there: leave the singing for music class, or stay after and see me. And guys—James and BJ—you better keep that drumming down, or you owe me recess." The compartmentalization of music was reinforced here: It was seen as having its appropriate time (the music period) and place (the music room). Under- standably, too many different musics at once are chaotic in a group of seventy or eighty children, but I found it intriguing that no one had considered a way of bringing music into the realm of mealtime as a means of focusing attention, coa- lescing behaviors, and socializing children in an orderly fashion—particularly due to evidence of its widespread coupling by children with their lunchtime social- izing.

After the second announcement, one of the monitorial assistants wheeled around and winked at me, saying, "This must be a bad day. We don't usually have so much banging. The weather, that's what does it," she said, blaming the unseasonably warm temperature on activating children's energies. I was wishing that the music teacher were with me to hear the rich musical collage I heard, and I vowed to tell her about it. While she, too, like the other teachers, deserved not to sacrifice her lunch hour in order to lead recreational singing in the cafeteria, I was hoping that she could be made aware of and figure ways of maximizing the musical moments of her children at their leisure.

Music at Cleanup

Within the cafeteria cleanup crew at Rundale School, one child is designated the official cleaner of each table; this position is passed around from child to child on a weekly basis.Their task is to take a wet cloth and wipe the table clean of crumbs and spills. In addition, two fifth- and four sixth-grade children are "hired" by the school to help clean up after the last lunch period: They spend a fifteen-minute period sweeping, clearing the trash, collapsing tables and benches, and pushing them against the walls of the cafeteria in preparation for the afternoon's use of the space for physical education classes. In return for these chores, they receive free lunches.

Over the four days, these aides worked efficiently and in somewhat musical ways. Some of the kinesthetic table-wiping gestures were beautiful to behold, as children employed grace or power to sweep, whisk, and brush their wet cloths across the table. One girl appeared to be painting, dabbing here, rubbing there, and then giving broad strokes across the table. A third-grade boy made clucking sounds as he wiped another table, and he used *ch* and explosive *p* and *b* sounds in a rhythmic chant:

He sounded this same pattern over several days. Another boy was whipping the wet cloth across the table, singing sea chanteys: "Blow the Man Down, Bullies" one day and "What Can You Do with a Drunken Sailor" on another day. He kept a whipping rhythmic motion in what sounded like a 6/8 meter, and I wondered whether he had equated his task to the swabbing of a ship's deck.

The six children in the after-lunch cleanup crew worked separately and together to clean the area. One boy swooped down under the tables, gathering napkins and pieces of bread and cookies, then tossed them into a trash can. His movements were graceful and quick, dancelike, not unlike some of the moves of a skilled basketball player. A fifth-grade girl used a dustpan to gather the trash under the table and then stood, staring, almost in a daze as she struck the metal pan against the metal rim of the can in a repeated pattern: ‖♪ ♩ ♩ ♩ ♪‖. The manual floor sweepers were operated by two sixth-grade boys. As they pushed and pulled, I heard one of them humming a syncopated melody on *mm* and *nuh*. The other boy worked quietly, save one time when the two boys produced a hocketed chant to the rhythm of their sweepers:

Connections

As the Rundale cafeteria had filled with children, so had the air of that huge hangar of a place filled with their musical sounds. Children made their own music "to dine by," and they carried on conversations as they ate that were alive with rhythms and melodious songs. Snippets of sound were pitched variously and were often organized as short patterns, then repeated incessantly, and there was rhythmic energy enough from some to incite even the most sedate of children. The few invented melodies I could capture were restricted in range, some with pitches no more than a third apart. Their preferred media songs (from films and TV) were of a wider range of pitches than their own creations and were often chromatic. The children had gravitated to the stylistic nuances of these popular songs, and as I detected the sliding of some of their young voices in, out, and around the pitches, I knew that the sound was intentional and not a result of their inability to strike at the pitch centers.

It was the extent and variety of their rhythms that struck me. Whether energized by their intake of calories or by the movement of their cleanup chores, the continuous rain of their rhythms could not escape my attention. From the syncopated tapping of a milk carton to the interactive exchange of the two sweepers, the rhythms the children emitted were precise, crisp, and constant. Some were performed vocally with syllables, while others employed rhymed and unrhymed words. The rhythms flowed invariably in duple meter, although they were not restricted to "four-square," even rhythms. Straighforward quarter-note pulses gave way to eighth- and sixteen-note patterns, irregular accents, interlocking patterns, and even a two-part progressive verse that featured two boys alone and together. Regardless of the activity in which they engaged, these children had rhythmic accompaniments of their own to sound and move to.

These impressions were with me as I looked up from my notebook to see the same two "sweeper" boys now huffing and puffing as they joined two others in pushing the tables against the wall. They were complaining, cutting up, joking. Then the rhythm was gone, and there was no more chanting to be heard. The last few minutes of cleanup had dissolved in the crew's scurry to finish the task and return to class. I was left alone to wonder about matters that had never before struck me so fully: the natural connection of eating with socializing, music, and movement, and the coupling of singing with the rhythms of work. Several of music's functions appeared with greater clarity than I had ever noted before, right within the culture of these children in their school cafeteria.

Riders of the C-Bus

Children spend an inordinate amount of time "in transit," on the way to and from school. For those who are car-pooled, radios, tape players, and CD players bring music to their ears almost automatically, from the instant the car's engine is started to the moment of children's arrival to school. These carpool children are wrapped in a cloak of sound, often loud enough to penetrate their thoughts and to interfere with conversations they might otherwise have. Yet in another type of vehicle, social and musical interactions among children are rampant. In cities, suburbs, and small towns, many children are daily riders of the bright yellow-orange school-bus—symbol of the American schoolchild for much of the twentieth century. Because there is no stereo system on these school buses, no mechanism for piping favorite tunes to passengers, children resort to their own devices for passing time and entertaining themselves while traveling. As the landscape rolls from one scene to another outside their windows, so, too, does a collage of music and conversation transpire.

I took four trips on the C-bus, one of five buses labeled from A to E that traveled from Meadowbrook School to one of the neighborhoods where children lived. I found my seat before the children boarded to go home in the afternoons, once in the front, twice in the middle, and a third time in the back of the bus. Despite introductions of me to the children by the teacher-mentor, at first a few of the older children appeared mildly disgruntled that I would trespass into this exclusively children's territory. My tape recorder sat on the seat next to me and my notebook was poised in my lap, ready for jotting as I looked, listened, and occasionally conversed with the children.

We followed the same route each time, up the hill from the school to a residential street, down a county road on which churches, shopping strips, and government buildings were located, and in and out of several subdivisions of homes—ramblers and split-level homes from the middle 1970s. The half-acre lots were grassy and lightly treed, some with flowery bushes and many with the April daffodils and tulips that bordered steps and walks. I saw a few swing sets and out-of-ground pools in the backyards, American-made cars and minivans in the driveways, TV antennae and even a few satellite dishes. These were family homes in working-class suburban communities, places where middle-of-the-road interests and mainstream values were proudly displayed. From one stop to the next, one or more children (and, in several cases, small "clumps" of children) jumped from the bus to cement sidewalks. I watched them as they skipped, hopped, and ran to the safety of their homes, their havens.

The People on the Bus

The C-bus was near capacity on the days I joined children in their travels. There were seats for forty-one, given the nine rows of two double seats (each separated by a middle aisle) and the last row of five seats that was stretched across the back. On each trip I took with them, I had a double seat to myself but there were few empty spots elsewhere. The children spanned the gamut of ages and grade levels, from kindergarten through the sixth grade. The majority looked to be of Euro-American ancestry, but about one-third were from African American or Asian American (mostly Korean and Vietnamese) ethnic cultures. They boarded noisily each day, talking, shouting, and singing as they climbed the steps and dragged their lunch boxes and backpacks down the aisle behind them. I noticed how none of the girls wore dresses; instead, they wore colorful pants and shirt sets, while the boys were typically in jeans or dark cotton pants and T-shirts. Several of the older boys looked somewhat disheveled in appearance, with half-laced high-tops, untucked shirts, and unzipped windbreaker jackets that hung unevenly from their shoulders; they gave the appearance of having spent some hard hours of hard play at school.

An interesting seating pattern showed itself to me, with little variation. There were no plans or charts which a teacher-monitor or bus driver might lay out for the children, but, as one fourth-grade girl explained, a free choice of location and partner with whom to sit was in operation "provided that you behave according to the rules." With few exceptions, the younger children sat near the front, while the older children filled the middle to back rows. Two fourth-grade girls invariably took the first row behind the bus driver, while the rest of the front-row passengers were children in the primary grades. Girls in the intermediate grades filled the middle rows, although three sixth-grade girls regularly squeezed together on one seat—against the rules—in the second-to-last row among the older boys. The proximity of certain children to each other allowed for particular genres of inter-active activities, such that while hand-clapping chants happened largely among the primary grade girls who sat together, and riddles and rhymes were popular among the younger boys, the older children were engaged in telling jokes, recalling sto-ries to favorite sitcoms, and sharing in school gossip.

Tina was the third-grade teacher charged with bus duty during the week of my observations, and I immediately noticed how firm yet good-humored she was at fulfilling her tasks: lining up the children, ensuring that they boarded the bus in an orderly fashion, reviewing the "rules" of the bus to the group, responding enthusiastically to the riddles, rhymes, and "knock-knock" jokes that the children put to her, and discreetly reminding a few children of her expectations for their improved behavior. Tina explained to me that the bus driver filled out regular reports for her on offenders of four rules: "No more than two to a seat, no standing while the bus is moving, no fighting, and no obscenities." She typically remained with the children until the last child was boarded, then disembarked with a smile, a wave, and a well-intended if trite "have-a-good-night" cliché.

The driver of C-bus was Julie, an athletic and energetic young woman in her early thirties with long auburn hail clipped back in a ponytail. This was her third year as driver of the same bus on the same route, with many of the same children. She claimed, "I'm getting old at this job, watching the kids grow into wise-crack smart-alecks," but then laughingly called some of the older children her "buds." Julie offered friendly or teasing comments for many of the children as they climbed on the bus: quips about their clothes, current sports events, and the musical instruments or art projects they carried on board. As she drove, she kept a watchful eye on children through her large rearview mirror and called out the names of the children on the verge of breaking one of the rules. Twice in the four days, she stopped the bus on the shoulder of the road to separate those whom she viewed as rowdy, "looking for trouble and fixing for a fight." The children seemed to regard Julie as a younger aunt or a favorite babysitter and were at ease and friendly with her. Her language was sometimes rough-and-tough, yet there was also a sincerity in her caring for her young riders that was not lost on them.

Rhymes, Riddles, and Songs

The C-bus children shared among themselves a vast repertoire of narrative forms, from rhymes and riddles to jeers, jokes, stories, and songs. The C-bus was the setting of a true "childhood underground": I sensed a certain bonding of children through the traditions they carried. This was a well-tended secret world separate from adults, where there was a deliberate exclusion of them from their world. I saw and heard what they, in essence, allowed me to experience; these occasions on the bus with them allowed me rare glimpses of a children as a folkgroup, people who share common values and worldviews (Brunvand, 1986; Dundes, 1990).

Among the most common of forms for both older and younger children were the jeers. Often loud and vulgar, jeers are often insults not intended as preludes to fights but as time-fillers and attention-getters that may even be shouted to friends with whom a jeering partnership has been established (Knapp and Knapp, 1976). In my observations, boys were more likely to shout jeers than girls at every age level. Many jeers were rhymed and rhythmic; some were pitched, while others sounded more like the typical rise-and-fall inflections (often settling on patterns of sol, mi, and la) of shouted or whined vocalizations. They included the following:

(1) Tattle, tattle, tattletale,
   Stick your head in the snail mail.
(2) Twinkle, twinkle, little star,
   What you say is what you are.
(3) Liar, liar, pants on fire,
   Go hang yourself on a telephone wire.
(4) Fatty, fatty, two-by-four,
   Can't get through the C-bus door.

Other jeers were unrhymed teases meant by children to annoy others or to fend off those who were perceived as annoying. Some were, despite the "rule," obscene, scatological, and with inversive elements; these were mumbled under the breath, hissed, or spoken by children facing the back of the bus (and thus out of the bus driver's range of hearing). In sending a child away from a seat he was saving for another child, one second-grade boy laid sideways across the double seat, saying, "Be like a tree and leave" and "Be like a banana and split." A fourth-grade boy was taunting to a girl his age:

God made mountains, God made lakes,
God made you, but we all make mistakes.

She immediately responded in defense, "Oh, go suck your toe to Mexico," then railed into a stream of obscenities that caused Julie to stop the bus, move her physically to the front of the bus, and "write her up" in a report to Tina, that week's school-bus monitor.

A number of riddles were shared, particularly by the younger children. A few of them sounded vaguely familiar, while others made me uncertain as to whether I'd understood them. Usually the receiver's response to them was not laughter but an immediate retort with another riddle, an undecipherable noise, or just a continuing stream of chatter.

Q: What did the pig say when he was grabbed by the tail?
A: That's the end of me.
Q: What do you call a friendly dinosaur?
A: A big fat idiot, like Barney.
Q: What's fat, rocky, and fruity inside?
A: Cherry Garcia (one flavor of the Ben and Jerry brand of ice cream).
Q: Julie dropped off three girls and one boy at one stop, and two girls and three boys at the next stop. At the next stop, she dropped off two boys. Then at another stop, she picked up five boys and three girls. At the next stop, she dropped off one girl and picked up three boys, and picked up one girl at the last stop. How many stops did the bus make?

I witnessed the telling of only a few formal jokes. One third-grade boy drew two dots on the closed fists of another boy. "What's the difference between these two rats?" He then drew a line with his black marker from the fist all the way up the boy's arm, explaining, "This one's got the longer tail." The victim rubbed the black line into one large smear, then responded with another joke. "Yeah, well, put your hand in a fist. Now raise your thumb and put your finger in and move it around. Now put your thumb back down. Thanks for cleaning my toilet." The two boys knocked into each other at the shoulders, then looked to me for my reaction. It seemed that these boys might have told these jokes before and were probably repeating them for my "benefit."

Little girls sitting together, across the aisle from each other or in the seat in front of another, often resorted to clapping games. In demonstration of their intimate friendship, these first- through third-grade girls chanted and clapped the rhyming verses they knew softly and with little facial expression; they looked almost in a daze as they spoke, staring ahead at their moving hands or partner's face. Often they clapped not only theirs (and their partner's) hands but also patted their laps, slapped their chests, and moved their hands to their eyes, foreheads, and necks in various gestures to reflect the words of their chant. More than once, and in several partnerships, I recorded these chants.

(1) I wish I had a dollar.
I wish I had a dime.
I wish I had a boyfriend
Who kissed me all the time.

My momma took my dollar.
My daddy took my dime.
My sister took my boyfriend
And gave me Frankenstein.

He made me wash the windows.
He made me wash the floor.
He made me wash his underwear
And kicked me out the door.

(2) Apple on a stick
Makes me sick,
Makes my tummy go
Four forty-six.

Not because you're dirty
Not because you're clean
Not because you kissed the boys
Behind the magazines.

Hey girl, want some fun?
Here comes Matthew with his pants undone.

He can wiggle, he can woggle
He can show you how to fly,
And I bet you fifty dollars
That you'll never see him cry.

(3) Three, six, nine,
    The goose drank wine.
    The monkey got tangled in a telephone line.
    The line broke,
    The monkey got choked,
    And they all went to heaven in a luxury boat. Clap. Clap.

(4) Fudge, fudge, call the judge.
    Momma's got a baby and he's a little pudge.
    Not a boy, clap clap. Not a girl, clap clap.
    Hard to tell, clap clap. But not a squirrel, clap clap.
    Wrap the diaper up and roll it up the stairs.
    First floor stop, huh. Second floor stop, huh.
    Third floor, doncha stop but take it to the top.

None of these hand-clapping verses were new to me, and in fact variants of each can be found in collections of childlore reaching back several generations (Abrahams, 1969; Fulton and Smith, 1978; Kenney, 1974; Withers, 1948). The girls chanted in rhythmic precision with one another, and as several others looked on, I realized that the observers might be learning from these models on the bus and would later imitate them. At one point, I asked the girls to repeat some of the words for me. They stopped, hesitated, and then one girl said, "Sure. But we have to sing it because that's the only way it goes. You can't just talk it." This was clear indication that the music was important—no, vital, to the lore.

I watched a quartet of fourth-grade girls chant, clap, and stamp a cheer that they had learned from watching cheerleaders at a recent basketball game. They were very much "in sync," as they explained their goal, timing their movements to coordinate with each other and with the rhythms of the words.

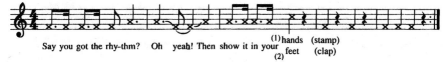

Say you got the rhy-thm?   Oh   yeah! Then show it in your (1)hands (stamp) (2)feet (clap)

Of the songs I heard on the bus, a few of them were parodies of songs in the traditional children's repertoire—a nursery rhyme, a Christmas song, a patriotic song. These three parodies came from one third-grade boy who performed to a captive and mildly interested audience of those nearby.

To the hexatonic melody of "Little Boy Blue":

(sung) Little Miss Muffet
Sat on her tuffet,
Eating her curds and whey.
Along came a spider
And sat down beside her,
(spoken) And said, "Yo, Sam, what's in the bowl?"

To the tune of "We Three Kings":

We three kings of Orientar,
Tried to smoke a Cuban cigar.
It was loaded. It exploded.
Now help us get off this star.

To the first two phrases of "The Star Spangled Banner":

Oh say can you see
Any roaches on me?
If you do, take a few
They're my gift to your dog.

One second-grade girl was singing into the wind that came whistling through her open window. I could not make out the melodies, but one led nonstop to the next one for over ten minutes. When I asked her what these beautiful songs were called, she smiled shyly and admitted that they were "madeup." "I don't even know them myself," she chuckled as she self-consciously ordered her hair, which had been tousled by the wind. Two first-grade boys were singing "The Farmer in the Dell" and were getting silly with the words: "The farmer takes a rat," "The cow takes a rock," "The horse takes a bed," and so forth. One afternoon, I heard several fourth-grade girls singing together the Scottish folk tune "Over the Sea to Skye," a few verses of "Froggie Went a-Courtin'," and "Hey, Ho, Nobody Home" in canon—no parodies, these performances, but the real things.

Many of the fifth- and sixth-grade children were recalling a TV show, a favorite video or film, or describing something that had happened that day. One sixth-grade boy had taken center stage for a few minutes, kneeling on his seat at the back of the bus. He was critically evaluating why Courtney Love (lead singer of the all-woman rock group Hole) had better songs than "old Madonna stuff. Her words are better. She's raunchy, and she's cool, too, because she can play besides just singing." I turned my ear toward two giggling sixth-grade girls who were looking at photographs in a fanzine for rock stars. Ogling a two-page color pull-out of So For Real, they were deciding which one of the singers they'd rather "be with": "I'll take that one over any guy in our class, or even at Kelly (the junior high). He's so-o-o-o-o cute." While I listened carefully at the back of the bus for chants and songs, I heard few enough songs to wonder whether there was an invisible wall erected about midway on the bus (as well as midway through childhood) that separated preteens from younger children regarding their willingness to perform, practice, and transmit musical and narrative forms. Most of the songs, chants, and riddles were coming from children in the primary grades and were absent from interactions among fifth- and sixth-grade children.

A Lone Listener

The expressions of children may well reflect societal purposes: What children say and do are at least partly linked with the social beliefs and practices of parents, teachers, older siblings, and other adults that hover nearby. Within schools, churches, the media, and other adult-supervised events, cultural transmission occurs through children's engagement in games, stories, songs, and other lore that have been selected (whether consciously or not) by adults as "the best," standard, or most representative ideas of a people. Cultural values are produced for and urged upon children by adults, and psychic structure is passed from one generation to the next through the narrow funnel of childhood as it is anchored into institutionalized settings. The fourth-grade girls who sang "Over the Sea to Skye" are illustration of engagement in a cultural expression that reflects what some adults—teachers, perhaps—deem to be vital knowlege, and a part of a large core that every culturally literate child should know.

Still, there is little doubt that in places like the C-bus, where children are set apart from adults, they express themselves authentically, creatively, and sometimes in purposeful opposition of what adults might wish. When they are left to their own devices—free to be silly, noisy, teasing, joyful, and obscene (or even belligerent), they generate words and actions spontaneously. They also accept into their lives what other children value and are willing to give to them. Most of what was spoken or otherwise sounded on the C-bus originated with children and encompassed their own inventions as well as the oral lore that has been transmitted by children to other children for multiple generations. The melodies of the little girl who sang out the window were made up by her, on the one hand, while the "Apple on a Stick" chant is part of a collective lore that has been passed from one child to the next for at least forty years.

The cheer ("Say you got the rhythm") was of particular interest for its source and probable means of transmission as well as for its rhythmic content. According to the girls, they had watched, listened to, and imitated the cheerleaders, and were copying their body postures and body percussion (clapping and stamping) as well. They performed the cheer with ease, yet also with great precision, every syncopation in its place, every body sound well-timed to the rhythm. Here was an orally transmitted "piece" that was not so much linked to the societal values of adults or to childlore traditions, but was instead something the children themselves had selected out of adolescent culture as worthy of their pursuit. It was fashionable—glamorous, even—to perform the cheer, and knowing how to perform it might have been for these children, powerless as they often are, a small piece of power for them to attain.

I often think about one of the older boys who wore his headphones on each of the four days I had spent on the bus and who had appeared unaware of and isolated from any nearby activity. He had slouched still and had stared silently out

the window most of the time, save the occasional moments when he had spontaneously joined in with the singers on his tape or drummed his fingers on some
surface to keep time or follow a rhythmic pattern. I wondered whether his
worldview would be lacking the childlike qualities of his contemporaries, due to
his detachment from the folklore group in his immediate environment, the children
on the bus. He had either graduated out of or bypassed the child-to-child conduit
of information that was occurring all around him. His oral lore was the adult
music of his radio or tapes, which was very much removed from the child-to-child
(or even adult-to-child) network typical of most children's experience. Perhaps he
was already slipping into puberty and was purposefully disassociating himself
from all who held even the thinnest veneer of their childhood traditions intact. Yet
while this boy may have been a marginal member of this folklore group, the
mainstream of children's culture was elsewhere quite evident among the riders of
the C-bus.

Mrs. Bedford's Music Class: At the Periphery

Even in the group-directed music class where they are taught en masse, children
are initiating music of their own making. At the start and close of class, and in
between their occasions to perform, children are engaged in creating and re-
creating music. Importantly, children are not the conglomerate whole that a sea of
same-age faces may seem to reveal; instead, they respond to and initiate their
music in unique and individual ways. At times, it is children's own internal music
that may spring forth, making audible what they may have earlier felt and heard.
At other times, it is a musical stimulus in the classroom that triggers their tapping,
bouncing, singing, humming, and clucking; a particular timbre, rhythm, tune, or
even a single sustained tone or constant pulse can motivate their musicking. Even
while class goals are set and instructional designs are activated, music is happening as a result of (and sometimes in spite of) the teacher.

Plymouth School was the site for my observations of children's self-initiated
music. My notes were gathered from six visits taken over a period of nearly two
years (the longest time span over which I scattered my observations), during which
times I spent entire mornings or afternoons observing three, four, or five classes.
The teacher and program schedule and mission remained fairly constant during
this time, in my estimation, although the children, repertoire, and instructional
strategies varied somewhat over the period of my observations. I found myself in
a corner of the room for these observations, often on the floor or at a desk chair,
looking, listening, and writing. I attempted to record and videotape my visits but
found the tapes only marginally of use, since some of the audio portions were
quite muddled. In the end, my jottings and actual field notes were of greatest help
in reminding me of the children whom I had observed.

Mrs. Bedford and the Plymouth School Setting

At Plymouth School, Mrs. Bedford had been a full-time teacher of music for eight years. She trained as a vocal/general music teacher in a state university program, studying applied voice and piano, and performed in a variety of choral ensembles through her four and a half years of study. She had been hired by the school district upon graduation to fill a midyear vacancy at Plymouth, and she proved through innovative programming from the start that she was a "team player," knowledgeable of both music and children, and capable of addressing the school's mission of "arts as academic enrichment." Yet as she explained, "I teach children musical skills first and foremost, but I'm aware of the need to interface my program with what the teachers are doing in their classroom." She was trained in the Orff method (Levels I and II) and had taken a summer course in Kodaly.

With two class meetings weekly for all children from kindergarden through the sixth grade, Mrs. Bedford defended what she considered her realistic goals: "They will have a repertoire of songs to sing, they will know how to tell the difference between Bach and Beethoven, and they will be able to think musically enough to create their own pieces. Through the second grade, I emphasize experience, but by the third grade, they're reading and writing music, some. Plus," she added with enthusiasm, "they will all be exposed to music from various American and world cultures." She confessed that she had to "drive fast and hard" to fit in the repertoire and experiences of her plans but assured me that "on our better days, we manage very well. My kids are mostly musically literate and performance-able [*sic*]." My skeptical self emerging, I wondered about the "worse days," when teachers and their students manage less well, if at all, and how she was defining and assessing the musical literacy and performance ability of her students. She hadn't mentioned her means of evaluation, yet she seemed genuinely confident of students' progress. I thought also of the 60 minutes of weekly music instruction she spent per class and gauged how minuscule it was when compared to the full 1,500 minutes (25 hours) of schooling weekly—to say nothing of children's outside-school exposure. How does a teacher make an impact when confronted with such odds? But Mrs. Bedford was bright, quick, and resourceful and possessed a certain missionary zeal about her work. By her admission, she also had support for her projects from her colleagues, so she might be well able to accomplish her goals. It could happen—it *does* happen, although sometimes against considerable odds.

Plymouth School is located in a middle-income suburb east of the city, one of five elementary schools in the district. It is a two-story building of dark-brown brick, built in the 1920s but with a wing added in the early 1960s to accommodate the booming population of children coming from the neighborhood's expanding families. Now the school has returned once again to its earlier population of about 350, and the "new wing" houses the library, a community preschool, a senior citizens' program, a small kitchen, and the music room. The children are largely Caucasian, although 18 percent are minorities, mostly African Americans. They live and play within a mile of the school, in yards and on streets lined with older maple, pine, and alderwood trees. At the edge of the school community are found a few churches, the public library, and a trickling of small stores leading to one of the area's large shopping malls, in the next suburb.

Mrs. Bedford's music room at Plymouth School is situated on the ground floor, beneath the preschool and just across from the senior citizens' center. It is a tiled room, much longer than it is wide, with one wall of windows that open to a parking lot and three walls of blackboards and corkboards. A grand piano sits in the far corner, and a set of choral risers are placed next to it. In another corner is an overhead transparency projector on a cart. There are four tables of Orff xylophones against the windows, and a display of feltboards and a butcher-paper tablet on an easel just to their left. A stack of carpet squares—"remnants," probably— are piled high near the door. Mrs. Bedford has acquired a variety of world instruments, too, which are displayed on the tops of cupboards and on shelves. These include two shekeres, three mbiras, several Native American drums painted with red, black, and turquoise geometric shapes, four flutes and one double-flute, tambourines, a large Irish bodhran, some rainsticks, Andean ankle rattles made from the toenails of llamas, and two slit-log drums. There are four conga drums and two kettle drums, which line the grand piano. A stereo system (tape, CD, and record players) and VCR are permanently lodged into one corner, and three shelves of books, recordings, and videotapes frame this "altar of sound."

Arrivals to the Music Class

I was fascinated by the entrance of children to the music room. Not surprisingly, by winter and spring (the periods of my observations), they had been taught an acceptable manner for their arrival and settling into appropriate places. Mostly, the children entered single-file, one head behind the other. Through the second grade, the younger children picked up carpet squares, while children from third grade on found a preassigned place on the choral risers. There were seating plans for classes of older children on the choral risers, while the younger children wore name tags that hung on yarn around their necks to identify them, given that their arrangement on carpet squares across the floor varied with every class.

Even while order prevailed, there were individual discrepancies in their manner of entrance. Certainly, there were musical arrivals, and movements across the floor that resembled dance. Many children walked, but at various tempi, while others shuffled, skated, dragged, or stepped in a light bounce into the room. A few of the younger children skipped or galloped; a little girl waltzed, another twirled, and one boy crept stealthily to his place, his carpet under his arm and his two hands curved in front of him like animal paws. Older children, particularly one of the sixth-grade classes, entered in groups of two and three, talking; several girls came in with arms wrapped over each other's shoulders. I was intrigued by the behavior of one fifth-grade boy, whom I twice observed entering the music room with his arms waving rhythmically above him, nodding his head, and rapping the same words from the same popular song, about "no dissing" his friends in the " 'hood."

More than a few children entered singing. Perhaps remembering the music of an earlier class, or anticipating what might be on the agenda for the coming period, a child might initiate a song, only to be joined almost immediately by a few friends. Some may have been unaware of their singing, as if it was unconsciously triggered— even though it was audible at a distance. I heard strains of "Tideo," "Sorida," "Over the Sea to Skye," "Uncle Jessie," "Mbube" ("Wimoweh," or "The Lion Sleeps Tonight"), and "The Battle Hymn of the Republic." I heard a third-grader scat-singing Bach's "Jesu, Joy of Man's Desiring," giving *doo*'s and *bee*'s to the pitches. Two fourth-grade boys were enjoying their mocking rendition of the theme from Schubert's "Unfinished" Symphony: "This is—the symphony—that Schubert wrote but never finished." Other tunes I could not identify because they were quietly rendered or seemed to converge with other melodies. Sometimes children clowned with a song they sang, delivering it in an unnaturally low or high range. Often children "conducted," waving their hands in exaggerated fashion as they sang, or "grooved" to their songs, by nodding and swaying. Usually the singing that commenced at the door to the music room was interspersed with talking and laughter; it was frequently carried on for two or three minutes while Mrs. Bedford ushered in the last children and made her way to the opening formal class activity.

Other musical arrivals were notable. Sometimes children passed close to the tables, and tapped or ran their fingers across the xylophone bars. Some would stop and try to get a tune going until Mrs. Bedford would urge them to their seats; I often heard Cs and Gs played as bourdons and ostinati rhythms. Occasionally, a few children would position themselves at the congas and slap a few strokes; they, too, were lightly admonished by their teacher. Some paused to shake a shekere or rainstick. Once, one boy swept past the musical instrument shelf and took an mbira to his corner place on the choral tier. He was feverishly twanging the metal tongues and did not hear Mrs. Bedford's call to order. His classmates turned to him, laughing, calling, and teasing, drawing him out of his daze. He smiled sheepishly and surrendered the instrument.

In the Midst of the Music Class

There was a predictability to Mrs. Bedford's music classes. Throughout the grade levels, she began by presenting four- or eight-beat rhythmic or melodic patterns that most children understood were to be immediately imitated. Patterns ranged from simple (♩   ♩   ♫   ♩   or sol-mi) for the very young, to more sophisticated patterns for fifth and sixth graders, including dotted rhythms and syncopated melodies in major, natural and harmonic minor, and dorian modalities. The rhythms were clapped and patted and the melodies sung on *la, loo, ah,* and *ooh.* Often, these patterns were derived from songs and pieces Mrs. Bedford was intending to feature in class that day. This five-minute warmup gave way to her announcement of "the plan" for the day: what concepts and skills they would learn and what musical repertoire they would perform and/or listen to. There was precision in the manner in which she articulated the lesson's aims, and also an enthusiasm that was infectious. There followed the introduction of children to a new song, which was often orally taught and segmented into a rhythmically chanted text (often accompanied by patting the hands to the laps) to which the melody was later applied. Then a set of ostinati were learned, also orally and kinesthetically, followed by the assignment of children to play these kinesthetic rhythms on designated bars of xylophones and metallophones or on various classroom percussion instruments. From the third grade onward, Mrs. Bedford notated the melody and its ostinati on the blackboard, feltboard or paper tablet, pointing to individual notes while she and the class sang and chanted while playing "in the air" or on instruments. A song and its accompaniment were usually the focus for about two-thirds of a class period, leaving just over ten minutes for (1) listening (directed, nondirected, or with movement or dance), (2) reviewing previously learned songs and pieces, or (3) viewing brief videotaped segments of a musical tradition or style. I observed no teacher-initiated creative composition or improvisation activities during my six visits, despite its advocacy by Orff specialists and its prominence in the professional literature.

Due to the high energy and good humour of Mrs. Bedford, children in the various classes were overwhelmingly attentive and involved as listeners, singers, players, and dancers. Still, there were a few outliers in every class. A few children appeared lost in thought, staring ahead, and nonparticipatory, but a few more were outwardly making their own music at the periphery of the class plan. During the warmups, not all were imitating what Mrs. Bedford presented: some children were supplying "answers" to her rhythmic and melodic questions, or improvising on what they heard. For example, one of Mrs. Bedford's rhythm patterns stimulated this response from a first-grade boy:

Another boy in the third grade patted a rhythmic response on his legs to one of his teacher's patterns:

In the fourth grade, one of Mrs. Bedford's rhythm patterns led him to his own rhythmic piece, which he slapped on his legs (lap), chest, and even the floor:

When Mrs. Bedford used the claves to play one pattern to a sixth-grade group, it erupted into a full-fledged rhythmic improvisation as a lead boy took the pattern and three others layered over him, patting their rhythms on their legs and on the choir tiers. I could not help but wonder what the sources of the other three patterns were, as they were unlike any I'd previously heard in Mrs. Bedford's class. Their rhythmic complexity was startling, and their syncopations, accents, and even silences were all skillfully executed. Interestingly, three of the patterns, including the lead clave pattern, were two measures in length, while the fourth pattern encompassed sixteen beats.

Interestingly, these and other rhythmic extensions or improvisations were typical in every class, increasing in frequency and complexity with age. Nearly all were initiated by boys. During these rhythmic occurrences, Mrs. Bedford took one of two strategies: she stopped, stared, and waited for the children to cease their rhythms, once sternly asking "Are you finished?," or she moved toward them while continuing the lesson, which typically (although not always) brought the musical extension or improvisation to a close. Of course, she had a plan to follow and goals to be met, yet I wondered whether she might do well to spin an occasional lesson from children's creative (rather than solely imitative) responses. She had mentioned her interest in developing their ability to create music, and I wondered whether she was missing opportunities for this to be developed.

The melodic material of her warmups triggered far less variation than the rhythm patterns. When Mrs. Bedford used solfege syllables (e.g., do-re-mi), children invariably imitated intact the syllables and approximate pitches. Her use of neutral syllables like *la* and *loo* were more apt to inspire some timbral variations when a few children in the upper grades chose to play with the "nonsense" syllable; they retained most of the pitch and rhythm content of a melodic phrase but sang in shrill and pinched tones, gravel-throated growls, or other similarly raucous qualities. There were times when children may have thought themselves to be accurately imitating a phrase but were in error. I sensed that even the stepwise or triadic patterns Mrs. Bedford sang were challenging to some children, enough so to attend more constantly to the imitation game rather than to develop elaborations.

Mrs. Bedford's oral transmission of new songs featured the breakdown of the whole song into phrases, or "chunks" as she called them, which were then repeatedly sung and imitated. The chanting of the text in rhythm was clearly appealing, judging by the full participation of children in the raplike quality of the exercise. Many patted a beat or rhythm in their laps while they chanted. Particularly when the text was syncopated, a mass of heads shook and nodded in a movement that emanated from somewhere near the top of the spinal cord. The chant-then-sing process did not vary; Mrs. Bedford did not discriminate by the age of the children nor by the extent to which the songs may have contained familiar, thus more easily learned, musical structures. Some of the phrases were complex enough to necessitate numerous hearings and opportunities to sing them back, but others were clearly (or nearly) learned in the first round. When she sang easily learned phrases four or five times, there were, with each successive opportunity, a greater likelihood for children's playful variation on the phrase. One notable example of this was one fifth-grade girl's changing renditions of the second phrase of the chorus to "Roll On, Columbia":

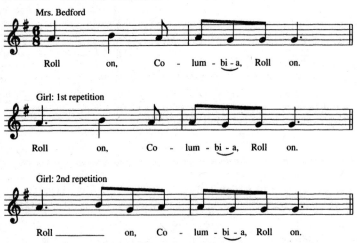

She sang these versions easily, gently swaying back and forth. She was not bored by the process but seemed instead to be secure and safe with the melody to be able to venture from an accurate imitation to a personalization of it.

Once a song was deemed "learned" by Mrs. Bedford, the introduction of ostinati accompaniment by their teacher triggered in some children more opportunities for individual musical engagement. As Mrs. Bedford presented an ostinato through oral and kinesthetic means, some children took to practicing it immediately. They patted on their laps, the floor, or the riser, made audible clicking and clucking tones with their tongues, and "played" it on imaginary instruments. For a few, their perpetual motion had them repeating the rhythmic movement even after Mrs. Bedford had moved on to another ostinato. When they were assigned to the instruments, many children could not resist immediately applying their movement patterns to the instruments. It was common for children to shake their maracas and shekeres, to jingle their bells, and to tap their hand drums, often holding an instrument up to their friend's (or their own) ear. At the conga drums, older children typically warmed up by "wailing," rapidly alternating their palms in a slapping motion to produce "rolls." As they settled into their ostinato, they tended to produce a subtle movement of the torso; once when a pattern had been internalized by four fifth graders, their drumming propelled them into a similar rocking movement backward and forward together as if they were all crewing for the same boat.

As for the xylophones and metallophones, children attempted to observe the class rule to play only on cue (lest they lose their turn). Thus, as they stood ready at their instruments, they frequently pretended to play, waved their mallets rhythmically in the air, and tapped the ostinato on the table or wooden frames of the instruments or into the palm of their hands. At Mrs. Bedford's cue, they were off—together at first, and then running at various individual tempi, their adrenalin pumped. Once their turn had been taken, however, and they were told to return to their seats, this was another cue for some to quickly pick out melodic riffs from familiar songs, to figure out variations to the ostinato they had learned, or to explore the range and timbres of the bars. For twenty, thirty, and forty seconds, some children lingered to play—until the next wave of players were up waiting alongside them, eager to take over the mallets.

A sense of rushing to the end characterized the final segment of Mrs. Bedford's typical class plan. The activities varied from listening or viewing a videotaped selection to singing familiar songs or moving in a free or choreographed manner. Fired up from singing and playing, or tired of sitting in the same position, children often appeared less attentive to their teacher's talking and her instructional thrust than they had been earlier in the period. On the other hand, perhaps they *were* attentive, but to their own "spin-off" from the activity. As Mrs. Bedford played the opening strains of Mozart's Symphony #40 (K. 440) to a group of third graders, many of them were "conducting" it, or tracing the rise and fall of its melody in the air, or singing it. (A brief description of Mozart and the symphony had preceded the hearing in this instance, but Mrs. Bedord gave no direction as to "what to do" on hearing it.) Their movements were truly beautiful listening responses. On one occasion, a second-grade class was listening to the "Winter" movement of Vivaldi's *Four Seasons,* and the class appeared divided between those who pretended to ride a horse-drawn sleigh and those who took to their imaginary violins, bowing rigorously (yet neither response had been suggested). On occasions when listening guides or charts were projected on to a screen, many children appeared little interested, looking elsewhere yet moving to the musical pulse or "drive" that sounded from the stereo speakers. When a fifth-grade class heard a segment of a Yoruba drumming ensemble, many began to bounce to the pulse, patting and tapping the rhythms they heard or that the music inspired in them. A videotaped snippet of Japanese *kodo* drumming produced similar reactions among a group of fourth graders.

My two opportunities to see a folk dance taught and learned were no less informative of children's musical responses. A Greek line dance, consisting of little more than a four-step "grapevine" that crossed front and then back to the right, brought varied responses from the sixth graders. Some were laughing as they tried unsuccessfully at first to master the footwork, a few boys were booming out the drum line with their changing voices, and a few more were singing the somewhat melismatic but very repetitive clarinet melody. A group of second-grade children danced "The Noble Duke of York" in two lines, and many were singing the melody that they had learned in an earlier class. I heard one boy working up a parody of the text as they lined up, retaining the same melody.

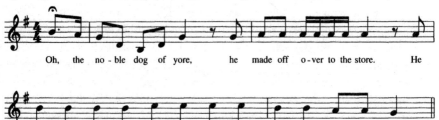

Oh, the no - ble dog of yore, he made off o - ver to the store. He

brought me back a Ta - co Bell, and then he took a snore.

As a first-grade class sang and played "Little Sally Walker" in a circle, I was struck by one little boy's pounding out of a four-beat ostinato on the floor in front of him:

It was not only steady, but the accents were inciting his rocking movement and that of several children near him. I watched a fifth-grade group review a West African dance they had learned the previous week (there was no further information on its origin to be found on Mrs. Bedford's "pirated" tape) and noted the extent to which the polyrhythmic texture of drums and a bell were amplified by children's own vocalized patterns as they moved. On phonemes like *buh, chee, dee, tss,* and *dah,* some were vocalizing the rhythms they heard, while others were inventing additional layers. This they did, most without missing a step in the circle dance.

When children were reviewing familiar songs, they usually sang with considerable vigor and enthusiasm: these were the moments of greatest musical unity in the class, when children functioned as an ensemble. A few times, the classroom teacher had stepped back into the music room, and the children then had an audience for their performance. The most cohesive singing happened at those times, when children best focused their energies.

Closing Shots

Mrs. Bedford usually spent the last few minutes of music class evaluating the progress and behavior of the children. In characteristic form, she democratically asked children at every grade level a series of questions, to which they were to respond affirmatively by raising their hands (and refraining from hand-raising if their response was no): Had they been good listeners? Good singers and players? Had they followed directions? Did the period "flow" (presumably without serious interruption or extensive admonishment)? In the presence of the children, she would stick a gold star on the poster-sized class-behavior chart for "the perfect class" and a silver star for the class with minor misses and transgressions. (She later explained to me that she rewarded classes with sufficient stars at the close of each term in ways that included candies, popcorn-and-video parties, and "free music" periods.) This was followed by calling children according to their "good sitting behavior" to line up along the wall, to await their teacher's appearance at the door to return to their classrooms.

Their "exit music" far surpassed the music they made as they entered, both in volume and variety. Particularly if their regular teacher was long in coming, and Mrs. Bedford was moving into her setup for the next class, children elicited a host of musical sounds. They hummed, sang, and even whistled the melodies they had heard or performed during class; this they did alone or together with others in front of or behind them. They leaned against the wall, danced, and hopped in place. They clapped and patted rhythms (and even tapped them on their friends' backs). Since they were lined up opposite the xylophone side of the room, they could not play them. Some stood alongside the shelves of musical instruments, and some of the bolder and more curious children could not resist turning the rainstick, shaking the llama rattles, or tapping the hand drums. From my vantage point, seldom did a single musical sound stand out among others, but the extent to which the children were musically engaged was nothing short of a phenomenon. I found myself silently applauding their teacher's allowance of "wind-down" time from her class but also wondered whether this could be just the *start* of their creative potential to make their own music.

The Toys and More Store

Amid the high-rise office buildings, department stores, and espresso shops that cram the downtown streets of this stylish city is lodged the architectural spectacle known as Toys and More. Although I'd heard rumors of this one-stop mammoth mart for children, I was nonetheless stunned at my first glance. As I rounded the corner, I was confronted by a glass-and-steel structure that rose three stories from the ground and that stretched half a city block wide; each letter of Toys and More danced in lopsided childlike scrawl above and below a bluish steel beam. I craned my neck upward to take in floor upon chock-full floor of animals, dolls, cars and trucks, bicycles and wagons: this was a world to its own of giant-sized bears, shiny red motor bikes, and pink frilly Barbies in pink frilly Barbie-houses. My eye caught the flashing blue and pink zigzags and shapes suspended off the indoor balconies of each floor, and movement of all kinds: a large carousel in the entrance was rotating a dog, panda bear, and gorilla on colorful wooden airplanes, a set of glittery red shoes were tapping atop an oversized baby-block, the head of a smiling dinosaur was bobbing off a wall, and a red-suited monkey was riding a unicycle on a tightrope that stretched the full expanse of the store. This was no five-and-dime store collection of playthings, no small corner shop of board games and do-it-yourself craft kits. I stood for awhile to marvel at it all, then I joined a stream of buyers and lookers entering through the wide glass doors. For a moment, I was Alice through the Looking Glass, entering a fantasy land in which children could once only dream to be. Toys and More was this dream, realized.

My premise for visiting the store was my hunch, based upon numerous casual observations, that children's musical behaviors at home and at play are at least partly stimulated by their toys. Folklorist Brian Sutton-Smith (1985) claimed that toys which children embrace are in fact emblematic of their interests and values as members of a cultural group. My first thought was to seek out musical toys, and to inspect them for their validity as tools for children's self-instruction in music. While this was my impetus, I soon turned toward another question: What were children's musical interactions, alone and together, with these toys? My observations included also "the sounds in the store"; even more than the visual, the aural ambiance of Toys and More was intriguing to me, since it was part of the overall experience for visiting children, who may spend an hour or more as captive audiences for the store's envelope of sound.

What I expected to learn from a single visit one Saturday morning in October proved unreasonable (due to my own wonder and sensory overload); I returned five times, including three visits during the peak post-Thanksgiving holiday season. My visits were two hours or more in length, and one visit had me there for over four hours, due to the kind assistance of two part-time floor clerks who demonstrated some of the musical toys for me. In my observations, it was possible for me to pass close enough to children as they explored toys, to linger awhile, and then to roam again to another play station, toy, or situation that appeared relevant to my questions. I also found stationary posts on benches set up principally for parents who watched their children in animated discovery of how a toy works. There was no tape or video recorder on these commercial premises, so I took to tape recording when I could and to jotting notes there and then drafting reports on my return home. What follows is a collage of these individual drafts.

The Sounds in the Store

From the ambient sounds of the street, I passed through the glass gateway to confront the three-story musical carousel in the atrium. As I watched the animals turn, I took in the sound of a calliope; it whistled a set of melodies to the repeated, arpeggiated chords of wooden and metal xylophones. The broken chords continued in much the same way from one melody to the next, and the treble voices of a small children's ensemble doubled the calliope's melody in singing one or two verses to complement the instrumental track. The addition of tambourine, woodblock, castanets, or a drum provided the only real timbral variance between pieces. In fact, the melodies ran together without rest, revealing their sameness of tonality as well as timbre in a cycle of songs that repeated every twelve minutes. From October through December, these melodies included the store's four-pitch theme song, "Welcome to Toys and More," and lively seasonal songs: "Jingle Bells," "Rudolph, the Red-Nosed Reindeer," "Santa Claus Is Coming to Town," "Up on the Housetop," "Jolly Old St. Nicholaus," "Sleigh Ride," and "Deck the Halls." At other times of year, the cycle was just under eight minutes, featuring the theme song, followed by "Happy Birthday," "If You're Happy and You Know It," "Old MacDonald," "The Eency Weency Spider," and a song which I could not identify but which resembled "It's a Small World." This carousel music was loudest at the entrance, but because all floors opened out with balconies to the atrium which contained the carousel, the music could be heard in any part of the store when no local sounds were competing.

The bobbing dinosaur head was one local sound that eclipsed the carousel music in a corner of the second floor. This smiling reptile delivered a minute-and-a-half monologue in a section marked off as "Zoo Friends," where stuffed animals of every size and type sat on shelves, in cages, and behind glass cases. He began with a loud "roar," then proceeded to sing a pentachordal melody (using do, re, mi, fa, sol) to the words: "The zoo's for me, as you can see, my friends and I, say 'howdy' and 'hi.' " A synthesizer of stringed sounds accompanied him. The dinosaur head proceeded to roar again, and then to speak: "My zoo friends join me in welcoming you to our zoo. Take a look around. They'd love to see you! And they'd love to go home with you, too." He laughed a deep laugh, introduced a few of the caged animals by name, and then sang a brief and repeating tune about life in a zoo; the only pitches were do, re, mi, and sol (and low sol). After a few more words about his happy life among animal friends, he said goodbye, roared, and then froze for a few seconds before repeating the same routine.

On the third floor, a giant keyboard mat was spread across the floor. The white (but not the black) keys, four feet long by eighteen inches wide, were activated when stepped upon, each one emitting a tinkling piano tone. The carousel music was clearly audible to me, but those who hopped, skipped, and jumped across the mat appeared unaware of any other sound but the tune they were creating. I heard mostly jumbled, arhythmic sets of pitches but detected a few attempts at familiar stepwise melodies: "Lightly Row," "Row Your Boat," "Go Tell Aunt Rhody"—the sort of melodies found in so many beginning instrumental manuals. I imagined that they played these on the keyboard because they had played them before on recorders, flutes, clarinets, and trumpets (and piano) at home or in school. One middle-aged man was successful in walking out all but the last three pitches of "Spanish Eyes"; because the keyboard spanned only one octave, he was forced to play an incomplete phrase. A young teen hopped down the scale for "Joy to the World," but she could not make the leap of five keys between "come" (the last pitch of the first phrase) and "let" (the first pitch of the second phrase). Most of the children seemed less intent on playing particular tunes than simply making sounds that could be heard by friends, siblings, and others who stood watching them; it appeared that the keyboard was less a musical instrument to them than a track for stomping out their energy.

I stood at the top-floor balcony, listening to many sounds that spilled out from the three floors to merge with the carousel music: the rumble of a motorbike on the first floor; the "thump-thumping" of a rap beat from the second floor's audio center, where CDs and tapes were sold; the meowing voices of *The Aristocats*, which played just behind me on a large video screen. I heard laughing, shouting, and squealing, too—children's responses to all of the playthings that had been so attractively arranged. The designers of the store had not short-changed the aural environment in their attempt to appeal to children's interests. The music and sound stimuli rivaled the visual displays for their clever and entertaining formats and for the variety of images they conveyed. Toys and More offered more opportunities to hear and do music in a single visit than many children have during weeks of in-school music instruction.

Musical Toys

I was eager to search out the musical toys I remembered from my own childhood: little toy pianos, plastic recorders, a harmonica. They were there but were nearly lost among the extensive "high-tech" music-oriented toys, instruments, and audio players.

Besides the giant keyboard mat laid out across the third floor, there were three other varieties of keyboards. A bright red miniature baby grand piano stood two feet from the floor to the top of its raised piano lid and contained thirty-seven wooden keys; the workmanship was by Kawai, a professional piano company, and the sound was soft and clinky but otherwise much like a piano's timbre. A second keyboard contained thirty-two keys, ran on AA batteries, and played songs or allowed children to create their own. These songs could be taped and played back, and a miniature microphone was available for (as the instruction booklet announced) "sing along fun." Still another keyboard was a pint-sized version of the giant keyboard mat, with white and black keys from middle C to high D which could be activated by stepping on them. The mat's transformer used four AA batteries and contained an amplifier. The box advertised nine "preprogrammed tunes of popular children's songs," from "Twinkle, Twinkle, Little Star" and "Itsy Bitsy Spider" to "Oh Susannah" and "My Bonnie." All three keyboards were remarkably well tuned and (not surprisingly) costly. During the holiday season, children swarmed around them, awaiting their turns to play or activate tunes.

There were recorders and "flutes" in neon colors, and harmonicas and small plastic saxophones; all were under plastic wraps and unavailable for play. Their packages recommended them for children from ages three through eight. The store's exclusive "Musical Band" set contained two metal cymbals, two plastic maracas, a recorder, and two double-disc tambourines, all painted in red, blue, and yellow designs, with rocking-horse motifs scattered here and there. A pro sound drum set "for serious beginners" was beckoning children and included the bass drum, snare, cymbal, and high hat, along with wooden and metal brush mallets. Next to it was a set of five practice drum pads that ran on electricity; a control panel allowed the player to set up various percussive timbres or to select from about forty rhythm tracks that ranged from "slow rock 1" to "funk." An "Electronic Rap Pad" (produced by LA Rock and Diversified Specialists, Inc.) produced four rap rhythms with the touch of a button which children could play along with on the two drum pads. The rhythms and timbres varied, as these first two demonstrate; while a bit "tinny," they were nonetheless appealing.

(1)

    c   d   d   d   c   d   d   d   oh   ch   oh   ch   oh   cl   cl

(2)

    c   d   cl   c   d   cl   ch   d ch ch   d ch c   d   cl

(c = cymbal; d = drum; oh = open highhat; ch = closed highhat; cl = clap)

Knots of children gathered around these drums on the Saturdays of the holiday season, listening to each other and eager to play.

Several toylike stringed instruments were intriguing, including a guitar that was similar in all ways to a "real" steel-string guitar except that it was smaller. A "soft rock guitar" for toddlers was made of yellow and red plastic and had eight buttons on the fretboard correspondent to individual pitches and to preprogrammed songs like "She'll Be Comin' around the Mountain" and "Old Paint." A "play-along violin" of brown plastic with a bow was fitted with three buttons, one for playing preprogrammed melodies ("Santa Lucia," "Greensleeves," "Ode to Joy," "In the Hall of the Mountain King" by Grieg, "Minuet" by Bach, and the theme from the second movement of Haydn's "Surprise Symphony"), a second button for altering the tempo of the songs, and a third for changing from one melody to the next. While the small guitar could be tuned reasonably well, the plastic guitar and violin were both sharp on their higher pitches, and there seemed to be no possible way to tune them. Additionally, I detected two interesting "variants" among the violin's pieces: "Greensleeves" contained a raised sixth in its minor melody, and the Haydn theme concluded its first phrase with a syncopated rhythm on the descending passage.

There were dolls that talked, sang, played music, and danced. "Baby Get Well" coughed, sneezed, and in a weak voice said "Don't feel good." "Limited collection" Barbie dolls were dressed in velveteen coats, masquerade dresses, sparkling electricity-lit gowns, and Rockettes outfits with swinging legs like the dancers of New York's Radio City Music Hall. One pretty little red-headed doll, made exclusively for Toys and More, spoke twelve phrases (two in French) and tunefully sang "Happy Birthday," "Jingle Bells," "Ring around the Rosie," and "Come All You Playmates" in a clear and strong soprano voice. "Really Rosie Doll," Marice Sendak's feisty storybook star, came complete with a video that featured music composed and sung by Carole King. "Wendy," in a choice of blonde or red curls, stood on her own (silent) dancing piano, her legs in position to hop out a melody on the keyboard. (Of the entire collection of over sixty dolls, there were just three dolls "of color"—startling, it seemed to me, for a store situated in a city widely known for its diverse, multicultural populations.)

In the audio center, three players caught my attention. A compact disc player in the brightest of neon colors was available complete with a microphone for sing-along; two little girls were trading phrases between them in singing "The Gypsy Song" from *The Hunchback of Notre Dame.* A "Hipster Stereo Tape Player," designated for ages three and up, was also decorated in colorful reds, yellows, and greens. It contained a built-in speaker and headphones for playing favorite tapes, for which many potential choices from collections by Disney and Warner Bros. were stacked in cases nearby. Children who wished to make their own recordings could do so with the "The Singing Machine," a set of black and silver equipment with two stereo tape decks, a five-band equalizer for better sound, two micro-phones, a cassette tape, and a booklet of lyrics from popular songs. The two tape decks allowed for children's playing and recording simultaneously. Although I passed this station frequently, set up and ready to play as it was, I was never able to observe it in use—perhaps because its somber casing made it appear more complicated and more serious than some of the other play stations. Along with the players, tapes, and CDs, the center also displayed videotapes and four TV-sized screens that played various classic and newly released animated movies and cartoons, as much for the parents' entertainment as for the children's.

I found myself amazed at how much more authentic and pleasing to the ear musical toys had become in a generation or so. The technology was impressive, that innocent little dolls could now sing in tune, that keyboards, guitars, and violins could play close to the timbres of their real-life models (if not always so well tuned), that rap rhythms could be laid out as tracks for children's imitation and rapped speech, and that even children could have their own home recording studios. My teacherly self imagined these toys in the classroom, thinking about how well they might stimulate the musical interests of children while also inspiring teachers to plan educational experiences around them.

Nonmusical Toys

Over 90 percent of the toys in the store were of the nonmusical variety, according to one clerk, yet the musicking that they triggered among the playful children was astounding. Even with the collage of programmed music selected by the store management, children made and moved to their own music or recalled familiar songs based on the experience in which they were engaged. It returned to me once more how musical children are—that they can respond in song and chant to one another as naturally as they speak and that the music that trickles or streams from them is spontaneous, effortless, and reflective of their experiences and thoughts.

The music was happening in many contexts. In the "Zoo Friends" section, children were petting, cuddling, and climbing on the plush and furry animals. I watched a young girl of about six dancing a small lion across the floor, all the while singing one of Simba's songs from *The Lion King,* "I Just Can't Wait to Be King." Another girl of kindergarten age was singing "I caught a rabbit, uh-huh," while cradling a very real-looking brown and white fuzzy bunny. A preschool boy was climbing onto the back of a large giraffe, squealing "I'm higher than any-body" to a spontaneous sol-mi-la melody. One small toddler watched as a six- or seven-year-old girl rhythmically pushed and pulled the chunky arms of the giant sitting bear, pretending to dance with him. When the older girl moved on, the two-year-old ran up to sing a greeting (on sol and a rather flat mi) in precisely the same tempo: "Hi, brown bear, Hi, brown bear, I love you, oo, oo, oo."

By a tree of puppets, a brother and sister team were enthralled with the diver-sity of animal-head hand puppets. For each one they tried on, they created a spon-taneous dialogue in a new voice that sounded as part speech and part song. As he donned a green rubbery and toothy head, the boy trolled a phrase from "Puff the Magic Dragon"; he later sang "Who's Afraid of the Big, Bad Wolf?" as he put on what was actually the head of a husky dog. His sister hopped a white and curly lamb on her brother's head to the tune of "This is the song that never ends," the chromatic theme to the *Lamb Chops Play Along* program. The boy then grabbed a Charley-horse puppet, and joined in singing and dancing his puppet to the rhythm of the song. The two of them carried on for over ten minutes in this way, conjuring up voices, words, and songs to suit each character.

A number of rocking or rolling animals seemed to incite children's singing and chanting. On a handpainted zebra rocker, a little girl of about three was sing-ing to the melody of "Clap Your Hands" (the first section of the Appalachian fiddle tune "Old Joe Clarke").

A toddler was scooting another zebra—this one on wheels—in several direc-tions; his melody on "la" was reminiscent of the first two phrases of "The Barney Song" ("I Love You"). A three-year-old boy was pedaling a covered wagon that was drawn by a wooden horse. He was joyfully yelling commands: "Go horsie," "Faster," "Giddyap," "Get 'em." When his mother pulled him off the wagon, his voice rang out a nursery rhyme in 6/8 time for a distinctively British (rather than western) style of riding, curiously out of character with the cowboy commands and pedaling rhythm he had established earlier.

This is the way the gen - tle - men ride: Trim, trim, trim, trim.

On the first floor, a small crew of boys was gathered around two adjacent train tables, one set up for Thomas the Tank Engine and Friends and the other for the Brio tracks, engines, and cars. They were preschoolers between the ages of two and five. All were intent on connecting one magnetized train to the next, talking in lower or higher than normal "train voices" to declare their past (or next) move, sometimes to themselves and sometimes to each other. Out of nowhere and all of a sudden, one of the older boys began to sing the *Shining Time Station* theme. The other boys paused, looked at the singer, and, quite remarkably to me, came staggering in to form a chorus of train singers while resuming their play. Then, just as they had layered themselves in, they pulled out until all that remained were once again the train-voice dialogues.

I heard no young musicians among the dolls, nor in the game section or where the Lego toys were laid out. In the area set aside for "amote controller" cars (as one boy called the radio-controlled engines), several children could not stifle their excitement as the turbo engines sped across the floor. However, these older boys and girls, aged about seven through ten or eleven, did not sing as they wheeled and jerked the high-performance sports cars. They rumbled, roared, and "vroomed" the sound of the engines, but I detected nothing that was pitched or that fell into a recurring rhythm. Several of the cars produced their own sound effects—swooshes, skids, and squeals—to blend polyphonically with what the children vocalized. One small boy stood mesmerized, watching the cars pass, and then to no one in particular spouted my very thoughts: "It sure sounds like race-car music here." I wondered whether the playing children heard it, too, the vocal and mechanical choral sound that blended like some *bruitismo* musical experiments with machines in the 1910s and 1920s.

Play is the Thing

In an area that specialized in toys for infants and young toddlers, the letters to four words were splashed across the wall in bright pink and blue polka dots: "Play is the thing." In slightly smaller print came this statement of the store's philosophy: "Play is the way children construct a world of possibilities and toys are their tools. Since every child is an original, so is the world they build to dream in with the help of toys." This was the essence of play theory espoused by experts in child development like Jean Piaget and Lev Vygotsky, a literature which the Toys and More management team obviously knew and found meaningful. This was the expression of the store's raison d'être.

To be sure, play is enhanced by playthings—toys—so the store's logo was relevant. Through my visits, I had become more aware of the roles that particular toys held in children's play. As the first consumer goods that children acquire, toys are implements of their socialization, problem-solving, and entertainment. I wondered whether modern, harried parents with little time to devote to traditional family activities might prefer toys that educate their children and that develop their skills of logic, language, imagination and invention, and motor and mathematical ability. On the other hand, I saw children as attracted to toys for what entertainment they perceive toys as offering them (for example, a doll that talks or a tape machine), what they can "do" to a toy (for example, manipulate the speed and direction of a racing car), or even what a toy may symbolize to them (for example, Barbie's glamorous career of fashion model or the sports car driver's fast life of luxury). As playthings, I recognized that toys might trigger the make-believe situations and social-pretending of play, and this fantasy might be a process by which children organize perception and interpretation to build social knowledge.

Of course, I observed with fascination how considerable were the musical aspects of children's play, such that so many little visitors to Toys and More could not play without musical utterances. If the toys spurred children on to construct their worlds, then music was a channel for their thoughts as well as a result of their thinking and doing. As much as the store planners had reckoned with the importance of an appropriate aural environment within their store, music was also a critical component of children's exploration of the toys and their socialization with one another. I did not doubt, either, that the store's environment as well as its toys were another piece in children's musical enculturation, an idea upon which parents and teachers could build.

Reflections

The six tales of children at musical play were drawn from various situations in which children typically find themselves: in the cafeteria, the music classroom, schoolyards, and (preschool) play areas, on the bus, and at the toy store. From descriptive accounts of the places where they gather and the people with whom they associate came floating a collage of images of playful children making music in a variety of ways. Sometimes consciously but more often unaware of the sounds they produced, children were singing, "rhythmicking" by way of their periodic, patterned sounds and movements, chanting and dancing their way through the many events that comprise their day. Their constant musical utterances, and their musical lore and repertoire, were certain testimony to the integral nature of music in their lives—whether offered as the result of painstaking deliberation or in the spirit of spontaneity.

Children through Their Childlore

Far beyond the "old-order" perception of children as not-quite-adults, in some amorphous stage, or in the process of becoming adults, is that of the folklorists and sociologists who recognize children for who they are in the present: a cultural group (or set of subcultural groups) all its own, with its own distinctive folkways (Dundes, 1965; Kline, 1995; Sutton-Smith, 1995). The beliefs and practices of children, held constant by them or in flux and evolving, define them and distinguish them from adults and adolescents (and also separate them from the babes-in-arms). Unsupervised by adults, children impose on themselves and enforce their own rules and standards. They develop their own channels of communication, their own vocabularies, and even their own dialects. Phrases like "alley, alley, in free," "eeny meeny, miney moe," and "until the day I die" belong collectively to children, while others, like "go for it" and "dissing," are adapted from the colloquial speech of adolescents and adults (and are preserved by children long after they have faded from fashion among their elders). Children practice various traditions and rituals that have been transmitted to them by other children (and also by adults and the media), and they preserve in their play (Schwartzman, 1978) those which they have deemed important to them. Their values are contained within their childlore; their knowledge and beliefs are gathered into the stylized genres of jeers, jokes, rhymes, riddles, rhythms, chants, songs, and singing games.

Childlore arises in fulfillment of various needs and functions. Although children may appear to be sounding off simply to hear themselves, there are often more explicit reasons for their engagement in orally transmitted lore—whether verbal and musical. They vent their emotions, letting off steam as they rhyme and rap, chant and sing. Whether repressed by the demands of school work or even social relationships which they may find difficult or unreasonable, some children find that their jokes, jeers, raps and songs serve as a safety valve for releasing their tensions. The windows of opportunity are opened in a music class or on a school bus for children who, when stimulated or given free reign, express themselves through the texts, rhymes, and melodies that they create or re-create, transmit, and preserve. For some children, their nearly constant need to kinesthetically expel their energy is accompanied by the music they make. Their lore also allows them a means of socializing with friends (or prospective friends) away from adult supervision, and they do so through their communal rhythmic "jams," jump-rope and hand-clapping chants and songs, and singing games. A few children signal almost ritualistically their arrival to and departure from a particular place (such as music class); still others may even use music to ease their work (as in the case of the cafeteria cleanup crew). Where adolescents and adults may prefer mediated music while they work (with the music of their favorite tapes, CDs, and radio stations piped to them through headphones, or from a central sound system), children are compelled to make their own music to fit their movements and their imaginations.

Children use their lore to deal with their personal feelings and their relationship with others. The child on the swing ("Alive, I'm alive"), the little girl standing in the pail of water ("I love to stay in the water"), and the boy on the rocking giraffe ("I'm higher than anybody") melodically proclaimed their thoughts to no one in particular. Many of the chanted and sung lines that children produced allowed them to comment on their relationships with friends and classmates. The gang of eight-year-old boys rapped on about their long-lasting friendship ("You and me, that's how it's gonna be"), while comparing themselves to "power (people) rangers." However offensive they seemed to me, the name-calling that the C-bus children produced in rhymed couplets (for the tattletale, the liar, and the fatty) were as frequently for their friends as for their adversaries.[8] Some of the jump-rope and hand-clapping chants had little girls referring to their imagined boyfriends ("Not because you kissed the boys behind the magazines"), while others feature members of the family ("My momma took my dollar . . ."; "Momma's got a baby . . ."). Not all mentions of "momma" or other family members may be in reference to their own personal situations, as some of these songs are simply parts of a long-preserved repertoire of childhood songs and chants. Still, the verbal content of children's lore reflected their historical, collective experiences and feelings, as well as quite personally situated thoughts.

The bulk of childlore may be conveyed through the low-key, intimate conversations children may have, but a considerable extent of it is found in the rather public performances children provide. Like stand-up comics, children can cleverly (if somewhat rudely) convey their thoughts through the jeers they conjure for poking fun at one another, as well as through the jokes and riddles they tell. An eager audience of other children can urge them on, and, buoyed by the laughter and encouraging comments, such verbal lore can soar to truly paramount performance heights. Their rhymes on all sorts of interest topics may take on rhythmic qualities as they chant alone or together in a public presentation of verse they are inventing or (more likely) re-creating intact. As well, their games can be wondrous to watch, these public displays that integrate childen's thoughts and sentiments into a Wagnerian *Gesamtkunstwerke*—a total and all-encompassing composite of staging, dramatization, choreography, and singing.

The Musical Parts of Childlore

Children's verbal lore is frequently embedded in rhythm and pitch, thus the childlore becomes "musical lore": songs, chants, dances, and musical games. They make parodies of the songs and poems they already know ("The Noble Duke of York," "Little Boy Blue," "We Three Kings," "The Star-Spangled Banner"). They convert their rhymes to songs and their speech to rhythms and recitative-like melodies. They are inspired (in unequal ways) by the popular music of the media, the seasonal, patriotic, and "school songs," and the music of their home and family surroundings. They use what music they know and make it meaningful and fitting for their own uses.

Children devise their own couplets and verses, and their own melodies and rhythms to accompany favorite activities such as jumping rope, clapping hands, bouncing balls, or circling together in ring games. Children who know the lore through its musical presentation often cannot conceive of it sans music. Stripped of rhythms and melodies, the rhymes, activities, and games are then viewed by children as not only "not the same" but also as less able to convey the messages or the symbols for which they were intended. The musical parts are integral to the lore as a whole and are not easily dismissed without children's own sense of the lore having lost its essence.

The musical components of childlore are rich in melodic and rhythmic formulae. Their melodies are typically comprised of steady quarter- and eighth-note rhythms, with occasional bouts of syncopations that pique interest (and add a moderate level of complexity). There are occasionally dotted rhythms, triplets, and polyrhythms, the last often occurring when children vocalize one pattern and clap another. The pitch content of their musical lore ranges from two-tone chants (often a variation of sol-mi) to full diatonic melodies, with numerous pitch-set permutations in between: tetrachords (some with rising chromatic passages), pentatons (gapped series of five pitches) and pentachords (stepwise sets of five pitches), and six-tone sets. Some pieces blend sung melodic parts with rhythmic chant, while a few chants with no exactly discernible pitch are nonetheless replete with a spectrum of inflections from low to high.

Despite the variety of these rhythms and melodies, children tend to adhere to the important formal principle of unity through repetition in the music they make. The relatively high redundancy rate of the musical content almost guarantees that the verbal message will not be overlooked but, rather, will be underscored and emphasized. After all, the lore of children consists of their knowledge and beliefs, however they are packaged. This musical packaging must never conceal the gist of children's thoughts and sentiments but must serve instead to transmit and preserve them.

Musical Utterances

To utter is to express aloud an idea, to vocalize the conscious or subconscious thought which an individual may have. Usually brief in duration, utterances may be comprised of spoken words, or words or syllables that are sung or rhythmically chanted. "Musical utterances" are essentially musical phrases that flow effortlessly from ideas somewhere deep within the mind's ear. They are indeed the (short) songs in children's heads.

Children often think aloud as they play; they orally emit thoughts relevant to the toys they are manipulating, the actions in which they are engaged, and the social interactions they are having. They can musically express their emotions, and they can communicate ideas to their playmates and friends in ways that pass for music even when they may not intend it as such. Children's musical utterances are typically quite brief: musical fragments, bits, and pieces. Partly because they are so brief, they are often progressive in form rather than organized into designs of similar and contrasting sections like some strophic song. Recitative-like, many of the musical utterances follow closely the pitched inflections and rhythmic nuances of children's exaggerated speech.

Through the course of my observations, children's musical utterances appeared frequently. Children called out each others' names, gave directions, and exclaimed about an event or phenomenon of importance to them in melodic or rhythmic ways. They joyfully expressed themselves, as in the case of the little girl on the swing who celebrated her freedom as she swung high in the air. They sang their brief tunes as they searched together for garden beans, as they played together in the sand, or as they ate some snack food that appealed to them. There were toys that incited their musical utterances, too: Robbie's wheel-rolling brought forth a melody from him, Tyler's overturning of the chimney of Lego blocks triggered Katie's teasing chant of reprimand, and the brother-sister duo's experimentation with animal-head puppets in the Toys and More store led to their spontaneous song-and-chant dialogue.

The musical content of these utterances varied, although many of children's melodies were somewhat narrow in range. A number of these melodic utterances were restricted to the interval of a third or a fourth, and a few were triadic from root to fifth, but several melodies even leaped a full octave. Rhythmic utterances, chanted words and syllables, were more rarely emitted than the melodic fragments, yet they were characteristically syncopated. The third-grade boy who rapped explosive consonants as he cleaned the cafeteria tables, the fifth-grade girls at the monkey bars who fused their two phrases into a single chant, and the fifth-grade boy who converted the jabs and punches of a boxing match into sound with movement—all these chants were rhythmically linked by nature of their syncopation.

In some circumstances, children seemed hardly able to function without their musical declamations coming forward. Particularly in the cases of children on the playground and in the preschool play yard (as well as indoors), children were spontaneously singing and chanting their sound bites. They were safe, satisfied, and fully at liberty to express themselves as they played, thus these were prime circumstances for nurturing their musical expressions. As I listened to their utterances, I marveled at what I presumed were the influences of parents, siblings, their friends, and the popular media (this order not necessarily reflecting the extent of influence). Whether spurred by socially contextualized interactions or by some force within them to sound aloud an idea or sentiment, children's musical utterances were springing from the musical knowledge they had stored within them from the experiences they have known.

Rhythmicking Behaviors

Akin to musicking, "rhythmicking" is the individual's engagement in some manner of rhythmic behavior. In various settings and under a host of circumstances, children rapped, tapped, slapped, and played their rhythms on themselves, on tables, chairs, desks, and floors, and on real instruments. They also bounced, nodded, and "grooved" to the sounds they made or heard, gesturing with their hands and arms or moving their entire bodies rhythmically to some external or internal pulse or pattern. Rarely were children silent and still; their rhythmicking behaviors were almost constantly evident.

There were simple rhythms, sometimes attached to words or syllables, sometimes not. The sideways dance pattern of the sixth-grade girls in the playground had been straighforward: a string of eighth-notes that cadenced on a quarter-note. The rhythmic movements of many of the children in the cafeteria were often a steady rain of pulses or their subdivisions, as were some of those of children in the preschool, on the bus, and in Mrs. Bedford's class. A good many were more complex, however. Even actions so basic as the bouncing of a milk carton or the licking of a lollipop had been executed in syncopated fashion. Robbie, the preschooler, had hammered with a stick the same dotted rhythm that he had heard his preschool playmates sing. One of the older girls in the cafeteria crew had produced with her dustpan a metallic-sounding syncopation, while the chant of the floor sweepers had been simple (although varied) until the closing syncopated tag, "if you don't want a kick."

Polyrhythms were also evident among these playful children. The chants of fifth-grade girls ("Jump down" and "Huh uh"), while simple in themselves, were rhythmically complex in their combination. The young boys rapped together in two syncopated rhythms for their "Power to the People Rangers" chant. Children in the cafeteria produced polyrhythmic movement as they moved various body parts simultaneously in different patterns. As two boys tapped with plastic forks, hands, and fists on their cafeteria bench and table, they created interlocking patterns replete with accents, syncopations, and longer and shorter durations. The eruption of the four-part polyrhythm in Mrs. Bedford's class, a response to her clave pattern, was perhaps the most startling of all rhythmicking behaviors—a truly stellar example of how children can channel their rhythmic energies into surprisingly sophisticated musical pieces.

Listening to the Children

The studied observation of children at play in unsupervised circumstances (or at least on the fringes of it) is a fascinating adventure for teachers and parents to know. Children live much of their lives following the maze of carefully conceived plans which adults invent, all too frequently with nary a nod to what children themselves may think and do when ungoverned and unseen by their elders. Yet if adults are to be responsible for designing plans for children's education and welfare, observations of this nature are of prime importance. For the very best plans which adults can muster for children without close examination of their knowledge, skills, and values can still be a considerable distance from the realities of what children may require for their further development as thinking and feeling individuals.

As a teacher, I know more now than ever that listening to and watching the children in their musical behaviors can be a transformative experience. As a result of such field experience (or fieldwork), my impressions of children's musical capacities are confirmed in some cases, denied in several more, and yet undecided in a few further instances. As my observations continue, I am finding that I can no longer espouse or impose universal principles on each and every child's learning schema without "going a piece" to know them. I am also finding that I am unable to teach a prescriptive lesson with the same confidence I once had that its channel of information will be appropriate for all children, in all contexts. Further, the music that was once described by some well-intentioned but remote-from-the-field curricular specialist as "the music every child should know" may not necessarily be fitting for children of every time and setting; other musical styles, particular pieces, and songs may emerge to take the place of some "canonized" repertoire.

As conscientious efforts are put forward for the sake of developing children's musical knowledge, it seems logical that attention is paid at the outset to what children already know and can do "on their own turf." Children are surprisingly accomplished listeners, creators, and performers and should be recognized as the source and the launch of designs for their musical education. Perhaps, by listening to the children who, while at play, are at least briefly beyond the direct influence of adults, teachers may be able to extend from what music the children manifest to the musical knowledge, skills, and values they can add to their young lives.

2
On Music:
Conversations
with Children

A Flexible System

Talk about music is a fact of life. Where there's music, there are people who talk about what it sounds like, how it feels, what it does, who makes it, and how (well) they make it. Further, as musical talk is a constant, it can also be studied. In 1979, Hugo Zemp suggested that "the ways people talk about music can be a significant datum of musical concepts, theory, and experience" (p. 29). In 1990, Jean-Jaques Nattiez laid out in *Music and Discourse* principles for the semiotic analysis of words about music. He claimed that through the "interaction between the ethno-information and analytical tools of the researcher," a thorough study of music could be had (p. 194). Words are documents of the ideas of those who make, listen to, and think about music, so they have been deconstructed, interpreted, and fit back together again, all in an attempt to understand music in its most comprehensive ways.

Yet despite interest in the application of a semiotics approach to music, children's discourse has not been the subject of much study. This is not surprising, for ethnomusicologists who employ semiotics will go for the "core," the central repertory of a culture, as it is made and thought by adults. Children are not typically bearers of the sophisticated traditions of an ethnic culture and are often—and inaccurately—deemed to be in early stages of musical enculturation and beginners in their musical training.[1] On the other hand, children constitute a separate (if broad) age culture, one that has been studied for years by educators and a fair sampling of psychologists and sociologists.[2] They are bearers of their own traditions and are sampling, retaining, or discarding the music that is within their environment. They are the products of the casual seepage of adult music or its formal transmission by adults, even as they also know their own repertoire of songs given them by other children or intended by adults for children.

As children are linked to age-based, religious, and ethnic cultures, they talk about the music and musical experiences that are important to them as members of these cultural groups. Using techniques that have been employed by Western scholars to study the music and culture of "other worlds"—Japan, India, and the Yoruba of Nigeria, for example—children and their music can be examined. Their musical works (both those they create and those composed or mediated works they accept, preserve, and transmit), their musical practices, and their words are worthy of careful attention. I chose to explore here their words on music, and a few of their musical behaviors and works as well. Perhaps the benefits of such explorations are, as Clifford Geertz had declared, "to aid us in gaining access to the conceptual world in which our subjects live" (1973, p. 24). What children say may at least partly reveal what children think.

In launching my conversations with children, I had in mind a set of global concerns. Issues which intrigued me, and for which I sought children's own words to enlighten me, included their expressed functions and uses of music, their aware-ness of the musical events within their home and school environments, their per-ceptions of their musical selves as singers and instrumentalists. I was curious about the means by which they received music at home—live or mediated, how they might explain their formal and informal methods of learning music, and how they might define music or particular musical styles. As well, I wanted to probe their own conscious efforts to create music and to understand something of the content of this music. I hoped to discover something of their musical needs and desires, partly by stimulating them to dream aloud their intentions to purchase musical "things." Children's own assessments of their musical studies at school were of interest to me, including indications of their reactions to specific types of instructional activities. Finally, I was curious to know something of children's long-range sense of how music would fit their lives.

In my view, any of these global concerns could be abandoned if the course of the conversation became redirected by a child's own expressed interests. I was unwilling to rigidly adhere to my set of guiding questions if a child was vague or uninterested in particular topics, or if he or she had other ideas to share concerning music. Sometimes I sensed that the guiding questions simply triggered the conver-sation or covered me when there were long lulls. I felt that the course of the dialogue could waver and zigzag some, as the spirit moved the child. Charles Keil's "idiographic" approach is relevant; like him, I was interested in the singular musical worlds of people, the unique configurations of music's meanings that vary from one child to the next (1994). Like him, I was willing to sacrifice some structure for children's substantive thoughts on a supposed "tangent." Perhaps such an approach cannot be deemed as highly scientific, nor precise or verifiable. Still, there was a system, albeit a flexible one, in which I worked on engaging children in these conversations.

In a search for the lived musical experiences of children, my probing might be seen as akin to some aspects of phenomenology. In this approach, the individual person (rather than a sample of the population, a school, or a culture) is the unit of analysis, and the lived experience of the individual as he or she tells it is examined as much as a text or description might be analyzed and interpreted (Heidegger, 1978). Phenomenology suggests that a phenomenon such as music can be investigated as it presents itself to the consciousness of the listening, performing, creating individual (Stewart and Mickunas, 1990). The interview is commonly employed to stimulate the reflections of the individual on experiences he or she has known, thus tapping in on streams of consciousness that come forward. Questions are optional or at least not rigidly adhered to, for interviews are intended to explore issues that may not have been preplanned but which may be operating in powerful ways within the life of the individual. Phenomenology allows the scrutiny of a single case—or a collection of single cases—for the purpose of understanding the lived experiences of the individual, as well as gaining deep knowledge of a whole people, a culture, and an epoch (Sartre, 1981). As in the view of phenomenologists, I saw each child with whom I conversed as incomparable and unclassifiable (van Maanen, 1990). I also reasoned that through the study of the personal revelations of each child, I might better understand the meaning of music in children's lives as a whole.

The fifteen conversations are dialogues between the selected children and myself, conducted over a period of sixteen months. They volunteered to talk with me, or were selected by their music or classroom teachers rather randomly (my only criterion, voiced to the teachers, was that the children be verbal, and able and willing to speak with me); I did not request musically interesting (or interested) students, or those that the teacher might deem "talented." The children knew that I was a music teacher, and a few knew that I was a visitor from the university. The fifteen children were drawn from mostly urban, a few suburban, and one small-town setting, yet all reside within forty miles of a large American metropolis. These children are between four and twelve years of age, with all but one preschool child enrolled in public elementary schools. They represent a variety of socioeconomic and ethnic-cultural groups and are a fair balance of both genders.

The fifteen were chosen from a pool of sixty-two taped interviews, sometimes because of topics I raised that children could articulate in coherent and clever ways, and other times simply because of novel views that they expressed.[3] I did not attempt to "stack the deck" by including only children who studied a musical instrument or who elaborated on their undying need for music in their lives. Rather, I wanted to present children that might reflect a wide gamut of musical attitudes and interests. I readily admit that such a selection process may appear messy to the more scientifically inclined, but I was pleased to exchange scientific rigor for the opportunity to present a handful of children who expressed their musical lives in fresh and fascinating ways.

Our conversations generally began with questions directed toward vital statistics, in order to discover a child's age, grade level, and family membership. Often, questions were soon directed toward knowing music's role in their lives: what they thought of it, how they used it, whether they viewed it as prominent. I attempted to be impartial to whatever opinions they offered, asking about but not becoming involved in the sentiments they shared, yet I recognize times in which I strayed and was drawn into the flow of the conversation or could not help myself from responding in teacherly fashion, voicing enthusiastic approval. Some conversations concluded in twenty or thirty minutes, while others noted here are the results of several visits. The dialogues may appear raw, although it should be noted that, in the interest of staying relevant to musical matters, they are sometimes scaled down from what I viewed as ramblings too far afield from musical centerpoints.[4] In a number of instances, I received quite explicit information about the children, their families and home environments, and their academic accomplishments and social behaviors at school through remarks made by their teachers, parents, or even siblings. These bits of information I was able to add to the opening descriptions, or to infuse within my own commentaries that follow. I admit to changing names of people and places in order to protect the identity of children, their teachers, and their families.

All interviews with children were audiotaped and field-noted. I converted all jottings and descriptions of children, the school, the neighborhood, and circumstances of the individual interviews into a draft of what transpired almost immediately, in most cases, but always within the first few days following the visit. Transcriptions of the tapes occurred somewhat later, sometimes a few weeks or even as much as several months past the interview. I chose to transcribe the taped interviews myself so that I could "jog" my memory of the child and be able to add my own margin notes for consideration. I was seeking to practice "inscription," defined by Clifford Geertz (1973) as the writing down of social discourse in order to turn it from a passing event into an account that I could consult later. These conversations *are* events, yet the commentaries are my attempts to clarify, interpret, or settle in to particular issues that were brought forward during the course of the interviews. The ideas I raised in the commentaries are not all-inclusive; another reader may find other moments in these conversations more worthy of contemplation. These commentaries are merely my own "spins," and they may help to launch others as well.[5]

The fifteen conversations are indeed "slices of life." They are glances at musical children at isolated points in time, each conversation its own "punctuated equilibrium point" (Frisch, 1990). I think they are too rich for the data reduction that is typical of social science research, although some patterns that emerge from this mosaic are worthy of our consideration and will be taken up in the reflections section that follows these conversations. But before seeking out the similarities of music thinking among this cross section of children, melding them into some type of monolithic archetype, these conversations need to be approached as they are intended: as portraits of individual children, unique and many-splendored as each child can be.

The Conversations

Michael

Mozart and trains are like each other: they're both fast, and they have clon-ductors [sic].

Michael is a second-year veteran of Firststeps, a combination day care–preschool in an urban neighborhood of renovated Victorian homes. He is four, a constant fiddler who wiggles and scoots, punching or bouncing a small pillow as he talks. A towhead even in early spring, his blond hair is bleached nearly white and is gathered in a small curly tail at the back. He was dressed in blue corduroy pants and a sweatshirt imprinted with trains. We were seated in the library, a small area near the entrance to the house-turned-school, blocked from the door by a low bookshelf. The library is stacked with soft blankets, pillows, and plush toys. Despite the coming and going of other children through the door, Michael appeared intent on telling me his ideas about music.

His teachers call Michael "the chatterbox" of the preschool group of eight children, not only for the rapid pace of his commentaries on cars, trains, dragons, and dinosaurs but also for the somewhat advanced vocabulary he boasts. Over the forty-five minutes I spent with him, he peppered his explanations with polysyllabic words like "recognize," "enormous," and "beautiful." His father is a junior partner in a law firm in the city, and his mother is an intensive care nurse at a nearby hospital.

Our conversation began somewhat musically. Michael had been playing with a hand-sized friction car when I arrived, and as we settled onto pillows, he found a large book over which he pushed the car continuously. The friction motor took on a pattern, "♩ ♩ ♩ ♪", to which he spoke the words "push that car," first soft and then louder with each repetition. Only when I began to chant "Mi-chael, hi" did he look up. He released the car, grabbed a pillow, and began to respond to my questions.

Q: Do you like music?
A: Yes, because it's usually so sweet. Especially when my mommy sings. *He hugged the pillow like a toy bear, slowly rocking it.*
Q: What kind of songs does she sing?
A: Well, lots. But "Bluebird, Go through My Window" is about my favorite.

His singing began well below middle C and sounded a bit gravelly, but it was in tune.

Blue-bird, blue-bird go through my win-dow. Blue-bird, blue-bird go through my win-dow.

Q: Is music ever not sweet?

A: Sure. But then I don't like it so much. Like when it's loud and low, and the bats and skeletons come out. Then it's not sweet; it's scary. *His teacher later explained that the children had watched* Fantasia *the day before on the classroom VCR player; thus, this was his reference to the segment of "Night on Bald Mountain."* Whenever I hear *that* music, I recognize it, and I see that enormous man with his huge black wings.

Q: Do you ever make music, yourself?

A: I'm a singer, like my mommy.

Q: What do you sing?

A: Favorite songs. "The Cat Goes Fiddle-I-Fee" and "Mulberry Bush." Let's see. Um, "Loop-Dee-Loo." I sing for myself, or for the people in my trains. One of my best songs is the Thomas-the-Train song. It goes (*he proceeded to demonstrate some of its melody, singing on* doo):

doo doo doo doo...

But don't ask me to sing anything from Barney. I don't watch him.

Q: I won't. Do you have any musical instruments?

A: I have a recorder, and a harmonica. We have a piano, too. And now I'm a violinist, but my mother isn't. *He had just begun to study violin with a Suzuki teacher; he had had four lessons.*

Q: What can you play on the violin?

A: Nothing, yet. But I could, if my teacher would let me. She's teaching me to hold the violin, and how to stand in a resting position, and to shake hands like this. *He took my hand and shook it up and down in the initial Suzuki rhythm of* "Mississippi hot dog": ♩♩♩♩ ♩ ♩ .

Q: Do you like violin music?

A: Sure. I play my violin tape when I go to bed at night. Or my mommy puts on my *real* favorite, Mozart's Fantasy. It makes me dream beautiful dreams. *This tape,* Mozart's Magic Fantasy *(Classical Kids, 1990), presents the story of a little girl and dragon who meet up with characters from* The Magic Flute; *much of the opera's music is excerpted through the story.*

Q: Do you want to be a violinist when you grow up?

A: Oh, sure. I would like to be an orchestra player, and maybe a clonductor [*sic*]. *He pointed to the train engines scattered across the front of him.* Trains have clonductors, too. You know, music and trains are like each other: They're both fast, and they have clonductors. Once, I wanted to be a train clonductor.

Q: Does your father make music?

A: He can't play any instruments. But we like to play our tapes together. He gets to listen to Willie Nelson, and then it's my turn to play *The Lion King*. Then he chooses Willie Nelson again. Willie's from Texas, like my dad. *He was punching the pillow as he spoke.*

Q: So you like Willie Nelson?

A: When I'm with my dad, I like him. I recognize all of Willie's songs, anywhere I hear them. When I'm with my mom, we listen to all the others— *Mozart's Fantasy,* my violin tape, and my favorite songs. And when the whole family is together, we listen to things like "Peter, Paul, and Mommy." Do you know "I Know an Old Lady Who Swallowed a Fly"? They do it funny. *He sang a verse of it, fast and loud.*

I know an old la-dy she swal-lowed a fly.   I don't know why she swal-lowed a fly. Per-

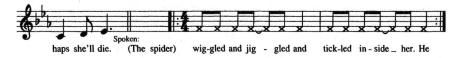

haps she'll die.   (The spider)   wig-gled and jig - gled and   tick-led in - side _ her. He

He chanted the last two-measure phrase three times, tapping his lap as he rhythmically spoke the words; each repetition was louder than the one before.

Q: If you could have any musical thing in the world, what would it be?

A: A violin. One that's big as me, and shiny, and that Ms. Lee would let me play. *He pretended to bow as he sang a melody based on the opening Suzuki "Twinkle" pattern.*

Commentary

The multiple channels through which Michael receives music are revealing of the diverse musical environment provided him by his home and family. The sources of Michael's music include his mother's singing (whether directed to him or not), musical selections and themes from videotapes and TV programs, and tapes of his father's own musical preferences. His musical diet is a blend of children's and adult's music, and folk songs, Western classical, and country styles. More than mere exposure, Michael's early musical experiences are allowing him to develop sensitivity to structures in several musical "languages" or styles. Regardless of the music he may embrace later in life, these musical sounds will undoubtedly stay with him. These are Michael's own musical wellsprings.

His mother's remembrances of such Anglo-American pearls as "Bluebird," "Bought Me a Cat," "Mulberry Bush" and "Looby Lou" have already brought him a small repertoire of tuneful melodies. These songs are many generations old and could well be the songs his mother herself learned orally in her own childhood (and which she has likely passed on to her son in that same oral tradition). Michael gave no mention of the games or movement that accompany these songs, but even as melodies and verse, they are valuable to him as favorite songs.

The traditional children's songs, sung live by his mother, are in direct contrast to the music his father chooses: the mass-mediated music of commercially produced tapes of popular country music. Michael's potential interest in country music in the years ahead may well be kindled by a seemingly casual yet consistent pattern of trading musical turns—sharing favorite tapes—with his father. When he spoke of liking Willie Nelson in the presence of his father, Michael may have been demonstrating the powerful influences of his father's preferences on his own. Both mother and father have claimed their musical territory and are active in the provision of their own personal interests to Michael's musical development.

Television and videotapes are vying for Michael's attention and receiving it. It is somewhat astounding to witness the staying power of Walt Disney's cinema classic *Fantasia*. Almost fifty years after its production, children like Michael are still entranced by the visual images that were conjured up by animators who could visually realize the structures and ideas of some of the great symphonic masterworks. Likewise, the animated series of *Shining Time Station* (featuring Thomas the Tank Engine) is a current favorite among preschool children, particularly boys, and its theme can be heard daily as a sign for the start and close of each morality story at the railroad yard. He mentioned no other television programs, yet there are also the themes and background sounds of other programs that may be sounding even as he devotes his direct attention to other playful experiences.

Michael's collection of cassette tapes are clearly important to him. *Mozart's Magic Fantasy* is one of a series of tapes produced by Classical Kids (including *Beethoven Lives Upstairs, Mr. Bach Comes to Call, Hallelujah Handel, Vivalidi's Ring of Mystery,* and *Tchaikovsky Discovers America*), which wrap the music of composers into a story about the composer or one of his works. Even by themselves and without the employ of the teacher's guides (Susan Hammond's *Classical Kids Teacher's Notes,* Toronto: The Children's Group) that are now available, these tapes offer children a taste of symphonic, chamber, vocal, and choral works by some of the most highly regarded composers of all time. With a tape recorder in his bedroom—and a selection of parent-approved children's tapes—Michael is able to receive music at bedtime or at play—be it Mozart; Peter, Paul, and Mary; or the melodies of his first volume of Suzuki music. The music selected by Michael's parents has clearly become Michael's music, particularly when he is making his own independent selections.

Repertoire aside, several of Michael's musical responses are noteworthy. Without provocation, Michael chose to sing several songs or song segments rather than describe them verbally—or to stop short of a complete response. His vocal range was lower, and, in the case of "Bluebird," dramatically lower, than the notated songs in children's song collections. Perhaps his mother sings in a low range and he is at home with her tonality, timbre, and tessitura. The "Thomas" theme, performed by a male singer, reached to a G below middle C in Michael's own performance of it, while even his rendition of the third song ("I Know an Old Lady") sat in a tessitura not frequently found before the age of eight or nine years. It is intriguing that while there are characteristic ranges for children's vocal development (Phillips, 1992), there are always exceptions. (On the other hand, if a song is perceived by a child as heightened speech, he may sing in the lower range of his speaking voice rather than to use the high head-tone pitches.) That he was able to sing in tune and in the same tonality from one phrase to the next is clear indication of Michael's somewhat accelerated stage of musical growth. Given the rich musical stimulation he is receiving at home—and, now, through the violin lessons he has begun—Michael's musical progress may well continue to exceed that of his contemporaries.

♫ ♫

Darryl
Mostly I just sing at special times, like when I'm happy because my family is all together, and we eat, and we sing, and we watch TV.

Darryl is a five-year-old kindergartener at Sloane Elementary School, a two-story brown-brick building in a middle-class neighborhood at the northern reaches of the city. The community's homes are small, sixtyish ranches and bungalows, some with hedges concealing their front lawns, others with small flower beds lining their walkways, and most with cement drives leading to attached garages. There are few stores or businesses in the vicinity, just street after winding street of homes interspersed here and there with a small park or greenway. Many of the residents are African Americans employed in professional and managerial positions, although white families live in a section that borders the city's historic botanical gardens. Sloane is "90 percent minority," principally African American, but with a sprinkling of Latino and Southeast Asian children as well. Darryl's mother is a fifth-grade teacher, and his father supervises a dry cleaning service. They live separately, but amicably, according to Darryl's kindergarten teacher.

Darryl wears his brown curly hair very short, and his light brown skin is without blemish. His Western-styled plaid shirt is tucked into jeans which in turn are tucked into brown cowboy boots. A pair of red suspenders completes his outfit. We were placed in a language arts room regularly used for tutorials for children with reading deficiencies and by "fast-track" children in the intermediate grades who work on the school newspaper. There were six oblong tables, each with six chairs; ours was closest to the window. Shelves of books framed the room, so that the appearance was more one of a library than a classroom. Darryl sat with an impish grin on his face across the table from me at the start, waiting for the musical conversation to begin. He was rapping rhythms with his knuckles and hands, humming and twisting in his seat as I inserted the tape to record him.

Q: What's music all about for you, Darryl?

A: Oh, you play you know those wood boxes that have brown bars that you hit.

Q: Xylophones. How do you hit them?

A: You hit them with mallets, hard mallets, and you hit them bars hard. Mallets are sticks with knobs on them. You have to learn how to play the xylophones, and Mrs. Matthews the music teacher shows you how. You hold the mallets like this—not like this. *He pulled two pencils out of his pockets. Holding one pencil in each hand, he rested his arms on the table, elbows out, and pressed the pencils' eraserheads together, point to point. His demonstration of an inappropriate performance position was with elbows close to his sides, the pencils parallel.* It's head to head. That's how. Then you start by hitting high C, and then maybe you play low C, and then the other bars. Did you know that some mallets have yellow yarn on them? But I like to play the ones with the wooden knobs.

Q: I see. So music is about xylophones, right? What else is music about, Darryl?

A: It's about stuff you do. Like drums, big and little drums. We mostly have little drums at school.

Q: What can you play on the drums?

A: I played lots of songs. Like "Mary Had a Little Lamb." It goes like this. *He sang on* loo *and* lee, *tapping the rhythm of the melody on the table with his index fingers. His rhythm was good, but the tonality rose or fell from one phrase to the next.*

lee loo loo loo loo loo loo   loo loo loo   loo loo loo

Q: Thank you for singing. So you like music at school?

A: Sure. Because it's fun. Especially when we go to the gym. I like the song "Monster Mash." We did it in the gym. We were jumping over the big orange cones, stepping around them, and marching in between them. And then the Ghostbusters was on, too. The music goes on and we get wild. *Later, I confirmed my suspicions that Darryl had confused physical education with music class. The two classes overlapped in his mind, perhaps because both are taught outside his regular classroom, and both feature music.*

Q: What about at home? Do you ever play music at home?

A: My sister Denita does. She's nine and in Mrs. Burke's room. She plays one of those things that sound high, with holes in it, where the air comes out.

Q: A flute? A recorder?

A: Yeah, a recorder. And Phonecia, my really big sister—she's twelve—she plays one of those long instruments, like a tube, that you put sticks in at the top. It sounds like a horn. *He lowered his voice, and moaned more like a cow than a horn—let alone a clarinet.*

Q: Is it called a clarinet?

A: Yeah. She puts her mouth on the sticks. She gets it wet by licking it, and then she puts it in this little holder, and screws it on the top. *He pantomimed the entire sequence as he spoke.*

Q: Do you ever play your sisters' instruments?

A: Not Phonecia's. But Denita lets me play. I can do "Jingle Bells."

Q: Could you do it for me? *When he nodded yes, I pulled out of my bag a recorder that was left over from a class I had taught earlier that day. He took it, pushed back his chair from the table, sat tall in his chair, and began to play. The melodic rhythm was accurate, but he did not have a sense of the blowing technique nor how to finger the instrument in any systematic way. Most of the pitches were the same: They had the high and squeaky quality of overblown tones.*

Q: Thanks for playing. Are you a singer, too?

A: Yes, I am. I also dance to my sisters' music. And to *The Lion King*. I always do. I like the part when Simba grows up, when he runs after Rafiki—the guy with the magic. I like when the wildebeests come. It sounds like thunder and lightning. There are drums, and those big banjo-things, and the harp. And Rafiki wipes Simba off when he just made him, on the tree.

Q: Maybe you mean stringed bass. They look a bit like big banjos.

A: Giant banjos.

Q: OK. And what do you sing?

A: *Lion King* songs. But also "Rock-a-bye baby, in the tree forest. *He sang slightly off pitch, but the melodic contour was there.* I forget it. But my mom, she sings that when she rocks me to sleep.

Q: Do you sing at any particular times of day?

A: Yeah. Mostly I just sing at special times, like when I'm happy because my family is all together, and we eat, and we sing, and we watch TV. There's my mommy, my daddy, and my two sisters and me. But my daddy's away a lot.

Q: What do you all sing?

A: Songs my mother knows, and my sisters. We sing commercials, songs from the TV, Christmas songs, "Happy Birthday" sometimes, church songs. I sing Barney songs.

Q: You do? Do you watch him?

A: He's my favorite TV show. He's my favorite animal. A T-rex. He's a dancing and singing dinosaur, too. Do you know his song? *He began a parody of "This Old Man," also known as "Knick Knack Paddywhack." It was very much in tune and in time.*

I love you, You love me, We wil be best friends, you see.

Q: I think I know it. So you must watch Barney pretty often?

A: I used to, when I didn't go to school. This year, I can't watch him so much. But I would if I was home. I like him much more than *Mr. Rogers* and *Sesame Street.* Because he's my favorite animal.

Q: Do you have any musical instruments of your own?

A: I have a toy piano. I can play "Knick Knack Paddywhack." My sister taught me, because she takes piano lessons. Denita does, and Phonecia does. When I get old enough, I'll play drums. Like Mrs. Matthews's drums, with mallets. I would like lots of drums, and I would move from one to the other. I would even play the Barney song on the drums. Like this. *He sang on* doo *the melody of "This Old Man" (or "Knick Knack Paddywhack") again, while tapping his fingers on the table. The rhythm was partly the melodic rhythm, and partly the beat; he fluctuated. I did not get the impression that he was aware that "the Barney song" and "Knick Knack Paddywhack" were the same melody, as he said nothing to that effect, although he had mentioned them in nearly the same breath.*

Q: Why would you rather play that song on the drum than on the table?

A: *He laughed and then, perhaps in his desire to articulate the extent to which he thought my question absurd, chanted a rhythmic response.*

The ta - ble's not an in - stru-ment. Don't you know?

And the top of the drum is light, and the mallet bounces off of it. It's like me on a trampoline. And the sound is much louder on the drum.

Q: Let's pretend your grandmother came and gave you lots of money. How would you spend it on music?

A: Um . . . two drums, and a shirt with little pictures of drums on it. I would buy three clarinets, one for me, one for Denita, and one for my mom. Then we'd have four clarinets in our family. We could all play together. Then I'd buy Barney shoes.

Q: I don't know about these Barney shoes.
A: They have batteries in it. They play Barney songs when you walk.
Q: Do you know any popular musicians, like Janet Jackson?
A: Never heard of her.
Q: No? What about Michael Jackson?
A: Is he on TV? Yeah, sure. I think I've seen him, but I don't *know* him.

Commentary

My first impressions of Darryl as we settled into our seats were not far off the mark of my final assessment. He was a lively child, one who seemed to enjoy music for the complement it offers to his own rhythmic energy. The music within him had come streaming out in some of his responses, as he sang or rhythmically tapped parts of songs or intoned the particularly expressive phrase, "The table's not an instrument." A "chair dance" continued through much of our meeting, with Darryl bouncing, turning, and twisting his body on the seat of his chair, while occasionally letting his hands, fingers, or hands sound a rain of rhythms. Yet even while he danced, he was mostly "on task," keeping his comments fairly focused on the musical issues.

Music permeates Darryl's home life: melodies his sisters play during practice on their instruments, lullabies his mother sings to him at bedtime, and songs that his family remembers when they are together. Clearly, his family values their roles as makers of music. That family gatherings are special to Darryl is poignant, as is his touching explanation of family activities as both cause and effect of his happiness. Their repertoire of TV themes, Christmas carols, and church hymns well may be exemplary of a newer type of "oral tradition" music that has largely replaced "John Henry," "Clementine," and other folk songs of old. Yet this music still transmits orally through the media or from person to person, through many repetitions, a musical heritage with which many Americans identify.

Darryl's view of school music is not only what is featured in music class but also the gym teacher's choice to accompany the physical challenges of rhythmic movement exercises. Recordings like "Monster Mash" and the theme from *The Ghostbusters,* although dated themselves, have replaced an older canon of pieces for rhythmic movement, classics like "In the Hall of the Mountain King" from the *Peer Gynt Suite,* the "Anvil Chorus" from Verdi's *Aida,* marches by John Philip Sousa, or symphonic overtures to once popular movies like *Star Wars* and *Close Encounters of the Third Kind.* Of course, in the early decades of the twentieth century, physical education teachers were trained rather extensively in eurhythmics, dance, and music;[6] through these courses, they developed their own musical sensibilities—and a wider selection of musical materials on which to design their lessons. For teachers with less formal training in music, it is no wonder that most select musical accompaniments to their lessons from personal collections of popular music, or from the "kiddie collections" that commercial companies mass-produce for easy listening entertainment. The development of stronger partnerships among teachers (all-subject classroom teachers and specialist teachers of art, music, or physical education) seems advantageous in many ways, not the least of which is for the purpose of knowing the best choices in instructional resources.

It is true testimony to the concept of idioculture that as Michael is uninterested in *Barney*, Darryl very much identifies with him. The T-rex is Darryl's favorite animal, and this is his stated reason for his attraction to the show and its music. Does Barney's paunchy and pudgy "cuteness" draw children to him? Do Barney's songs, many of them sentimental parodies of traditional children's songs, also provide a "hook" for preschool children that *Mr. Rogers* and *Sesame Street* do not? Children's TV has teetered between education and entertainment aims since television's inception, but the enormous popularity of *Barney* in the early 1990s was clear testimony to the media's power to produce (and the public's willingness to accept) programs with little informational substance that fill (even, "kill") time which children could otherwise spend in more enriching ways. In this case, I am referring not only to the trite musical matter of the *Barney* program, but also to the banalities of plot and characters that comprise the shows. Still, the dinosaur projects a lovable image to young children, so much so that it would seem reasonable for parents and teachers to advocate that his producers develop in him a greater intelligence. Barney might be refashioned in order to motivate his millions of children to share in ideas that reach beyond his "cotton candy" persona.

By extension, greater monitoring of children's shows at large for their educational content should be an adult responsibility. The advent of the V-chip (Denby, 1996) and TimeSlot (DeGaetano and Bander, 1996), both intended to block particular shows and viewing times from children, will aid in this monitoring. The recent rating system devised by the television industry is intended to guide parents in the selection of children's programs; Labels are assigned to programs based on the extent of violence, sex, and offensive language contained within them (TV-Y, all children; TV-Y7, children seven years and older; TV-G, general audience, including children; and another three labels that designate parental guidance, parental caution, and mature audiences only).[7] But I also dream that parents could have access to an "LCD-file," a directory to children's programs of sentimental drivel for the "lowest common denominator"—that is, programs of the most passive sort with little educational value for children. Parents would consult the list, then find other things for their children to do rather than patronizing these programs and their products.

Like many young children, Darryl is intrigued with musical instruments. His descriptions are uniquely colorful and show his interest in the way in which musical sounds are produced. He has learned from his music class experiences: he understands the function of mallets on xylophones, differentiates between the soft and hard mallets (and has his preference for the latter), can model the appropriate playing position, and discriminates high C from low C. He also knows from observation that a drum struck by a mallet will create a louder sound than the surface of a table, and he has observed the effect of the mallet bouncing lightly off the head of a drum. His pantomime of preparing a clarinet for performance, complete with the wetting of the reed "sticks," is further evidence of his intense interest in instruments and their music. Darryl is motivated to play, and there ought to be a way to harness his strong interest. For a child who talks a great deal about drums, and who would buy with his grandmother's money "drums, and a shirt with little pictures of drums on it," holding off on instruction until the traditional age of nine or so (typically in the fourth grade) seems a long stretch for Darryl, who would find lessons gainful *now*.

Darryl's singing ability is similar to that of many children his age, in which tonality between melodic phrases wavers some, although melodic contour is in place. His rendition of "Knick Knack Paddywhack" was far better than his "Mary Had a Little Lamb" or "Rock-a-Bye, Baby," perhaps due to more extensive exposure to the first melody through the Barney parody, his sister's playing of it, and his own casual attempts to play it on his toy piano. Such an outcome demonstrates how repeated listening and practice hones skills, even for one so young as Darryl. What he may have lacked in pitch accuracy, he most surely made up for in his ability to keep the pulse or to tap or play a melody's rhythm. Musical traits do not necessarily develop side by side, or hand in hand, and one (in this case, rhythm) may lead to another (melody) in the final assessment. For Darryl, it is too early to tell, and he has a few years before his musical talents blossom fully. In the meantime, his continued singing, "playing" of rhythms, and listening can be nurtured while these traits develop and mature.

♫ ♫

George

So with whistling, you've got to change tones once in a while, and with drumming, you've got to change from just all shorts to longs and shorts. That's when it's music, and not just sound.

George is "six years and two months old" and "right at the end of kindergarten" at a modern suburban school at the far east side of the city. The homes there are bi- and trileveled, many with large glass windows for viewing the blue-green lake, with its lining of colorful sailboats. As a result of his parents' divorce, George spends alternate weeks at his mother's lakeside home and his father's condominium across town. His mother is employed in computer sales, and his father Kevin is an electrician who plays guitar in an occasional country-western band.

George has long sandy hair that hangs loosely in waves; they frame his fresh, round face. He smiles a wide smile easily and often, revealing missing teeth in four places. He wears a navy blue wool sweater with a green turtleneck under it, green denim pants, and a horse on his silver belt buckle. His shoes are brown leather, slightly scuffed, with two Velcro-strip fasteners. We sat cross-legged on the floor just outside the music room and were undisturbed by the light traffic between classes. Once the voices of singing children came wafting out as the door opened to admit two latecomers to music class, but the acoustics of that room were of sufficient quality to muffle most of the musical sounds during the remainder of our conversation. We spoke for just thirty minutes, but he kept on a musical track for most of the period.

Q: Do you live near here?

A. A little bit, because I live in two houses. One, I live far. One, I live close. Because my parents are divorced. My father is the one who lives far. Actually, I have two dads, my dad Kevin and my dad Bob. *He seemed to be waiting for a reaction from me, or for further questions regarding the marital status of his parents, but I turned to the subject of his houses instead.*

Q: So you live in two houses.

A: Uh-huh. I spend a week and a week: one week with my dad Kevin in his condo, and one week with my mother and my dad Bob in their house. Back and forth. I have my own bedroom in each place. I have one baby brother at my mother's house, but I'm the only kid at my dad Kevin's. I've been living in two places since kindergarten, since I was five. It works pretty well, and I have loads of toys in both places.

Q: Do any of your toys make music?

A: *He hesitated, then chuckled.* My puppets make music, when I tell them to. They need me to supply them with songs. And there's a piano at my mom's. It's flat, and you can set it on the floor or on a desk or table. It's a plug-in type. It's just got black and white keys, maybe about forty of them.

Q: What do you play on the piano?

A: I sometimes play "Old MacDonald," or I can make up some of my own music. But I don't have words to my music. Nobody knows my music but me. *Again he chuckled, and then formed his thumbs and forefingers into large Os, which he placed around his eyes like a pair of binoculars.* Sorry. You can look and look for these songs, but you won't find them. And I can't let you hear these songs. What I mean is, they're *private. He cupped his hands to his mouth before speaking the last phrase.*

Q: So I shouldn't expect you to share them with me?

A: Not if they're private.

Q: Do you have any other musical instruments?

A: Well, first of all there are guitars. My dad Kevin and my dad Bob play. They don't play together, because they don't live together. My mother married my dad Kevin, then they broke up because they didn't get along too good. My dad Bob doesn't play too good, but my dad Kevin does. He plays in a band. He has a black and white guitar, and a bass guitar. I like the bass guitar because it sounds strong when he plugs it in. And I want to always listen to it in my chair, with ear muffs. It feels cool.

Q: Lots of music in your life.

A: Yes, and I have whistles, six of them. They're not the "toot-toot" kind, but the kind that go high to low and low to high when you slide the silver stick. *He demonstrated the movement of the metal rod on his imaginary slide whistle, alternately raising and lowering the pitch of his voice on* whoo *as he imitated the movement.* I love the *feeling* of music, especially when it goes from low to high. It makes my tummy tickle, kind of like going up on a rolley [*sic*] coaster. I also have two harmonicas, one in a box and one without a box. They're about this big. *He framed a space of about three inches wide with his hands.*

Q: How do you play the harmonica?

A: Oh, you go *zhee zhaw zhee zhaw. He was puffing his cheeks and chest in an out and releasing great amounts of breath as he spoke the syllables.* I can't really make the sound: it's thicker than whistles. The thing that's neat about harmonicas is that you can blow in or out and still get a sound. With the whistle, the only time you get a sound is when you blow out. That's because the harmonica has a metal piece inside that moves every time you breathe on it, and when it moves, it makes music. So you have to remember to suck in, and not just to blow out. *He repeated his earlier* zhee-zhaw *demonstration.* I painted one of them red.

Q: How did you learn how to play the harmonica?

A: I just figured it out. I like to play some of the Michael Jackson songs. When he comes on TV, I just get my harmonica and dance around and play with him. He doesn't play harmonica, of course, but it could fit, anyway.

Q: Is Michael Jackson one of your favorite musicians?

A: Well, I like the way he dances. It's not easy to sing and dance at the same time, but it's important to do both if you want to be a good musician. I usually dance when he comes on—his music just makes you want to. It takes coordination to dance *and* sing, but since I can play the harmonica and dance, I should be able to sing and dance, too. My dad, Kevin, you know, even saw Michael Jackson, for real, one time. He can dance, my dad, jumping up, doing the splits, sliding his feet along.

Q: When you sing, what do you sing?

A: I sing "Abiyoyo." I learned it at my preschool, and I love the story even now. I also know "Puff, the Magic Dragon." I close the door to my room, and I play the tapes for these songs, and sing along. You might say that I practice these songs. I do. How much do these big tape recorders cost? *He pointed to my tape recorder but did not wait for a response.* I'm saving my money and would really like a larger and louder tape recorder. Starting this week, I get two instead of one allowance. All I have to do is take out the trash, dry the dishes, and sometimes walk the dog. I get two dollars a week. I get two dollars at my dad's, too, just to clean up my room. What I really want is a tape recorder with a radio in it. And a CD. And more tapes, probably, and CDs. But I'd also like more whistles.

Q: Can you whistle without an instrument?

A: Of course. Some people whistle with two fingers in their mouth. *He demonstrated, barely inserting his fingers, and produced a windy sound with no pitch. As if to apologize, he explained,* I'm still learning.

Q: Do you think whistling is music?

A: Yes. But whistling comes from yourself, like singing. Instrument music is different, because it's not really sound coming first from yourself: it's sound through metal pieces, or wooden parts. So whistling and singing are close music, and instrument music is kind of far from yourself.

Q: Can you describe the whistling sound?

A: Now, the whistling I'm talking about is not just a straight sound *(he whistled on one pitch)* or the wavy "chirp-chirp" sound of a bird. That's just sound. Whistling music has to go to different highs and lows. *He gestured with his hands the highs and lows of the melody he was whistling.* All music needs to have highs and lows.

Q: Can drums make music?

A: Well, in the case of drums, music has to do with longs and shorts. Drums that just bang . . .

. . . on and on are not really making music. A loud clock can do that. Drums make music when you have something like this:

So with whistling, you've got to change tones once in a while, and with drumming, you've got to change from just all shorts to longs and shorts. That's when it's music, and not just sound. *He shook his head, obviously pleased with his explanation, and awaited my approval.*

Q: How do you know all this?

A: I figure it out. I listen and figure it out.

Q: So do want to learn to play instruments one day?

A: Well, I really want to make instruments. Like at my dad's, I can go to his tool shop and make things. I'm making a whistle now, with a white plastic tube and a thing that will slide inside. I also am making a flute from a wooden tube. I'm drawing the holes, so that my dad can drill them open. And next week, I'm going to make wind chimes. I've been watching them getting played in the music class, and they're beautiful. But there's too many kids in my class, and too few times to play, so it's better that I have my own.

Q: Are you learning things in your music class?

A: Hmmm. Well, yeah. Some. I like music class OK. But I've got lots of music right at my two houses.

Commentary

Few young children possess the insights George holds on music and musical instruments. He is musically precocious, a quick learner of the mechanics of musical production via homemade instruments and other instruments in his possession, and clever in his explanations of what sounds constitute music. He spoke with an air of confidence and self-assurance, demonstrating at times skills of logic and articulation that would be the envy of any teacher. His enthusiasm was testimony to his genuine interest in various acoustical qualities of musical sound, and his comments were lucid and made more understandable by an occasional gesture or vocally produced "sound effect."

His father (Kevin) appeared to be an important influence on George's musical interests. The bass guitar Kevin plays offers his son a visceral listening experience, as he vibrates to the low pitches his "ear muffs" receive. The popular dance moves Kevin can execute with finesse are enough to impress George; they have stimulated his son's interest in learning to sing and dance simultaneously. But it is Kevin's tool shop where father and son can collaborate on the creation of the slide whistle, flute, and wind chimes of their dreams, that has provided George with his greatest musical pleasure to date. Perhaps George has seen and heard his father on stage in the act of performing music with his fellow band members (although he did not say); this, too, would be likely to prove a powerful influence on his musical choices. Still, these other influences were undoubtedly shaping the musical ideas and attitudes George holds.

Several of George's comments are of the "stop in your tracks" variety. He referred to his puppets as toys that make music yet teasingly suggested that they can be musical only through his direct assistance. He understood his musical power over them, but he may also have used them as means through which to express himself. Children often play musically with their puppets, singing songs that they would not otherwise sing yet unembarrassed to sound them through their hand-sized musical mediators. Puppets make excellent "props" for timid singers, providing a kind of defense or shield for children who may feel uncomfortable, or even naked, without a little friend through which to send their music. George appeared to know a musical use for his puppets, reflected in his comment that they "need me to supply them with songs."

George's sensitivity to music's physical nature emerged a number of times. As he described the sound of his father's bass guitar, he slipped in the comment that "it *feels* cool." Later, he chose a roller-coaster image to convey the feeling of a tummy tickle as his slide whistle ascends in pitch. Still later, in his description of Michael Jackson's performance style, George emphatically stated that song and dance belong together and that "it's important to do both if you want to be a good musician." His valuing of music is innately connected to its kinesic quality—a sensual feature too often ignored in more cerebral discussions of music's merits. Music has drive and energy that links the ear and mind to the bodily self and that can provide a more encompassing sensation than the purely mental or controlled emotional. It is nonverbal, often unconscious, and physical, as George has fully discovered.

Music can be as personal and private at times, as it is social at other times. George explained that "nobody knows my music but me." Perhaps he could not recall or name the melodies he plays on the piano, particularly if they are word-less. They are his own songs, unique, and not to be found anywhere else but within him. He appeared to relish the privacy of them and even drew a ring of mystery around them. He might have shared his music with me, but he did not; clearly, it would have been difficult for a six-year-old to share them by describing them. On the other hand, he might truly intend his music to be heard only by him—a statement to be rightfully honored.

Not only was his definition of music revealing of a thoughtful child (sounds that "change tones" and that consist of "longs and shorts"), but equally so were his views on instrumental music ("sound through metal pieces, or wooden parts") and on whistling and singing (sound that "comes from yourself"). George further extended his separation of instrumental music from whistling and singing by call-ing the latter "close music" and describing the former as distant ("kind of far from yourself"). From this point, he led to a discussion of different kinds of whistles (straight, wavy like the chirping of a bird, and the more musical highs and lows that he perceives the slide whistle to be capable of making). When asked how he had arrived at these rather profound thoughts, George did not hesitate to respond: "I listen and figure it out." His explanations were a revelation of how well a young child can reason, how logically he can think.

His only mention of music at school was a comment that saddens the heart. George has fallen in love with the sound of wind chimes but, as is too typical, had not had much opportunity to play them in a class with few instruments, lim-ited time, and many children. On the bright side, he saw that his was an abundant musical life "in his two houses" away from school, providing him with a certain fulfillment in his early life. At least for now, there are avenues beyond school for

George to take in serving his own musical interests; would that others could have such opportunities on the outside.

𝄞 𝄢

Carrie
Some music helps the stories along. Like I might be more frightened of the dinosaurs in *Jurassic Park* when I hear the powerful music that plays on it.

Described by her first-grade teacher as "precocious," six-year-old Carrie is an unusually tall girl, big-boned and strong, yet graceful. She wears her brown hair in a braid that is wrapped around itself at her neck, with short, curly wisps that frame her light brown face. Carrie speaks through the gap left by the two front teeth she has recently lost, and her bright eyes are expressive of the events and emotions she conveys. Her blue wool jumper is accented by a gold turtleneck shirt and gold tights, a fitting outfit for the brisk autumn day it is.

Carrie's mother volunteers as one of the school's handful of reading aides. She, too, is a large African American woman, gregarious, who laughs easily. She spoke to me once of the hardship the family has endured since her husband, an aeronautics engineer, was paralyzed in a car accident two years earlier. "The children have coped well," she concluded, "and Carrie has become her father's best friend. 'C'est la vie', Carrie says, and we've all learned to adjust to our new life, amazingly so." Education and schooling are important in this family, if judged alone by the M.A. and Ph.D. degrees held by Carrie's mother and father.

The school in which we met is a low and sprawling building with three wings, built during the development of this middle-class suburb in the late 1960s. A bit worn through its three decades of use, the halls and rooms were covered with indoor-outdoor carpeting on floors and halfway up the walls, muting the ambient sound while also providing a sense of uniformity and coalescence throughout the building. Carrie and I met on the ramp to the back door of the music room, concealed from those who pass by a four-foot wall. We sat side by side on the floor, leaning our backs against this wall and stretching our legs out to the full wall we faced. While this made eye contact more difficult, Carrie turned toward me each time she wanted to make an especially meaningful statement.

Q: Do you like to sing?
A: Yes. Because I like music in general, and because all of my friends sing with me, and because I like Ms. Donaldson. *Ms. Donaldson is the music teacher who meets three times weekly with each of the primary-grade classes.*

Q: Why do you like Ms. Donaldson?

A: Because she's really nice. And she feels like a mama or a brother to me. I like her singing voice. I'm not very good at it, myself, but it helps to hear her sing. I'm good at "Gilead" and "Pizza Pizza Daddy-o." But not all of the songs.

Q: Do you sing in your first-grade class?

A: Well, I know one song that my teacher gave me: "Out in the Garden, the Spider Web." *She turned to me, began to pat a steady beat on her lap, and sang to the melody of "Up on the Housetop."*

Out in the garden, the spider lives.
How much help to the gard'ner he gives!
Capturing insects that crawl and fly,
Ten, twenty, thirty, forty, fifty, oh my.

Spin, spin, spin, building a web.
Spin, spin, spin, eight busy legs.
Out in the garden, looking around,
Capturing insects without a sound.

Her s sounded like th through the space of her missing teeth, and she changed tonalities between phrases, but her tempo did not falter.

Q: How did you learn that song?

A: We practiced it in our class. We're studying spiders, and my teacher always likes to put a poem to a song. And then we take the poem, which turns into a song, home to our family. We're supposed to sing it to them. I do.

Q: So you do sing at home?

A: I do. But my mom doesn't, much. She's mostly nonmusical. She doesn't know as many songs as Ms. Donaldson. My brother sings, and while he doesn't really teach me his songs, I hear them from him, and I can memorize about half of them.

Q: But does your mom ever sing you a lullaby?

A: She did, some, once. But I also have a lullaby tape that I listened to when I was three until I was five, and it always put me to sleep. I could sing those songs to her. They are short songs, but I don't remember them all, except for "La-la-lu" and "Rock-a-Bye, Baby." My mother only sang to me when I was teething.

Q: How do those songs go?

A: You don't know how they go? *Genuine surprise was registered on her face.*

Q: Just get me started. *She sang "Rock-a-Bye, Baby," in tune within and between phrases, and I joined in to sing it with her a second time.*

Q.: What songs does your brother sing?

A: Things he learned from Ms. Donaldson. He's in the sixth grade. I learn parts from lots of songs he sings. He thinks I don't know them, but I do.

Q: What's your favorite song?

A: That's hard to answer. *She laughed.* Lots of them. And I don't really have a favorite TV show, either. Except that I do know a TV show that sings just songs, something like *Wee Sing*—something. But now that the schedule for TV shows changed, I haven't been watching it. When it was on, I sang all the way through the program with them.

Q: Do you like to dance?

A: Well, yes, but just when certain songs come on. Dance music comes in all kinds of ways. My mother doesn't dance at all. She sprang her back—actually, her hip. Well, she almost broke it. But she can walk with a cane pretty good. So if I dance, I might dance with my friends, but not with my mom.

Q: What kind of dance music do you like?

A: *She waited to answer, obviously pondering the question.* That would be hard to answer. I like all kinds, depending on how I feel. You couldn't give me dance music I wouldn't like.

Q: What will you be when you grow up?

A: Well, I like music, but I've been thinking about being a ballerina, but then again, maybe a baseball player. But I was also thinking about being a teacher. Music would be just for fun when I grow up.

Q: How can you become a ballerina?

A: Only with practice. That means if you do it once and you mess up, don't stop, keep doing it. Then you'll be good at it. Lots of things I have to practice— not just dancing like a ballerina. You know, I was also thinking about becoming an artist, or maybe being an actor. *She turned fully toward me for the first time, and I knew she was eager to describe her interest.*

Q: An actor?

A: Because I act really good. I play by myself, with imaginary people.

Q: What kinds of imaginary people?

A: Friends. And I just play by myself, and pretend. I normally pretend that I'm myself, and I pretend that there's different kids in the room. Like maybe Jenny, and Marguerite—because she's in Illinois. Yes, I'm me, but I pretend I'm talking to them. And we go places, like to movies, or sometimes we're the characters in our favorite stories—like the *Madeleine* stories, you know. *She spoke with such certainty that I could not refuse her gaze and merely nodded my agreement.* Mad about Madeleine *is the collection of classic stories of the little Parisian girl and her friends by Ludwig Bemelmans (New York: Viking Press, 1993), a favorite of little girls since 1939.*

Q: Where do you act?

A: In my room. I also listen to music there.

Q: What do you listen to?

A: Normally, I hear music on TV in the family room. But I also take my mom's tape recorder and play *Wee Sing* tapes by myself in my bedroom. *The* Wee

Sing *tapes are a collection of traditional songs of children, from "Row Your Boat" and "Twinkle, Twinkle, Little Star" to "Mary Had a Little Lamb" and "Farmer in the Dell."*

Q: What kind of music do you listen to on TV?

A: There's all kinds of music on TV, on all kinds of shows that we watch. We have a huge TV. There's one movie that my brother and I like, with lots of tunes on it. It's called *Jurassic Park.* It's still like the movie if it didn't have music, but some music helps the stories along. Like I might be more frightened of the dinosaurs in *Jurassic Park* when I hear the powerful music that plays on it. *She made a face, as if she were terrified of some image she had conjured up.*

Q: Let's say that you grandmother gave you $25 to spend on music.

A: Never! I've never had that. The most she ever gave me was $15. See this? *She pointed to the space where her two front teeth had been.* "That's when I got the $15. But if I ever got $25 for music, I would get tunes from some of my favorite videos, like *Jurassic Park.* I'd get my own tape to listen to, because my brother would not like me taking his. He'd kill me. And he's tried to strangle me, anyway, and drag me around the wet schoolground. But I'd also get a trombone, and a flute.

Q: You'd like to play an instrument?

A: Yes. Either one of them, or a saxophone. Did you know that the president of the United States plays a saxophone? But he isn't very good at it. He doesn't practice enough.

Q: Is your father a musician?

A: Actually, he's disabled, and he has to sit in a wheelchair. He really doesn't have time to sing. *She let out a long, audible sigh, and waited a moment before continuing.* He stays at home, but he does go out once in a while with us to movies—the ones on the big screens for the public.

Q: What movies do you see together?

A: Well, I'll tell you one we won't see. *Pocahontas.* Not at all. We don't have one Pocahontas thing in our house. Hmm-mm. *She shook her head in a deliberate way, as if to underscore her disdain.* She had so many gimmicks. She just wasn't very true. It's a real story, except that Pocahontas was younger than the movie, and John Smith really had a beard, and things like that. I've even wondered whether the tunes were for real. I don't think so.

Commentary

Carrie is an unusually expressive young child, both in word and in gesture. She is also clearly attracted to the expressive arts and to thoughts of becoming an artist, actor, or ballerina. She used a variety of tones and inflections in her speech and did not shy away from accenting her words with various facial grimaces of surprise, shock, or disapproval. She seemed pleased to tell something of her world of imaginary people and of her favorite videotape—another imaginary world (of dinosaurs). Yet she was also able to talk about the very real world in which her disabled dad, tempestuous big brother, and "mostly nonmusical" mother live.

It was disconcerting for me to hear a six-year-old child evaluate her own singing as "not very good." Who told her so? Against what models was she judging her own voice? Perhaps her music teacher's, or one of the singers from her tapes, TV shows, or "big screen" movies? Carrie's voice is typical of children her age, soft, in a moderate range within the middle- to high-C octave, in tune within the phrases (although changing tonalities between some of them), and rhythmically steady. Despite her critical assessment of her voice, she did not hesitate to sing and even admitted to singing some songs well—quite possibly some of her favorite songs.

Carrie's teacher's use of poetry and song to teach concepts illustrates music's function as a memory aid and an enhancement to the learning of nonmusical concepts. Not only did she sing the spider song for me, but as she admitted, she took the song, verse, and concept embedded within the verse home to her family, where, according to the teacher's instructions, she performed it. It is intriguing that "Up on the Housetop," a seasonal, composed song, had undergone a transformation to something resembling a folk song, with its transmission by the teacher to her students in the oral tradition. This parody of a familiar song is not unlike children's own playful alteration of verses belonging to patriotic and seasonal songs (for example, the Battle Hymn of the Republic's "Glory, glory, hallelujah! I hit my teacher with a ruler!" See "Riders of the C-Bus" in Part I for other examples of parodies). As parodies are enjoyed by children, they also attract the attention of teachers such as Carrie's who seek provocative ways of stimulating children's grasp of information.

Carrie is a young member of the video generation. Yet despite the visual appeal of her favorite stories on film, she was keenly aware of the "powerful music" that carries these stories. Film music is like the programmatic music of some symphonic poems, its qualities and forms determined by the plots, characters, and events on which the composer may be commenting (Frith, 1988). Carrie is drawn to the programmatic messages of the music and is mesmerized by it.

Another conduit of songs in Carrie's life is her brother. While she clarified that he does not intentionally teach her his songs, she explained that she learns them by listening. Again, the oral/aural learning process is evident: As he sings, she hears, learns, and memorizes song "parts" for half of his repertoire. While this pair of siblings may not always be on the best of terms (note her descriptive words for their relationship—"kill," "strangle," and "drag me around"), Carrie is nonetheless learning a set of songs—and much more—from her older brother.

Among the most striking of the children's comments are two that Carrie made about practice, and music's role in her future. Instead of the more technical definition of practice as "systematic exercise for proficiency," Carrie used words that reflected her own experience. Her definition implied errors she may have made in developing a skill but also underscored her understanding of the concentration and perseverence inherent in practice that eventually leads to the necessary refinement of that skill. That she was able to transfer the meaning of the word from her first mention of it in reference to becoming a proficient dancer, to "lots of things," was an indication of her ability to value and take stock of the discipline inherent in achieving a variety of goals she may be setting for herself.

As for Carrie's remark that "music would be just for fun" in her adult life, I could not have hoped for a more lucid comment on music's meaning in children's lives. Since music can be made even more "fun" through formal training, so that she might be able to know the pleasure of a fuller intellectual understanding of music's many manifestations and the joy of performing these musical styles well, I earnestly hope that there will be a strong and enticing educational program in music available to her. Carrie's astute observations of music, family, school, and popular films (and even the president's lack of musical accomplishment!) are telling signs of a bright and musical child ripe for development.

♫ ♫

Ramnad

I got a check from my grandfather in India, and I'm going to spend it on a whoopee cushion, and a clarinet, and a Mozart tape.

At age "six and three-quarters," Ramnad, or "Ram," is a wisp of a child who is nearing the end of first grade at Waterside School. The school is a two-story building of brown brick, its wide hallways paved with bright red and green tiles and lined with children's art—in cases, on bulletin boards, and covering nearly every space in between. He does not live in the school's affluent neighborhood but is dropped off and picked up daily by his parents, who have selected it for its reputation as a center (although not a magnet school) for science and computers; the city operates on a policy of "school choice." His own neighborhood of modest homes is a blend of first- and second-generation Indians, Koreans, and Eastern European professionals, located about a twenty-minute drive from the school in typical morning traffic. His father is a technician at one of the city's hospitals, and his mother is a civil engineer.

We met at a table at the back of Ram's first-grade classroom: it was recess for his class, but he chose to stay inside to talk. There were quarter- and eighth-note patterns on the blackboard, and ostinati and borduns printed on large sheets of paper and stuck to the walls surrounding us. Even as I was settling into the ambience of the room, Ram had begun talking. He was explaining that his name is Indian, because his dad and mom were born there, "but not me or my brother," yet he was quick to note that "I lived in India when I was two, for ten days." His wide brown eyes were serious, and he remained in a straight—almost rigid— sitting position at the edge of a wooden chair for twenty minutes. Ram looked directly at me as he volunteered information relevant to his musical life, and he seemed almost to anticipate some of my questions. Not only did he begin the conversation; he needed no prodding to carry it to its close.

A: I'd like to talk with you about music. Mr. Martin said I could, and that you'd tape-record me. That's OK.

Q: By all means, let's talk.

A: You know Mozart? That makes you work better.

Q: Tell me more about it.

A: If you put on Mozart while you're working, it makes you smarter and faster. And one time, when a teacher played Mozart for students in college, they became smarter. *His large brown eyes widened even more, as he studied my own startled response to him, so surprised I was to hear this from him.*

Q: How do you know?

A: My teacher told me that. My mom knows this, too.

Q: Your music teacher?

A: No. Mr. Martin, my first-grade teacher.

Q: Do you know what Mozart music sounds like?

A: I was *just* going to tell you. It sounds like violins, and soft and light. *He paused, looked up to the ceiling, and spoke as if he were thinking aloud.* Maybe there are guitars, but I don't think so. It's definitely softer than most music, and not as fast, either. If I was listening to Mozart, I would not be jumping around or dancing. I would be working. Maybe I'd be writing, or doing math. I might be writing words, but not necessarily having to do with Mozart. It's just that Mozart would help me do better. *Without taking even a breath, he switched subjects.* Can I tell one thing about India?

Q: Sure. Please do.

A: They have a lot of music in India. And Divali, it was yesterday. There's lots of lights, food, and music. People listen to the music, and then they eat, and there's fireworks. That's about India. My brother might bring his clarinet to India when we go back there, and play real Indian music. He's twelve. But you know what? Indian music is not the same as Mozart music, even though they play violins in India. I don't feel like working when I hear Indian music. *He had strung all of these sentences together on a single breath, speaking rapidly but enunciating well.*

Q: What do you feel like doing when you hear Indian music?

A: I feel like playing, or singing, or sometimes—you might think this is weird—praying. We sing and play at our weekly visits to the temple each week. But there's this one instrument in India where you get some bowls, and you fill water up in them—all the way to a mark—and you get some sticks, and you can make different musical tones. You can play songs on these bowls. We don't have that here. But my dad used to play them when he was young. You put the bowls in a circle, or in a line, and you just play. I've tried it, too. *His reference was to the folk instrument called a* jaltarong, *a semicircle of porcelain bowls played with mallets, each tuned to a pitch of the pentaton.*

Q: What other kind of music do they have in India?

A: They have violins, as I said, and pretend guitars. We wouldn't say that they're real, but Indians think so. These guitars have more strings, and they're bigger.

Q: Are you thinking of sitars?

A: Yeah. Sitars pretending to be guitars. But they sound different. I like them in India, but I'd rather hear guitars here.

Q: Do you like music class here at school?

A: *His only considerable hesitation in responded to my questions occurred here. He looked at me, rolled his eyes, and then looked again.* Hmmm. Well, it's a little long, and they sing too many songs. Maybe someday I'll bring my recorder to music class. If we played more instruments, I would like music class more.

Q: Do your parents play?

A: No. But my mom would love to play Mozart on the violin. I think she's about to take some lessons. My dad just sings Indian songs when he's cooking. They speak Hindi. They're not about food. Probably, they're about holy things. But he sings them just when he's at the stove, making curried chicken and rice. I like hamburgers just as much.

Q: Can you sing any of these songs?

A: Yeah, but it's really confusing, and I always forget, because I think about American songs. They're on my mind. *Now his forehead took on a few worry wrinkles.* I know that I want to learn my dad's songs, but I was born here, and so my songs are mostly different than his.

Q: What do you play on your recorder?

A: I can play "Old Saint Nick." I can read some music from my book—it's like a picture of the music—but I learned this one just by trying it out. I thought about learning some Indian songs just to surprise my dad, but I don't have enough notes on my recorder.

Q: Not enough notes?

A: Well, he sings notes I don't even have. *He may have been referring to the microtonal quality of some of the music, or of standard Indian tunings, neither of which is typically (or easily) produced on a recorder.* There's only ten holes in my recorder, including the one at the back, and I know that my dad sometimes sings more notes than that. Plus, we're pretty far from India, so maybe that's why it's harder to play.

Q: Why?

A: Because I just don't hear the Indian music enough. My dad doesn't cook every night, and when he's not cooking, days can go by when I never hear any Indian songs at all. In India, I would hear Indian music all the time. But I'm going to Bombay with my family in January, when it's hot there and cold here.

Q: Do you ever listen to music on tapes or CDs?

A: Yes. I play a tape of Christmas carols a lot, even when it's not Christmas. You know what? I got a check from my grandfather in India, and I'm going to spend it on a whoopee cushion, and a clarinet, and a Mozart tape.

Commentary

Ram is a product of a bimusical experience (Hood, 1960), in that there are two cultural streams influencing his musical sensitivities. His father brings him the spiced folk melodies of his youth in Bombay, but the Western musical culture of his surroundings plays a pervasive influence on his sensibilities. Moreover, there is the broader bicultural implication of these two forces, as Ram hears both Hindi and English spoken among members of his family and in the extended Indian community, is as at home with curried chicken and rice as with hamburgers, and accepts the celebration of Divali and Christmas as somewhat equivalent festive occasions—highlighted blocks on the family calendar of events. Unless the connection to his parents' mother country is reinforced through extended visits, or the Indian-American community is a particularly strong presence in the next few years of his childhood, the bicultural-bimusical scales may be tipped in favor of an increasingly mainstream American profile for Ram.

Remarkably, some researchlike reports in education and the arts seep into the popular media stream of newspapers, magazines, and TV features. Ram has picked up what his teacher has learned about the supposed power of Mozart's music to increase students' concentration level and thus to raise their scores on standardized intelligence tests. This is stunning information, particularly in its converted form as a type of oral lore that is passed to children at home and in school. In fact, the reinterpretation of the findings of Frances Rauscher and her colleagues (1994) on music's impact on the improvement of spatial reasoning skills many times over has produced a myth regarded more as "immutable truth," one that has been widely embraced by musicians and made known to the public at large. Unfortunately, the research from which this modern American musical myth has arisen is taken from a single observation of a relatively small number of students: one setting, one sample, one analysis.[8] The dangers of inference of this result (that Mozart makes you smarter) to a larger and more general population should not be taken lightly, however, as even a second setting or observation of the same population could potentially produce different results. In larger terms, opposing results could immediately deflate and even adversely affect the myth on which so many musicians are currently riding. While educators typically cling to research that appears supportive of their work (recall the excitement, ca. 1980, regarding the right-brain/left-brain dichotomy,[9] a cautious review of the circumstances of the research should precede its acceptance.[10]

But what if Ram is convinced that Mozart will indeed make him smarter? (And of course, what if, through replication, the results stand firm?) Ram, his family, and his schoolmates may then listen to Mozart more regularly and may develop a taste for the music that extends beyond its current acceptance as a stimulant of more intelligent thinking. The music may lead to their personal renewal and transformation, outcomes that are far beyond the Rauscher group's extramusical findings on one small dimension of a complex, multi-faceted construct called "intelligence." There is much to be gained by the "Mozart makes you smarter" belief, so long as the bubble does not burst and the thesis is not found vacuous.

Variety is a constant in Ram's musical life. There are the two prominent musical styles in his world, and pieces that ranges from Indian folk songs to "Old Saint Nick." Music is used by Ram and his family in various ways, too, from the songs that accompany meal-making, to music selected for listening because of its potential to stimulate intellectual development, to music for worship—as in the case of the *bhajans* (devotional songs) that are sung by groups of devout Hindus on a regular basis. There is also variety in the instruments to which Ram has been exposed (his recorder, his brother's clarinet, the *jaltarong* of his father's first culture, and the sitars which he calls "pretend guitars").

Ram's own interest in playing the recorder is unusual for a first grader, particularly in that he has independently begun to play songs from Western standard notation (which he calls "a picture of the music"). He is perceptive in his statement that some of his father's songs do not fit within the tones he is able to sound on his recorder; Indian traditional music is likely to be ornate and replete with pitches that lie "between the holes" of the instrument. He understands that learning music in the oral tradition requires extensive listening and that he is simply not going to be as enculturated through his father's irregular singing of these songs as he would were he to live in India, where "I would hear Indian music all the time." As for singing his father's songs, he claims that the American songs he knows may interfere with and even supercede his learning of "the other" music.

Ram's view of music class at school is cautiously given, it seems, because he knows that I am a music teacher. Yet there may be some truth to the matter of music instruction that appears lengthy to children like Ram, who might instead prefer the variety (of styles, activities, and approaches) to which he has been accustomed on the outside. At the very least, a blend of instrumental music with the singing of songs may be the balance that improves his attitude toward school music and that brings the music for which he is so highly motivated on the outside into the classroom.

♫ ♫

Lisa

Just like I don't sing too much at school, or my brother either, my mama y mi papa don't sing when they work. So we save up our songs for when we go home.

Lisa is seven and in her second year at Ivanhoe Primary School. Only kindergarten and first and second grades, many of them constituted as ESL (English as a Second Language) classes, are housed in the school. According to Mrs. Tanner, her classroom teacher, Lisa's family moved to the city after five years as migrant workers in the fruit orchards of a neighboring state. Both her mother and father grew up in a small town near Guadalajara in central Mexico but followed several members of their family to El Norte in search of greater economic promise. Now living in one of the central sectors of the city, Lisa and her brother board the same bus bound for separate primary and intermediate schools in the district. Their father sees them off each morning before his own departure for the central market, where he unloads produce trucks; their mother has already clocked in as a chambermaid at a downtown hotel.

Mrs. Tanner volunteered that Lisa is "progressing slowly—more slowly than most of our children"—in the acquisition of an English-language vocabulary and grammar. Despite the fact that she was born in the United States, her family and the Chicano communities in which she has lived have steeped her in the language and cultural traditions of her parents' homeland. Even at school, she frequently speaks Spanish, seeking out two other little girls who have moved with their families from Mexico. Home, church, and community events in which she and her family participate seem to have impressed upon her the primary importance of Spanish as the lingua franca, the necessary language, in her world.

Lisa is dressed in a lavender and pink striped T-shirt with matching lavender pants. Her anklets have small lace fringes, and she is wearing white patent-leather shoes with straps. Her hair is long, dark, and wavy, and her large dark eyes hold a glimmer of playful mischief. Lisa was seated in a student desk that faced my own in an empty classroom as we began to talk. She was wiggling already, her feet kicking back and forth in the air, not reaching the floor.

Q: What do you think of music class here at school?
A: Well, I like some sounds. I like that sound. *She pointed toward the music*

classroom, referring to the sound of brass instruments that flowed from the music room's open door down the hall. It's a . . . a football sound. It's kind of low for a football sound, maybe, but that's because we're not right by it. Maybe it's a parade sound, far away. A *fiesta.*

Q: Do you have any instruments like that at home?

A: No. Yes. *She shook her head back and forth, and up and down.* There is a horn on my bicycle that goes:

It's a good sound. I also like the sound of what we do in Mrs. Tanner's class. We go *qua-qua-qua,* and we move our hands like this. *Mira. (She formed her two hands in the shape of a duck's beak, opening and closing it while she sang the song and then chanted the pattern several times in succession.)*

Q: What is that song?

A: About a duck. That's what I know. *Throughout, as now, Lisa constantly wiggled as she talked, swinging her legs and playing with her hair. Yet, although she was active, her reception of my questions was delayed; she was hesitant, or responded in conflicting ways.*

Q: Do you remember any other songs that you sing at school?

A: Yes. You pat your hands and clap your hands. You go "Che Che Koolay." We sing this song with Mrs. Tanner. But I sing *en mi casa . . . mi* house. You don't know these songs. *She sat back, folded her arms across her chest, seemingly satisfied with, if not smug about, her statement.* They are Spanish songs.

Q: So you speak Spanish?

A: I do. That's what we talk at home. My brother is ten. That's how we talk, in Spanish. And sing.

Q: Does your daddy speak English?

A: You know *pocito?* A little? My mama, she talks in Spanish, always. I talk in Spanish at home, and English at school. I learn English *aqui.* Here.

Q: You said you sang songs at home. What songs?

A: Spanish songs. Like this one. *She began a lengthy song of over two minutes, without pause. Several phrases were clear:* Como quieres?, A mi me gusta, Eres tu, *and* Un amor. *She frequently repeated these phrases, many of which consisted of just two or three pitches. The syncopated rhythm, the romantic text, the repetitious melodic and textual phrases identified it to me as a popular ballad—or a pastiche of several ballads. She was in her own world as she sang, with accents coming and going, and dynamics that ranged from barely audible to loud and forceful. Her eyes closed for the soft parts, as if she was singing something no one else should hear. She concluded with a syncopated pattern on* ah, *repeated three times, and punctuated with* no no *at the end.*

Q: How did you learn that song?

A: *Mi mama y mi papa.* And the tapes. But some of it is my own parts. I can do some more. You want to hear?

Q: Of course.

A: *She tapped her lap as she sang. Some of it was lost to me, and to the tape recorder as well, as she turned her head from side to side and swiveled in her seat. She was animated, and sang with vigor and enthusiasm.*

A   mi me gus - ta _____ a mi me gus - ta a   mi me gus - ta _____ a mi me gus - ta a

mi me gus - ta _____ y pue-de suer - te a   mi me gus - ta _____ y pue-de suer - te a

Near the end of the song, she leaped an octave from low to high, again sounding a syncopated pattern on ah *and* no.

Ah   Ah Ah Ah Ah Ah Ah No No   No   No No Ah Ah Ah Ah No No

Q: Did you make this song up?

A: No. I mean yes. I mean I know it, I made it, me and only me, mostly. It's from here, and here. *She pointed to her head and her chest, a gesture that I took to mean that the song she had made up had taken both her thinking mind and her feeling heart.*

Q: Could you sing it in English?

A: It could be. It goes, "I like go, I like go, see my hair like this." *She appeared to be making up words to her earlier melody, but she struggled with the rhythm, then laughed and was embarrased when she discovered that it did not fit.* No. It's not working this way.

Q: Do you know any other songs? The Spanish sound is very nice.

A: There is music on tapes and videotapes at *mi* house. But it's in Spanish. I know two English songs. Go like this. *She moved her hands in front of her face, palms out to me, waiting for me to imitate her. As I did so, she began clapping her own hands on "1" and my hands on "2." She smiled when I matched her movement, and she began to chant something in English that appeared to be spontaneous and new to her, mixing text phrases. Still, she stayed with the pulse she had set.*

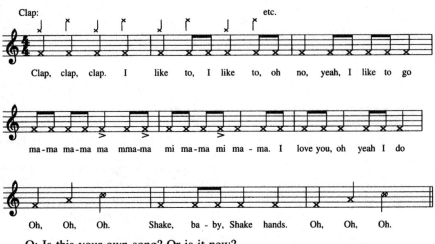

Q: Is this your own song? Or is it new?

A: Yeah. I like to sound, I mean, to sing. It will get better, the more I sing it. We sing in my family. I like to dance, too. My daddy goes like this. *She stood and wiggled her hips, laughing.* My mama, she goes—*She rotated her shoulders several times around, laughing more.* We got tapes from Mexico.

Q: Would you like to make music, even when you're older?

A: Yes, I like coco drums. And to sing.

Q: Coco drums?

A: You know coconuts? Coconut shells? We sing and dance at my house, and sometimes we play drums. When *mi tio* Ignacio was here, we really had good coco drums. Before, we live in a small house by the river, where the apples are. I was still small. We live here now, not far, over there. *She pointed in the direction of her home.* My mama makes beds, and my daddy, he works on a truck.

Q: So you sometimes make music together?

A: Yes. Just like I don't sing too much at school, or my brother either, my *mama y mi papa* don't sing when they work. So we save up our songs for when we go home.

Commentary

While Lisa is not a fluent speaker of English, she was able to communicate through a sparse vocabulary and a functional grammar on which she can hang the words. She speaks mostly in present tense and mixes in a Spanish word now and then. Much of Lisa's verbal communication is enhanced by the gestures and facial expressions she employs, which gives emphasis and greater meaning to some of her words than others. Since Spanish is the language spoken at home (perhaps due partly to her parents' minimal need for language in the manual labor of their day jobs), Lisa has little opportunity or motivation to practice and extend her facility in English. While she could be conversing in English with her older brother, or learning through the media of TV and radio, she gives no indication that she has pursued these channels; her only mention of the media in her home were the Spanish-language tapes and videotapes she claimed as sources of her songs.

Her response to questions of her musical interests were seasoned with the music itself. She honked like a horn, quacked like a duck, and then launched into performances of songs and chants that combined parts of popular melodies in personal ways. As Lisa explained it, one song included "my own parts," and of another song she said, "I made it, me and only me, mostly." These descriptions were not further clarified by her, but the melodies might be interpreted as musical composition "in progress," songs that were emanating from those she has heard many times before but were taking new shape through her organization of melodic and textual phrases. The chant, "Clap Clap Clap, I Like To," appeared to be more spontaneous than the Spanish-language songs, as she dropped phrases like "I like to," "mama," "I love you," and "shake, baby, shake hands" into a steady duple-metered speech rhythm of quarter- and eighth-note patterns. Lisa's discovery that the translation of a song from one language to another is worthy of contemplation: After her failed attempt to fit the new words to the same rhythm and melody, she exclaimed, "It doesn't fit." How often is this the case with singing translations, when music or language—or both—suffer? Or when, in order to retain the melody in its original form, the meaning of the text is altered?[11] We who lead children in group singing or who are involved in directing children's choirs should give our attention to retaining the retain textual meaning in translations of foreign-language songs to English. Perhaps an even better solution would be to steer our children toward singing songs in their original languages while also helping them to understand what the songs mean.

It is obvious that Lisa finds immense enjoyment in her music. The songs of her parents, her tapes and videotapes, and Mrs. Tanner's classes—all of these elements comprise her musical life. She remembered the Akan song from Ghana, "Che Che Koolay," as readily as the song "about a duck." Neither the Akan nor English are first languages for her, yet she sings both songs with vigor and rhythmic drive. She also became lost in some of it, too, closing her eyes to keep herself in her own musical world. Like Darryl, Lisa is a chair dancer; her songs were laden with gestures, and her body continued in constant motion throughout our conversation.

Certainly, Lisa's strong attraction to music could be used for her own linguistic gain as well. In much the same way in which she has selected out particular phrases from Spanish language songs to form new ones, or has even taken phrases from her spoken English to insert into a speech rhythm, Lisa could be made more competent in her speech through the design of a song-oriented language curriculum. Mrs. Tanner's careful selection of songs for English-language vocabulary, concepts, and structures might offer Lisa a treasureload of words and ideas. Then, with further guidance, she might practice her comprehension and articulation of these words through their incorporation into rhythmic speech and songs. Thus might music become an instructional device to enrich her communication skills— while Lisa would still be free to pursue it as an avenue for her own personal expression.

♫ ♫

Ramona
Sometimes when I'm sleeping, I think that I'm Janet Jackson. Sometimes I move around like her. Akila and Pumina, my cousins, we all dream about making a music video.

Ramona lives "down the block" from Hillgrove School, in a city neighborhood mixed with wooden two-story double homes, multilevel apartment buildings, convenience stores, taverns, and a sprinkling of fast food restaurants. There are billboards on the building walls and rooftops that advertise cigarettes, hair care products, cars, and the latest films. There is litter in the streets, graffiti sprayed and splattered randomly, iron bars on windows and doors of various establishments, and orange "block watch" signs in the front windows of homes. Numerous gangs of youths, including branches of the L.A.-based Cryps and Bloods, vie with each other for turf in this rough-and-tough district. Apart from those who reside here, most of the city stays off these streets. Yet this is a neighborhood in want of the attention of the city's planners, with parents who wish for the safety and care of their children, themselves, and their places of residence. Hillgrove School rests peacefully on a small hill overlooking the neighborhood, seemingly oblivious to the storm below.

At seven, Ramona is a gregarious second grader, quick in delivering opinions of her family, school, and musical life. Although she has four siblings, she does not offer reasons for their various locations, nor does she clarify her exact relationship with them. Her own immediate family consists of her mother, a licensed practical nurse, her grandmother; and her fifteen-year-old brother, Jamal. Ramona is close to two young cousins who often "stay over."

On the day of our conversation, Ramona was wearing a pink-and-white striped pullover sweater that matched her pink stretch pants, both neat and fitting to her small form. Her brown hair is parted in the middle, fixed in two larger braids and one smaller one, all fastened with pink hairclips. She is not shy but immediate and certain of her remarks, maintaining eye contact with me through our visit. We sat face to face in a large storage closet crowded with boxes of books, school stationery, and stacked chairs. The vocal inflections of Ramona's speech ranged from soft to boisterous.

Q: What kind of music do you like?

A: Lots. *She paused to ponder, scratching her head with her index finger.* I like jazz. When flutes, violins, and saxophomes [*sic*] play, not necessarily together. Saxophomes are actually my favorite instruments.

Q: Do you want to learn to play the saxophone?

A: Yeah. Once, when I went to the bathroom last year, I went through the gym, and I saw some fifth graders playing sax. They played so pretty, that's when I knew that I would learn sax when I'm that old. I would like to do piano sometime, too. I'd need a piano teacher, though. *She raised her eyebrows, and her eyes sparkled with an idea about who might teach her: me!* Do you play?

Q: I do, but I don't teach piano. What would a piano teacher teach you?

A: She'd teach me what my fingers should do. *She spread her fingers in front of her on an imaginary piano in the air and "played."* This may sound strange, but I'd like to play "You Are Not Alone." That's a Michael Jackson song. I'd like to play the new song by Janet Jackson, too. Plus, I would like to learn the gospel songs we sing in church.

Q: Does your mom make music?

A: She sings. *She slowed her speech, and stretched each syllable of her next thought, speaking more loudly than before.* I mean, she really sings. She's one of the loudest singers at our church on Sundays. My mom likes to listen to Michael Jackson and Janet Jackson. My mom, she used to have all his videos. She could-a had a lot of money by now, but she threw them in the garbage. *She threw her hands down, then folded them in her lap, squinted her eyes at me, and spoke in the hushed yet dramatic tone of a stage whisper.* I don't think you'd like to listen to my brother's songs.

Q: Why not?

A: Because they have cussing words in them. *She waited for my response, but I tried to hold an even and noncommittal expression.* When he's at home, my mother says that he's not to play them. My gramma, too. Even though he's fifteen, he has to listen to them. Snoop Doggy Dog has just too much cussing. If Jamal wants to, he can listen to it on his Walkman, but he's not allowed to play it on the family stereo. Not alone, and not with his friends. It's too loud, and it sounds angry all the time. *She put her hands on her hips and bobbed her head forward and back as she spoke, altering both the tone of her voice and her dialect.* Jamal, he think he all grown up. No way, Jose! I really don't like his music. Do you like rap?

Q: Some of it is fine. Is Jamal your only brother?

A: I have an eleven-year-old sister, Stacy, plus Jamal. She lives with my aunt.

And also, there's Lionel—he's twenty-seven, and Jimmy, he might be thirty or forty. He's old. *I sensed that she was not completely sure of the ages of these two brothers and may have been pulling numbers from the air that sounded "old" to her.* "But Jimmy's got a different mother, but we have the same father. But just Jamal, the fifteen-year-old brother, he lives with me, my mom, and my gramma. Plus two of my cousins stay over a lot.

Q: Do you have just one stereo for listening to music in your home?

A: No. We have three: my mother's in her bedroom, the family one, plus my brother's Walkman. The family one downstairs is really mine and my gramma's— but she doesn't listen to it. When my cousins bring their walkman, I listen in my bedroom. *She shrugged her shoulders, as if it didn't matter.*

Q: Do you ever make music at home?

A: Yeah. One time, we had pots and pans and spoons and stuff—my mom, gramma, my cousins, and me, and we be banging on them. It was at night, on this holiday, when they throw confetti, and there be a whole bunch of people, and you can make lots of noise. And we went—*She patted on her lap while she chanted.*

bang   bang   bang   b'   dang   dang   dang

We also had one drum, and my mom, she say "You could play, you could play" to me. And I did. I went:

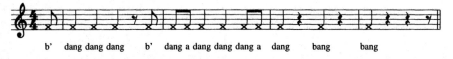

b' dang dang dang   b' dang a dang dang dang a dang   bang   bang

Q: Do you ever see musicians on TV?

A: Like when Janet Jackson jumps on the roofs of high buildings? Or when Michael Jackson pretends he's in a different country, and stuff, or wears high heels? I watch it, but I don't like some of it. I like Janet Jackson more than Michael. Janet is really a woman, and Michael isn't, but he sometimes acts like he is. Michael sometimes does stuff that's nasty. *I sensed that she would have enjoyed elaborating on this for me, but I did not press it.*

Q: So you like Janet Jackson?

A: Yes, I would like to be on a video, like her. Sometimes when I'm sleeping, I think that I'm Janet Jackson. Sometimes I move around like her. Akila and Pumina, my cousins who stay over sometimes, we all dream about making a music video together. My eleven-year-old sister has a friend who looks like Janet Jackson. Sometimes I wish that I could wear her clothes. She's so pretty.

Q: Would you still like her video even if you turned the sound off?

A: Yes. Even without the music, the video's great. Because I already know the music, but I don't know the dancing, and I want to learn the moves. But wait.

She stopped and shook her head. I guess I'd have to have the music, wouldn't I? To have something to dance to. *She emphasized the last word.*

Q: What if you could not get music—on your TV or stereo?

A: That's OK. This is the way my day goes. *She cocked her head from one side to the other, back and forth, as she listed her typical activities. Her voice took on an almost singing, melodic quality.* I come home from school, go up to my bedroom, change, have a snack, go outside and play in our yard, come in to eat my dinner, play with my toys, watch some TV, and then go to bed. But I like music, OK? Singing songs that I already know, and learning new ones. Like at my cousin's funeral, we all sang "Silver and Gold," my whole family—my mother, gramma, my cousins, aunts and uncles, my sister and my brothers. Daniel was a teenager, he was sixteen when he died. He got shot. But my whole family got together, and we sang.

Q: How did the song go?

A: Well, you start with singing "silver and gold" over and over again, and keep doing it. And then you go, "Woke up this morning, feeling kind of down, put on my hat" and all the rest. *She slid in and out of pitches as she sang, and from one syllable to the next.* There's no instruments. We just sing and clap, and move side to side. It's funny, because I didn't know that song until my cousin's funeral. But I heard it, and could just join in and learn it, so now I sing it all the time. Even in school, to myself. Even in my sleep.

Q: Are there instruments that could play?

A: I guess there could be. But our voices are our instruments, and the clapping we do is like the rhythm to go along with it.

Q: What do you think of this music here in school?

A: I like it. It's so nice and pretty. And the teacher is really nice. I like the song we're doing now. "Bluebird." We play this fun game: You like form a circle and then one kid, a bluebird, goes under other kids' arms, in and out, and picks another and another one and another one to be a bluebird too, by tapping on your shoulder. Do you know "Bluebird"? *She proceeded to sing the song, changing tonalities three times. She rendered a bluesy flourish to the final descent.*

Blue-bird, blue-bird, go through my win-dow.   Blue-bird, blue-bird, go through my win-dow.

Blue-bird, blue-bird, go through my win-dow.   Oh, John-ny aren't you ti - red?

Like that.

Q: Nice. So you like making music with your friends?

A: Oh, yeah. We do hand-clapping songs. Some of them my mother doesn't like me to do. Like "Down Down Baby." Sometimes at the part where the white boy is, we say "spank your behind." It goes like this. Hold your hands up, and I'll do it. *She took my hands, positioned one with palm up and the other palm down, placed her own hands over or under mine, and chanted "partner, up, together" in a three-beat motion, encouraging me to follow her patting her hands on "1," then again in a vertical position on "2," and clapping our own hands on "3." Then she sang softly, almost in a whisper.*

Q: Who do you usually do that with?

A: Well, I do it with my cousins, some friends, even my mom—except the part about the white boy. She'd ground me, for sure.

Commentary

Ramona's "live-in family"—mother, grandmother, brother, and occasional cousins—does not remotely approach the historical two-parent, two-children family ideal. To further distance her from an older "all-American" image of family, her father, sister, and two of her brothers (quite possibly step-siblings) are scattered across several other households. It is a confusing picture, yet Ramona registered no outward concern; she showed every indication of adapting well to her family situation. Living in the midst of a gangs-and-graffiti zone, again Ramona showed no apparent worry about her own well-being—not, at least, in this fleeting conversation. Seven years old is just barely the "age of reason," however; it is quite possible that she will soon come to understand the potential dangers of her neighborhood. For now, her life is toys and TV, going to school and coming home to play in her yard. Music is woven in and around her various activities, from the songs of Janet Jackson and her famous brother to the traditional singing games, along with a repertoire of gospel hymns from her weekly visits to the Mt. Lebanon Baptist Church.

Like so many children, Ramona has her musical fantasies. She would like to study piano and learn to play the saxophone. With her cousins, she has dreams of doing as Janet Jackson does—singing and dancing, with all of the glamourous trappings of the star system surrounding her. Her school music program may provide her with sax lessons, but formal piano instruction will be harder to come by there. As for the video dream, this Alger Hiss rags-to-riches saga is the American fantasy shared by millions of schoolchildren and realized by very few. Further, unlike more predictable career tracks, the pathway to such stardom is random and in no small part due to tremendous serendipity. Still, these musical fantasies are akin to the fairy tales of brave princes and beautiful maidens that have engaged children for eons. The names and appearances of the leading characters change, but the potency of these images as role models for children cannot be denied.

The music Ramona made during the conversation shows her ease and comfort with highly syncopated rhythms and vocal elisions that slide in and out of principal melodic tones. She sang "Bluebird" in an entirely original way, notable for her probably unintended changes of tonality and for its blueslike flourish at the close. Her rendition of "Down Down Baby" was polymetered, as she sang in duple but clapped a hand pattern in triple. Some of the African American musical idiom showed itself in her music in fresh new ways.

There was a certain attraction to the sensational in Ramona's remarks. She pointed to the "cussing words" in her brother's angry rap songs, to Michael Jackson's occasional performance of "stuff that's nasty," and to the phrase in her street song that would mean trouble if her mother heard her: "I said, hey white boy, don't be shy, I'll spank your behind, and make you cry." Ramona teeters on the edge of the forbidden, and if unconcerned, she is still vaguely aware of the violence and the sexual inuendos that comprise her mediated world. Ramona was testing the waters in our conversation, curious of the reaction she might receive from me. I presented no threat, as I was not an authority figure to her, just a visitor passing through. She might have pressed further, probing the margins of appropriate, acceptable topics, had I allowed it, yet I tried to steer us along the straight-and-narrow of a proper school decorum. At the time, this seemed the appropriate choice to make, yet I wonder what insights I missed as a result of "holding the line."

Ramona initially claimed that she could accept life without music, but then she went on to explain her fondness for singing. Her enthusiasm was visible as she described her music; "Silver and Gold" had so captivated her as to have her singing it "even in school, to myself." While she attempted to explain that a music video without the music is a viable possession, particularly given her goal of viewing it to "learn the moves," she retreated from that point as she thought aloud of the critical link between music and dance ("I guess I'd have to have the music, wouldn't I?").

Music holds many meanings for Ramona. While most of the music in her life is vocally oriented, she recalled one holiday (New Year's Eve, perhaps, or the Fourth of July) when she and her family produced rhythmic music with kitchenware. Then, music served a festive occasion for celebration, even as the music for her cousin's funeral was the antithesis: somber sounds for mourning the deceased one, while buoying up members of the family and creating a sense of solidarity among them. Ramona's life seemed musically involved: She plays games, she dances, and she dreams—much of it to the accompaniment of music.

<hr>

♫ ♫

James

Lots of the music at the Flashes and Dragons games don't have words. It's brassy, almost like march music, or it's rock music without words. I normally like words with my songs, but not at games so much.

James will be eight on Columbus Day and is in the third grade at Wilson Road Elementary School. The school is situated in an open valley on the borders of a small city that grew up around its own colorful history of fishing, canning, and ship-building. It is a one-story redwood-and-metal building with large windows and skylights, built six years ago to accommodate children of largely professional families who were taking up residence in the new development of executive manor homes. James's own parents are cofounders of a growing biotechnology firm, both with advanced degrees in the biomedical sciences.With spacious lawns and playing fields, modern playground equipment, a sparkling cafeteria, and an impressive library collection, the school resembles a well-endowed private academy. Perhaps the circular drive leading to and from the grand entrance (complete with a rock-and-flower garden and small fountain) adds to this impression.

But though the school may appear a bit pretentious, James is not. He looks to be the type of boy that might wear his baseball cap backward and, in a different time, would have had a slingshot lodged in his back pocket: the classic American boy-child of a bygone era. His light brown hair is tousled, and his nose shows the spread of a September sun's last splash of freckles. He is dressed in a horizontally striped rugby sweater of blue and green, which he wears over green corduroy pants. He speaks with a slight rasp but spouts a rich vocabulary of visual images and insightful observations that distinguish him from other children his age. We sat on a bench that was literally outside—outdoors from—the music room, one of two rooms in a portable barracks-like structure across the parking lot from the school. We were shaded by trees, which also served to mute the sound of cars passing in the distance.

Q: Do you like music?

A: A lot. I like the music class here, too. We do "Zudio" in a really upbeat kind of way, jazzy-like.

Q: How does it go?

A: *He snapped his fingers on the off-beat while he sang the opening segment in a raspy but in-tune voice.*

Here we go zu - di-o   zu - di-o zu - di-o   here we go zu - di-o   all day _ long.

You can move back and forth while you sing. We play instruments, too.

Q: Like what?

A: Oh, eggs that go *sh-sh-sh-sh,* and thick sticks like this. *He patted on his lap.*

We play a steady beat on the drum, too. I like to play the instruments, and work the lights for some of the songs that we sing and play, so that the music has the right mood.

Q: In what way?

A: Scary music can be scarier with the lights out. Sometimes we even have a kind of strobe effect, when I turn the lights on and off to the beat.

Q: So you're the "lights man." Do you like to sing and play, too?

A: Oh, yeah. I think I sing well. On pitch, you know.

Q: Do you sing outside of music class here at school?

A: No. Well, we do the flag song, but that's not really music, I guess. It's the salute. *He placed his right hand across his chest, and began to recite.* I pledge allegiance to the flag of the United States of America. And to the republic, for which I am [*sic*], one nation, under God, invisible, and justice for all. Invisible. That's a joke. It's "indivisible," not "invisible." *He seemed unaware of his substitution of "for which I am" for "for which it stands."* We try to do the salute every day, after lunch. We do it standing up. Someone lifts the flag, and we stand in front of it. So that's not really music, but it's a little like a song.

Q: How so?

A: Well, we all perform the words together, at the same speed, listening maybe to someone who knows it best, like the teacher. If we don't stay together, the salute is no good. That's kind of true whenever a group of people sing: they should stay together in rhythm, at the same tempo. *There was a earnestness about the manner in which he explained the similarities, as if he felt he should defend his position.*

Q: Do you ever do any kind of music outside on the playground?

A: *He shrugged his shoulders.* Some girls do. I play soccer when I can. I do music at home, though, and at church. I sing in a choir. Every week. We sing "I am a Promise, a Possibility." That's in front of the whole congregation. It's interesting: I never get frightened, even when some of my friends forget the words or the melody. My mom says that sometimes you can only hear my voice.

Q: Do your mother and father like music?

A: Yes, some. At home, of course, not at their company. My mom likes to sing a lot when she's working in the house, or wherever. She sings songs that we don't sing in school, songs that she knows from records. She likes the Beatles, songs like "Eleanor Rigby." I like it when she sings "Crocodile Rock." That's Elton John, and I really like him. That was his greatest hit.

Q: Do you have any musical instruments at home?

A: Yeah. Some wind instruments that my parents got when they were in Peru. My father and brother play trumpet, and I will probably study it in two years. Maybe we'll play trios then. But my dad will have to brush up on what he used to know, because he's been busy at work and not practicing for a long time.

Q: How does your brother sound on the trumpet?

A: He sounds pretty good. He can do the Dragons tune. *On na, his raspy voice delivered a syncopated melody, sung twice.*

na   na na   na na   na na _____   na na   na na   na na

He can do "Hot Cross Buns," too, but the Dragons tune is much cooler. He actually was reading an exercise from his book, but it sounded so much like the Dragons tune that I recognized it and started singing it. Then he realized what it was that he was playing. The second part goes:

na _____   na na _____   na na _____   na na

I've never been to a Dragons game, but I know the tune.

Q: How do you know it?

A: I watch them on TV. *He had picked up a few stones from underneath the bench and was popping them in the air with one hand and catching them with another.* That's their signal tune, as I call it. It's when you know the Dragons are playing. I don't like their new jerseys. The sign on it is the *ugliest* I've ever seen, really. *He shook his head in disgust.* It's brown, and says Dragons, and it has a sick, really sick-looking dragon on it. It's too bad. The older jersey was much better—better colors, better dragon. They just always have to change things, like the Rockets and the Hawks did.

Q: Have you ever gone to a baseball game where music plays?

A: You mean the Flashes' games? Yeah.

Q: Do you ever hear any music at the Flashes game?

A: Yeah. They have their theme, too.

Q: Do people ever sing or chant at games?

A: Well, they do "the wave." People get up and sit down again, all the way around the ballpark." *He stood up and sat down, in demonstration of the wave.* I guess that's not really music, but it's cool, the way it goes around and around the stadium. *He gestured in a large circle to indicate how quickly the wave could progress.* People do yell and "scream-sing" during the wave, sometimes. They do:

We   will,   we   will   rock   you.

But lots of the music at the Flashes and Dragons games don't have words. It's brassy, almost like march music, or it's rock music without words. I normally like words with my songs, but not at games so much.

Q: Do you ever listen to classical music?

A: Yeah, we do that. My brother and I got to sit in the front row at the children's orchestra concert a few weeks ago. That was on a Saturday. Basically, my parents just dropped us off, and we got to hear the orchestra play, um, let's see, Dvorak, Copland, and Mozart. There was a piece by this guy, Holst, too, that had lots of percussion. The violins sounded good when we were that close, too.

Q: So you like classical music.

A: *He nodded, then stopped, and slowly enunciated his next statement.* And I'd like it more if I could hear it live.

Q: Do you know lots of songs to sing?

A: All of them, or just parts? If it's all, then probably about thirty. But I could sing you parts of about a hundred songs. My best one is "Crocodile Rock." I know all the regular kids' songs, too, the old ones like "Mary Had a Little Lamb," "Twinkle, Twinkle Little Star," "Yankee Doodle," "Skip to My Lou," and "I've Been Working on the Railroad." Add to that the songs from school, from choir, and from my tapes, and that's at least a hundred. My family has loads of records, mostly rock and jazz, and I have thirteen tapes of my own. *In another visit, I recorded the songs he knew in full (all verses), including fourteen from his tapes, particularly those popularized by Raffi and the* Wee Sing *series, seven Christmas carols, two patriotic songs, six songs from his church choir repertoire, three camp songs, and nine songs from his music class at school, for a total of forty-one songs. He knew "parts" of twenty-four others.*

Q: You mentioned jazz music and rock music. What's the difference between them?

A: The rock is like, you rock and roll. The jazz is more swinging. It's smoother than rock. Rock's rocky, louder, and pretty choppy. Jazz makes me want to sit and listen, or eat and talk. Rock just makes me want to get kind of crazy, to run around. It's fun.

Q: Is kids' music different from grown-ups' music?

A: Sure. *He nodded his head vigorously.* For one thing, kids' music is on tapes, and grown-ups have records, or maybe CDs. But that's not all. Grown-up music is probably harder to listen to, because you're supposed to sit there and not move. Some kids' music is pretty silly, especially when they make voices sound like animals. Chipmunks! I don't think so. There's Raffi. I used to listen to him a lot, and I went to two of his shows. But I wouldn't anymore.

Q: Why not?

A: Aw, he's for little kids. Like in kindergarten or first grade.

Q: So what do you listen to now?

A: Now I listen to Elton John, when I can. I saw him live, and it was so cool. I went with my dad. The background was great. There were dancers on stage, and movies on a screen, and lights. We sat pretty far back, on the side, and we couldn't always see. People were just rocking out, putting their arms up in the air. *His own arms went up, and he rocked from side to side.* But we could sure hear him. He could play piano, guitar, you name it.

Q: When you finish school, do you know what you will be?

A: A veterinarian. I love cats and dogs. We're getting a golden retriever.

Q: So you don't want to be a musician?
A: Not for a living. I like animals more than music.

Commentary

Music and "not-music" was a theme around which some of James's thoughts revolved. When asked whether music "happened" at school, he first referred to "the flag song" when describing the Pledge of Allegiance, then reasoned aloud why it might pass for a song: "We all perform the words together, at the same speed." He understood that the pledge paralleled musical performance as he knew it, since it involved ritual (standing still, facing the same direction) and required ensemble behavior (following a leader, staying together in rhythm). The music/not-music theme returned with his description of the wave, a fan-initiated ritual requiring the well-timed rise and fall of bodies in sequence around the circle of stands framing a ballfield or court. While he described the wave in response to the question of whether singing or chanting is heard at sports events, he then doubted himself but in the next instant rationalized why it might pass for music: "People do yell and 'scream-sing' during the wave, sometimes." James was struggling with issues that tug at the heart of many esoteric ruminations on what constitutes music. He seemed to suggest that not just the sound but also the "trappings"—the contexts—make music the event that it is. He was coming to terms with some of the culturally determined factors of music as performance and group participation, utilizing his eight-year-old logic and experience to define music as human expression.

He was also descriptive of specific musical styles. He opined that jazz is "more swinging" and "smoother" than rock music, creating in him a mood of listening and contemplation (or eating!). To James, rock music is "rocky, louder, and pretty choppy" and capable of inciting him to "get kind of crazy, to run around." That he can differentiate between them is a beginner's response to these styles, but to be able to describe as lucidly as he did how they differ is quite a remarkable feat at so early an age. Perhaps the words James employs are not the syntactical grammar that one might expect a few years on, but they do clarify the feeling and mood of the styles (which may well be their musical essence). Continuing his pronouncements on musical genres, James distinguished between children's and adult music, noting not only what he perceived as different technological packaging (tapes for children and records and CDs for adults) but also underscoring the challenge of listening to adult's music: "You're supposed to sit there and not move." He was critical of the effect of sped-up voices intended to sound like animals, calling it "silly," and dismissed Raffi's music, to which he once listened, as music "for little kids."

James brought focus to the music listening experience when he described his attendance at a children's concert. He remembered the composers of the programmed pieces and commented on the quality of the violins from his vantage point in the front row. When asked whether he liked classical music, James did not hesitate in noting the condition on which he would like to hear it more of it: *live*. Musicians and educators have known for a long while that there are compelling reasons for hearing music in person, in concert, as it is made, and despite the advances of audio-technology, many still pay premium prices to hear music of their preference (or that they are curious to know more about). A trip to symphony hall for a children's concert is often programmed into a school schedule as a once-only endeavor; it may be the major excursion for fourth-grade classes, for example, never to be repeated in their school years. Yet there are chamber groups, community ensembles, and competent young musicians in training at colleges and conservatories that may be looking for an audience of potential music-lovers. As important as an audience is to performers, so too is a live musical performance important to this MTV generation of children—music that can be seen as well as heard. Of course, there is also the logical connection of children today as music patrons tomorrow; this realization should inspire the scheduling of multiple concerts for children each year.

While James is musically perceptive, skilled, and experienced, he has decided for the moment that he will be making his living with animals rather than music. His singing voice, although a bit raspy, is strong and sure, his rhythm is excellent, and his repertoire is wide and varied. His musical memory appears keen, and so was his ability to identify a familiar melody from the motif of an exercise in his brother's lesson book. He may follow his plan to study trumpet and may already be gaining insight on technique and the discipline of practice as he observes his brother at work. James is aware of music's uses as entertainment, emotional expression, physical response, and the validation of civic, social, and religious ritual. He enjoys the musical "sideshows," too: the lights he sets to accompany his class performance of a Halloween song, and the stage effects and audience reactions at an Elton John concert. Indeed, to him they are not sideshows but integral to the musical experience. While music may settle into the periphery of the life James makes for himself in the future, it appears to be an attractive feature of his young life now.

♫ ♫

Beth
My grandmother is the one who gives me music.

Beth's musical tastes are unusual for an eight-year-old girl; she is undoubtedly one of few third-grade children (or anyone else under sixty, for that matter) who knows so well the historic movie music of which she speaks. Mrs. Armstrong, her music teacher at Bailey Road School, helped to draw a profile of Beth in school and at home, beginning with an assessment of her "keen sense of pitch and strong singing voice," with its occasional coloring by way of a "premature vibrato." She described Beth as highly verbal, analytical of the music presented in class, and full of questions about musical pieces to which she was especially attracted. Without prompting, I learned from Mrs. Armstrong that Beth's parents were both affluent and distinguished in their work; her father is a widely published humanities professor at the university, and her mother an expert in international law. They regularly host parties at their home for visiting scholars in their fields and for artists sponsored by the museum and the chamber music organization on whose boards her mother serves.

Beth was keen to tell about her favorite music and had given up her recess to do so. She is petite, with curly black hair, and wore a red- and blue-checked jumper. Her red turtleneck sweater coordinated with her red tights, and black patent leather shoes added the finishing detail to this well-groomed little girl. We were in the music room for our chat, sitting in two chairs that face out to the front lawn of the school. There were cars passing, and the crossing guards were standing duty for the children who walk home for lunch. Within view as well were the middle-sized graystone colonials and several Tudor homes on the far side of the street that characterize the neighborhood. Once she learned from Mrs. Armstrong that "a visitor would be coming to talk with children about music," Beth had continuously requested time with me. She appeared shortly after the recess bell, out of breath from her run to the room and flushed with excitement.

Q: So you want to give up part of your lunchtime to talk?

A: Yes. I like singing. *She wiggled to the back of the chair to adjust herself for a lengthy "armchair chat," her legs now outstretched and parallel to the floor.* My grandmother likes Nelson Eddy and Jeannette MacDonald, and she introduced me to "Naughty Marietta," and that's when I knew how great they were. I listen to them all the time now.

Q: How old were you when you first heard them?

A: About six. Now I'm eight. I love the soprano. My grandmother says that I am a soprano. But the only thing is that I can't reach the high C—yet.

Q: Do you want to be a singer?

A: Yes. I *am* a singer. *This she declared with an air of confidence, rising slightly in her chair, holding her head higher.* I listen to movie singers. Like Jeannette MacDonald. Different kinds. My grandmother buys me movies every time she comes. We watch them together, and then she leaves them with me when she goes. I watch them until I know all the songs that Jeannette MacDonald sings. I have "Naughty Marietta," "Rosemarie," "Girl of the Golden West," "Maytime,"

"Bittersweet," "Sweetheart." How much did I do so far? "I Married an Angel." I might have missed a few.

Q: Can you sing any of the songs from these movies?

A: I could hum a mounty's song. *She took a breath, then let it out, apparently reconsidering her readiness to perform it. She shook her head.* I'm still learning it, though, so maybe another time. You know, most of these movies were made in the 1930s. My grandmother was young, and my mother wasn't even around yet. My grandmother had a chance to be in *I Married an Angel.* But she decided she didn't want to. She was living in Chicago. She put in her name, and they picked her, but she's . . . I don't know. She was a fan of them, and she probably wanted to be in the movie, but was embarrassed. If I had the chance . . . well, I'd probably be embarrassed, too. But I'd stick around and get their autograph.

Q: Does your mother like Jeannette MacDonald and Nelson Eddy?

A: No. Not my mother or my father. Just me, my grandmother, and my brother, a little bit.

Q: What music do your parents like?

A: Oh, violin and piano music, the symphony, chamber music. *She waved her hands in the air, giving emphasis to each of these genres.* They're not against my movie music, but they don't know it either. And I like their music, too, but it's not what I'd choose to listen to first. I mean, I take piano lessons and my brother studies violin, but classical music is just not my first choice.

Q: How old is your brother?

A: He's thirteen. He's having his bar mitzvah on Saturday. He's going to become an adult. It's a kind of special day for a person in the Jewish religion. So we'll have a big party. My brother won't be in school on Friday. They'll be testing him on Hebrew and stuff, so that if he passes, he gets to be bar-mitzvahed, and we have a party. You'll be interested in this: They have music at the bar mitzvah. Both during temple and afterwards. At temple, the music's from a cantor. But I'm also going to go up, in front of I don't know who—*(she lifted her shoulders to indicate her uncertainty, and then tilted her head upward, as if looking for an answer from on high)*—and I'll be singing a Hebrew prayer for my brother.

Q: All by yourself?

A: Yes. I'm a singer, as I said. My grandmother taught it to me, and she remembers it from a long time ago. *As if she had just remembered something she had wanted to tell "the visitor" from the start, her face brightened.* I have a favorite song I'd like to share with you. It's a love song.

Q: Please sing it.

A: It goes:

Oh, Rose-ma-rie, I love you. I'm al-ways think-ing of you.

She then resumed her speaking voice to say: No matter where I go, I'll always be by you. Like that.

Q: Will you sing that at the party after the temple ceremony?

A: I doubt it. My brother and all his friends and the bigger cousins will be going to Fun-Zone. All of my family will be over, including aunts and uncles. I may put the videos of Jeannette MacDonald and Nelson Eddy on for my cousins, and maybe we'll all sing with the videos, although they don't know the songs. I could teach them, though.

Q: Will your grandmother be there at the party?

A: Yes, she'll be staying with us all week. But she may be upstairs with the grown-ups.

Q: Do you like other kinds of music, too?

A: Well, I know other music, but no, I don't like them as much. Nothing's as good as these songs. My favorite of all is a song called "Lover, Come Back to Me." Also, "Blue Moon." There's another one, when Nelson Eddy is bought by Jeannette MacDonald, and he is her servant. I forget the song.

Q: Do you have tapes of this music?

A: I have tapes, CDs, videotapes—you name it. Oh, there's a great song called "Ah, Sweet Mystery of Life." It goes:

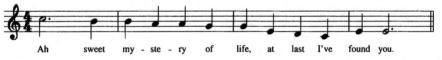

She sang with all of the chromatic detail, and even with the wavering vibrato characteristic of the style. They sing "Trump, trump, trump, [*sic*] the boys are marching." And from *I Married an Angel,* there's "Have You Heard I Married an Angel?" And of course, there's "The Indian Love Song," "When I'm calling you-o-o-o." *For each of these snippets, she sang, her hands folded gracefully in front of her in a style vaguely reminiscent of a position popular for salon-style singing of the 1930s. She maintained a vibrato and was able to leap the large intervals with ease.* These are all famous songs, you know.

Q: I know. Do you wish these songs were taught in school?

A: *She smiled, as if to lighten her response.* Well, they couldn't be. Hardly anybody knows these songs anymore. Not Mrs. Armstrong. Not my friends, although I think they're curious about it.

Q: But you do.

A: Yes, I'm holding onto them for when there's really, literally, nobody who knows these songs. In a way, I'll be like a museum, keeping them. And when people get interested in this music from past history, they can come to me.

Q: Does your family know what you know about this music?

A: Not my father or my brother. My mother doesn't even sing. My grandmother is the one who gives me music.

Commentary

When I asked Mrs. Armstrong whether there was ever "room" in her curriculum for showcasing the movie music of Beth's preference, she looked aghast and perhaps in wonder of my intent. "Are you serious?" she remarked, then adamantly stated that she would never teach "Hollywood music," due to the poor vocal modeling it would provide—"to say nothing of the trite stories" with which the songs are associated. She defended her position by describing the musical content of her curriculum: songs and singing games she considered to be vocally appropriate for third graders, and listening selections from the orchestral repertoire that she programs into her lessons. Playing the devil's advocate, I asked whether she ever gave any emphasis to American popular music or whether her teaching plan for instrumental art music ever gave way to vocal art music or music of the theatre. Mrs. Armstrong explained that she teaches a three-week (six-lesson unit) on popular music in the sixth grade, "when they start listening to rock," and that she has an abridged script-and-song version of Menotti's *Amahl and the Night Visitors* which she offers to her fifth graders as an example of opera. Although I did not ask, I also wondered whether children's own personal musical interests should play a part in the design of the curriculum. Could any of these points—children's musical interests, or the initial study of American popular music, multiple styles of vocal music, or music of the theater—argue a place for Jeannette McDonald in a third-grade music program?

In some ways, my discussion with Mrs. Armstrong proved as fascinating as my conversation with Beth. Rather than peripheral concerns, her ideas on valuable music conflicted with her student's, with their ideas crossing at the junction of two "canons," two repertoires. The critical question that surfaced was "Which music is valid and worthy of study in a school music curriculum?" I could not cast aside Mrs. Armstrong's comment on the age at which children begin listening to pop/rock (sixth grade). In fact, popular music is prominent within many children's environments, from their infancy onward. The preference for listening to pop/rock increases with age (LeBlanc, 1988), so that by adolescence, children are encased within the mediated musical worlds that their headphones provide. Still, these preferences are a result of the gradual development of children's taste for mass-mediated popular culture. It would seem that while intensive study of popular music may happen later, some bits and pieces of it can be wedged into a curriculum from the earliest grades. Rock music, just one of the particular types of popular music, has its own individual aesthetic, history, and substreams: Rock music is urban folk music, valued by children and adults as much for its message and its social significance as for its musical content. Why should it be dismissed as unimportant or irrelevant to the curriculum?

Musical pieces, styles, and traditions can often be cross-referenced by the teacher in a curriculum so that their niches are found in various ways. Should she wish, Mrs. Armstrong could easily give a nod to Beth's cinema music through a unit on music for the theater. This large category could encompass music for stage (musicals, operas, and operettas) and music for media (film, TV, videos). Jeannette McDonald and Nelson Eddy could be put in perspective for Beth and her "curious" classmates so that the widespread use of music in many times and places to tell a story could be better understood. The tangents of curricular development of this theme are quite considerable.

To Beth, all musical genres before and beyond the cinema songsters of the 1930s are currently out of her scope of interest (she seemed relatively unexcited about her piano lessons or temple singing), while Mrs. Armstrong cannot see any reason for the curricular inclusion of "The Indian Love Song." I am not advocating the Eddy-McDonald duets as a staple curricular item at any level, yet the passion that one student holds for a particular musical style may be reason enough to find a way of situating it within a program. To allow Beth's music to play a "cameo role" in a music lesson, even by way of a ten-minute video clip, is to acknowledge the current state of her musical mind, her musical thoughts and interests. It might spark discussion among her classmates as to why this music is important to Beth now and why it was so popular in her grandmother's time. Such a brief exposure could hardly function as a model of musical performance, as models take time to be observed and then imitated (Bandura, 1986). Thus, Mrs. Armstrong's concern about deterring her children from developing a particular type of vocal timbre may be largely unfounded.[12]

But if Beth were granted permission to share her music in class, would that lead to a rash of cameos? Would every other child then wish to show and share a favorite music, or a musical style once important to their own family elders (parents, grandparents, aunts, uncles)? Frankly, that strikes me as a delightful class project, one that might lead children to know their own family music, and perhaps a greater selection of other musical traditions as well. Such a project would serve well to inform the teacher of the musical sources and surroundings of her children. "Cameos" can result from children's oral histories of their families, complete with taped interviews and the collection of historical "artifacts" (78s, LPs, eight-tracks, sheet music, instruments, photographs), all of which could be successfully conducted and prepared for presentation by children as young as second or third grade. Family members might not only serve as informants but also assist the child in the collection process. Classroom teachers and music specialists might even co-conspire to achieve their children's successful pursuits of their musical wellsprings.

Beth has the opportunity for considerable exposure to art music in her home, due to her parents' interest in "violin and piano music, the symphony, chamber music." Indeed, she studies piano and hears her brother's violin practice sessions. Still, she has chosen her current interest despite her sampling of other musical styles. But what of children who have no choice but to claim the single musical style they know as their "favorite," with no opportunity to compare it with other genres? This would seem to be one of the explicit purposes of even a time-limited curriculum in music: to minimally bring students into contact with the music they have not experienced elsewhere. It is for this reason that Mrs. Armstrong feels obliged to provide some variety in the songs and musical styles she features. She knows and has canonized a selection of songs and works; all teachers do. She might find it refreshing, however, to learn how other musics interface with those she has singled out for lessons with her children.

Beth is a literal treasureload of songs from a historic American era. She is by her own admission a musical museum, encouraged by the enthusiasm and devotion of her grandmother to her interests. She claims singing as something she truly loves, and she sings well. I wondered whether she could be starting on a course toward her continued development as a fine lyric soprano, a singer inclined toward the world of the theater. Perhaps her current musical passion is "just a phase she's going through," yet her pursuit of the genre is a manifestation of one child's musical values that is worthy of note in the development of curricular content.

♫ ♫

Manuel

I stand on the other side of the drum from him, and right after he plays, I play. We just go back and forth. That's how I learn.

At nine, Manuel is a tall and husky boy, dressed in black jeans and a sweatshirt with the imprint of a fierce two-headed dragon on the front. He appears older than his fourth-grade classmates, his hair cut very short and brushy, with wire-framed glasses that darken each time he looks toward the window. One of four children, Manuel lives with his family in a district of two-story apartment buildings. Many of his classmates are apartment-dwellers like him; the school's neighborhood sprang up around a large shopping mall, developed in the 1960s to serve the city's south suburban population. Many of the families work at the mall: Manuel's mother and father are employed in the maintenance of the mall's indoor spaces and surrounding grounds.

Downing Elementary School is just two blocks from the mall and is framed by the neighborhood's yellow-brick apartments on three sides. It shows signs of twenty years' wear without renovation: soiled spots and foot-traffic pathways on its gray-speckled hall carpeting, clusters of tape marks left on walls from art projects that had once been posted here and there, and the occasional yellow-brown ceiling tiles discolored by water damage. For our talk, Manuel and I walked the short distance from his classroom to a closet of sorts, one that had been converted into the music teacher's office. We each took chairs that faced the teacher's large desk. The sounds of children singing and playing percussion instruments bled through the wooden sheetboard walls and over the walls (there was at least two feet of open space between the makeshift wall and the ceiling); these sounds sometimes distracted Manuel from the first questions I posed to him. He was reserved, speaking softly during most of the thirty minutes we were together. His posture revealed much of his anticipatory attitude: he sat tall, straight, and near the edge of his chair. But he was intent on conveying his thoughts, and he soon found a fuller concentration and a more relaxed posture and was able to turn to a freer discussion of his music.

Q: Do you like your music class here at school?

A: Yes.

Q: Why? *Drums were beginning to pound, and maracas were shaking through the sheetboard.*

A: Because we learn how to play, like those instruments. *He pointed to the music room.* And we learn how to read the notes.

Q: What do you learn how to play in music class?

A: Those instruments. Hear them? *He pointed again to the room, where a full-size percussion battery of drums, rattles, and claves was performing.* A few small percussion instruments. But I play the drums, too, but not here. I have a special music teacher away from school. He comes to my home.

Q: What kind of drums?

A: The normal kind. The kind that you see in a band. Snare, bass, cymbals. Some conga. You don't see my type of drums in school here.

Q: Do you play with mallets?

A: Yes. *He was rhythmically pressing the palms of his hands into his legs, emphasizing the underlying beat of the percussion music that continued to sound in the next room.*

Q: How long have you played?

A: What?

Q: How long have you played the drums? *He seemed to be tuned to the rhythms next door, not my questions.*

A: About two years, since second grade.

Q: So you have your own drums?

A: Yes. My dad bought me the drums. I bought the sticks myself. My dad gave me the money. But to get the money, I have to help cook, or go to the store to get some of the groceries—stuff like that. So once a week, I get ten dollars. That's how I got the sticks. *The music continued in the next room, but now Manuel was oblivious to it and centered on telling me more of his musical self.*

Q: Have you always wanted to play the drums?

A: Yes. One of my friends has drums. He's twelve and in the sixth grade. But we go up to his house—my family knows his family—and I've watched him for a long time. So finally I got to take lessons myself. With the same teacher.

Q: What kind of music do you want to play?

A: Well, I'm starting to learn rock rhythms. But I also want to play sad rhythms.

Q: Sad rhythms?

A: Yeah. It's like this. *He placed two hands on the teacher's desk in front of him and tapped.*

It doesn't sound like rock and roll. Rock and roll is much harder-sounding. *He tapped more forcefully this time in demonstration.*

Q: How does your teacher teach you?

A: He uses my drum. I watch him play. I stand on the other side of the drum from him, and right after he plays, I play. We just go back and forth. That's how I learn. *He came to a pause, as if to end his discussion there, but then rushed his next thoughts at a quicker tempo.* My teacher says I'm coming along. He makes me say things while I play. Maybe "1211, 2122," or drums words like "par-a-did-dle." I always start playing with my right hand. *He held it up.*

Q: What is your favorite music?

A: Right now, I like Hope to My Heart. They play rock and roll. I like rap music OK, too. No matter what music, I always watch drummers to see what they are doing. One of them wears a jacket with a picture on his back of a drummer with seven drums. Most drummers have long hair.

Q: You said you sometimes play conga drums.

A: Yeah, sometimes I do. We have one at home and I've beat on it for a long time. Congas don't play rock music too much. Players don't need to use sticks. You use your hands.

Q: Does anyone in your family play music besides you?

A: Yeah, my uncle plays guitar. He's good. He plays a Spanish style, like from Mexico. He mostly plays sad songs, and sings while he plays. *He looked directly at me for the first time.* Do you know "Guantanamera"? That's the kind of songs he does. My mother plays trumpet, and my dad plays guitar and vilheula. My brother—he's twelve—plays trumpet, and my ten-year-old sister plays clarinet.

Q: A whole family of musicians.

A: *He beamed, yet was bashful, lowering his head a bit.* Yeah, people say we're got a lot of talent in our family.

Q: What if you didn't have these instruments and you all didn't play music?

A: Well, then it would be quiet, too quiet. My family wouldn't have as much fun as it does now, when we get together and play. *His description was flowing now, and he needed no prodding from me.* We play different parts. Me, I play kind of a sad part, and my brother plays a happy part. Trumpets always sound happy to me. My uncle plays romantic songs really well, you know, about love. We do mariachi music, and play for birthdays, and when someone's getting married.

Q: What songs do you play?

A: Oh, lots. We play "La Bamba," and people start dancing. We're too busy playing, so we can't watch them. I have to watch my drums, or I'll miss my part. Once, I looked away from my sticks and I messed up the whole piece. We got lost. I try to concentrate on what I'm doing, and relate to the other players. One of our best songs is "Dance of the Ghosts." We sing it in English, and we really get going at it, then we stop. *He gave a rather slow, sneaky turn of his head left and then right, and held his hands out frozen in the air for dramatic effect.* People think it's over, and they start to sit down. That's when we start playing again. It's a trick, and it works every time. People like it. They dance harder when the music starts up again. *He was chuckling to himself, obviously pleased with the effect the band had devised—and how well it worked on their dancing audience.*

Q: How are you set up to play?

A: We play right on the dance floor, or in someone's basement for a party, or a church hall. Sometimes we're even on a small stage. I'm in the back. We have microphones, too. We play music from other countries: Mexico, Spain, Brazil, Australia or Austria, or somewhere. People dance either in partners or in one large circle in front of us.

Q: Do you get paid?

A: Yeah. About seventy dollars.

Q: Altogether?

A: No. *He appeared stunned that I would imagine so little a fee, and then almost disdainfully proud.* Each of us get seventy dollars.

Q: Did you always play the drums in your band, even before your lessons?

A: No. Before I started with drums in the second grade, I used to sing in the band. Just sing. But I like the drums more.

Q: You said earlier that you liked music in school. Can you explain why?

A: *He paused to think, then began slowly into what seemed more like a soliloquy, talking aloud on related and not-so-related issues.* Well, music here is fun. I'm getting to learn more of the sounds, different sounds, and to read notes. I might even try some of the music I learn here on my drums, you know, singing while I play a rhythm that works with it. Here in school, we all sing together— everybody sings in a circle on the floor. When I'm playing with my family, we're usually separate from the rest of the people, sometimes even up on a stage. We're the musicians, and they're the dancers. Here, we all sing and move and play together. Still, in school, there's a lot less dancing than there is at the parties. We're not supposed to get out of control here, but it's OK at the parties. They really dance. I hope to form a band with kids my age, kids that live in my apartment building. We know a lot of the same music, and could be good, if we get a head start. That's what I'd like to do when I grow up, play in a band.

Q: Do you ever do music outside of parties and school?

A: Hmmm. Some. Yeah. At church. We sing Spanish music: "Dios para vida." It's pretty hard to sing by myself. We have violin, three guitars, saxophone, trombone, and a drum at church.

Q: Sounds a little like a mariachi band.

A: No. It's not as fast. Definitely not party music. I can't play that church music.

Q: Why not?

A: I just don't know it so well. It's mostly played by old people.

Q: So what are you doing with all of your allowances and band money?

A: I'm banking it. *Although he had been serious for most of the conversation, at this point he smiled.* No, not really. I'm spending it, too, to buy more music to play. I'm going to get "Inky Binky," and a book about the famous rock stars.

Commentary

It is astounding to recognize the nature and extent of performance in which a child can be musically engaged outside of school. Particularly when his initial demeanor had been so gentle, modest, and unostentatious, Manuel's performance experience came as no less than a shock to my system of "pigeon-holing" nine-year-olds as inexperienced (as well as unsophisticated) musicians. Yet here was a young boy who had been performing as a singer in his family band since second grade and who now accompanied his parents and uncle (as well as his older brother and sister) on drums, providing much of the rhythmic vitality essential for music to which people are expecting to dance. So disbelieving was I that he could manage his part in even an amateur ensemble that I requested a tape from him of some of the party music he plays. I found myself convinced of his ability in the opening bars, as I became aware of my own body moving to the grooves that he and his family had set.

What had begun as a slow and almost belabored question-and-answer routine turned fuller in description as Manuel became progressively more drawn into relevant discussion of music's place in his life. His description of his family band's music, its personnel, and its audiences were intelligible and at times insightful. While he had not yet developed a vocabulary to describe music's moods and effects much beyond his assignment of "sad" and "happy" to timbres, genres, and even rhythm patterns, Manuel was able to articulate some of his band's repertoire and to describe with enthusiasm his future musical plans in the formation of his own rock band.

Manuel is devoted to music. He wants to learn to play and to read music, and he recognizes that his lessons and his music class can each provide him with these skills. His description of the drum lesson provides a somewhat typical image of beginners' lessons, in which the master teacher models performance techniques as the student watches, listens, and then attempts to imitate him. The addition of vocalized mnemonics helps to solidify the rhythm pattern for the beginner, whether words, numbers, or even semantically meaningless syllables are chanted. This image is a cross-cultural one, too, as fitting to this American schoolboy's lessons as it is to novice musicians in India, Japan, Ghana, and Indonesia (Bakan, 1993–94; Campbell, 1991b). In Manuel's lesson, the use of the same drum, with the teacher and student facing one another, provides a rapid back-and-forth follow-the-leader sequence that no doubt is shaping Manuel's technique and repertoire of rhythms.

As for the music class, Manuel sees himself learning "more of the sounds," which may be variously interpreted as styles, particular melodic or rhythmic components, or instrumental timbral qualities. Perhaps "more" is significant here, as Manuel may be claiming the potential of the school music class to develop for him a broader knowledge of music—music that is beyond beyond the rhythms of his drum lessons and the repertoire of his family band. He thinks aloud the possibility of applying rhythms on his drum as an accompaniment for the songs he is acquiring from a vocally oriented school music class; he sees a link between these venues. No doubt, the musician that Manuel is becoming is a combination of his lessons and his musical education at school.

Yet Manuel is also learning as he listens to his twelve-year-old friend play, as he observes rock drummers on television, and certainly "on the job": by playing. His family band's repertoire is a mixture of Mexican-oriented mariachi songs and dance music and ballads sung in Spanish from a variety of sources ("Mexico, Spain, Brazil, Australia or Austria"); he may be unsure. He mentions his uncle's "Guantanamera" style (a Cuban freedom song popular in Mexico), "La Bamba" (a *son jarocho* from Veracruz first popularized by Ritchie Valens), and his family's English and Spanish renditions of "Dance of the Ghosts." He knows about the element of silence and surprise comeback in a performance, the "trick" of a fake ending to a dance piece which is then started again, serving as a reprise—and a certain means of energizing dancers to the satisfying close. Indeed, he is learning the tricks of a band's trade.

Even as he plays the older music of Chicano family gatherings and dance parties, Manuel is reaching for his star: becoming a drummer in a rock band. He has already eschewed the "ethnic" conga drums for the "normal kind of" drums found in a rock band. He watches drummers on television "to see what they are doing" and has observed not only how they play but also what they wear. With the boys who live in his apartment building, he is planning to form a band: "We know a lot of the same music," no doubt with practice sessions where he and his friends alternately teach and learn from each other (Campbell, 1995). With his allowances and band earnings, he is collecting "more music to play." Unlike most children his age, Manuel is already setting a course for realizing his music dream, hanging his hopes on the star shining for him in the world beyond his childhood.

♫ ♪

Lateesha

I might be reading or playing with my puppy or something, and then slowly, I start getting into the CDs my sister is playing. That's when I start singing.

Lateesha is new this fall to the school, having moved from a small community near the state capital. She is ten years old and in the fourth grade. Early in our meeting, she was recalling her first three years at John Glenn Elementary with fondness, particularly her friends Joy and Simone whom she left there, and her third-grade teacher, Ms. Brennan, who often enlisted her as her after-school helper. She remembered also her kindergarten class in Washington, D.C., and her pre-school years when the family lived there with her grandmother. Wellington School is her third elementary school, and decidedly her last, she claimed, although she admitted that "the family could possibly move again when I get to middle school." For Lateesha, her home is "all girls now"—her mother, a fourteen-year-old sister, and herself. "My father lived with us in our last house, but he had another house here—which is the one we're living in now." The "girls" moved in when her father, an economist, moved to Hong Kong for a two-year consultancy. As she explained it, "The Chinese people want to know what we're doing here, so he'll be advising them. We won't see him for two years."

The family's frequent moves and her father's extended departure do not seem to have outwardly affected Lateesha. She bubbled with opinions and seemed genuinely interested in talking about her life, her friends, and her music. She is small and graceful and wore green corduroy pants with a yellow T-shirt hanging over them, and black tie-shoes with rubber soles. Her brown hair is arranged in many intricately braided rows across the top of her head and down to the nape of her neck, a model of the African American fine art of hair design.

In this urbane neighborhood of new condominiums, restored homes, and fashionable shops, the school was an anomaly. The halls were missing floor tiles, the paint and plaster was peeling on several walls and ceilings, neon lights were out or flickering arhythmically, and a drinking fountain leaked a slow puddle not far from where we were sitting. Colorful fingerpaintings, cutouts, collages, and poems handwritten in large cursive style donned the walls, brightening the otherwise drab environs. Lateesha and I were seated at a table placed in an alcove at the end of the hallway, in a place where teacher's aides sometimes meet with small groups. We faced each other, Lateesha straight and tall at her chair, her hands loosely clasped in front of her. Even while there was activity in constant flow around us, she was able to concentrate and respond quite directly to my questions.

Q: What's your favorite subject at school?

A: Reading. We have groups, and I'm in the highest group. I read easily. *She looked down for a moment, an indication to me that she had not intended to sound boastful, and then went on.* I make mistakes, but not big ones. I know the words when I read out loud, but I also get nervous.

Q: How many classes do you have outside your regular classroom?

A: I have PE, reading, and music. Art used to be outside *(the regular classroom),* but we don't have it anymore.

Q: What part does music play in your school activities?

A: I like singing. I'm in the honor choir here at school, besides music class. I have a low voice, an alto voice. This is my first chance in the choir, but I sing a lot at home. Usually, my sister is doing her homework, and she likes to play music while she works. I might be reading or playing with my puppy or something, and then slowly, I start getting into the CDs my sister is playing. *She began to move her head forward and back, as if dancing to music she had suddenly conjured up.* That's when I start singing.

Q: Who's your sister?

A: She's fourteen. Her name's Benita. She's at Tabinatha. They call it "Tabs." She's in the ninth grade.

Q: What is your favorite music?

A: I like Coolio. He raps. He's on MTV, and he's always on KAKE. I listen to KAKE alot. My sister likes Coolio, too. He raps with four other people, but he's the leader. The rest of the people in Coolio are in, like, the background. They don't sing the main part; Coolio does. They're kind of like, *after* Coolio. They follow him. They sing different things than what Coolio sings, too. He's my favorite for rapping. But singing, that's someone else. *At this point, she leaned forward and spoke more softly, in a reverant tone.* Whitney Houston. She's got a new song that'll be in a movie, like "I Will Always Love You" in *The Bodyguard,* but not that same song.

Q: What do you like about Whitney Houston's style?

A: Everything. Her voice—it's so high. She can also wear anything and look beautiful. In this video, she wears regular clothes, like she was going out shopping. They're much more relaxed than what she wore in *The Bodyguard. She slapped her hand flatly on the table.* Why can't I think of the name of her new song? You'll be hearing it a lot, probably.

Q: Does she dance when she sings?

A: In some of her songs, she dances, and in others, not. In this new song, since it's a sad song, she doesn't dance. But she gets all over with her high voice. My sister doesn't like Whitney Houston the way I do. I have hanging in my room pictures of Coolio and all of his group, and one of Whitney Houston. I have Janet Jackson, and Big Papa, and Faith. I share the room with my sister, but my pictures are around my desk and bed.

Q: Do you ever listen to music played by an orchestra?

A: Not really. *She eyed me suspiciously, and then the gaze passed.* I'd rather listen to singers.

Q: Is there any music that you can't listen to in school?

A: The teachers are not allowed to let kids listen to rap music in school. The board says so. *In fact, the school's PTA passed a motion last year to this effect, according to Lateesha's teacher.* Not rock music, either, or even oldies. The only music you can listen to in school are classical music and kids' music, stuff like Raffi. *She made a disapproving face.* You can listen to rap and rock outside, but not on the school grounds. When we have indoor recess when it's raining or cold, if kids listen to rock music on their Walkmans and get caught? They have them *(the Walkmans)* taken away and put in their teachers' boxes *(by the recess room monitor),* and then the teachers can decide whether or not to give it back to them. Sometimes, our teacher calls kids' parents to come get it. Most of the kids, if they're playing rap or rock, play it softer than they like, but then they can listen at recess and not get caught. I don't know why they bother: it's not the same, soft. The whole thing is cold, because we do rap in our music class.

Q: You can't listen to rap in school, but you do rap in the music class?

A: Well, it's kind-a rap. It's not really got a beat. But we can do it, because the words are safe.

Q: No bad words?

A: Yeah. No bad words. Like we have this one. *She began to move her head again, as if she was hearing some internal beat. She chanted:*

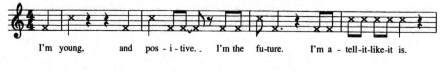

I'm young,   and   pos - i - tive. .   I'm the   fu - ture.   I'm a - tell-it-like-it is.

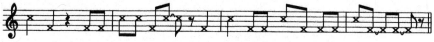

No-one's   gon-na stand in my way. __   My   eye's on the prize, I'm gon-na   stay that _ way. __

Q: Nice.

A: It *is* nice, but I can't say that it's the rap we hear on our Walkmans.

Q: Do many of your classmates have Walkmans?

A: About half of my class have their own Walkman. Everyone has a CD player at home, maybe a few don't. I share our CD with my sister.

Q: Would you want to play an instrument?

A: Well, they have a band here at school, but that's all. I might like to play something else, but then, I'm kind of careless with my stuff, so it might be better that I didn't have an instrument. I might wreck it. And besides, I'd probably have to pay for it myself. Every month I get fifty dollars—my dad sends it for me, because my mom only pays for stuff that I really need. And so I pay for everything else from my dad's money. That's why I'd worry that if I bought an instrument, I might wreck it, and waste my money. Or my puppy might chew it up. She's only five months old. Basically, I use my money for food, Coolio tapes, and toys. And I want to get Whitney Houston's new tape. I really need to get new headphones, too.

Q: Does your mom sing?

A: Yeah, to music in the car. She listens to really soft music. She has a pretty good voice. Sometimes we all sing, mostly in the car. My sister usually chooses the station because she sits in the front passenger seat. Sometimes it's a contest between my mom and my sister, deciding what we'll listen to. And sing to.

Q: Do you like to dance?

A: Mm-hmm. We dance at sleepovers. One's called "The Tick," and it's really slow, and you like, move your . . . um . . . right here—*(She stood up, pointed to her hips, and began to weave in a figure-eight motion).* You go really slow, and you make this tick-tock move. And there's others, like the tootsie roll and the butterfly. The tootsie roll goes like this. *She rolled her hands forward, while her feet were parallel, moving sideways.* Now, the butterfly is really hard. I can't really do it. You have to start from the top, and then go all the way down. It's really hard.

Q: How do you learn all of these dances?

A: My sister. She goes to dances at Tabs? *She took her seat again, and she was now clearly conveying an excitement that wasn't there earlier. The flavor of her language changed slightly from what it had been.* She usually brings some of her friends back over after, and then they be turning the radio station on, and then the songs that they played at the dance will be on, and they do the same thing they be doing at the dance. There's actually a song called "Tootsie Roll," and the rhythm for doing the dance is on it. My sister's friends don't really teach me, but I usually learn by just watching them. Charmina—she's one of my friends—she has an older sister, but since her sister is older than my sister, Charmina actually teaches me to dance, too. And when my friends that don't have older sisters want to learn, they can just watch us. I'll just do it, even on the playground just to be funny, and then they see me and learn it.

Q: What will you do when you grow up?

A: I'll be in school for a long time, because I'm going to be a doctor. But really, music is important to me, and the number one thing I'd like to do is to become a singer. A doctor is the last thing I want to be, only if I can't be a singer, or an actress. No matter what I do, I'll finish my four years of college first. And if I get old, and nobody likes my music anymore, and I can't get another job, and I don't got a degree, I'm not going to be a grown-up still going to school. Singer, actress, doctor—in that order.

Commentary

Like many children, Lateesha shows the influences of the media and an older sibling in the musical choices she makes. She described occasions on which she has been nonchalantly involved in various nonmusical activities, when the sounds of her sister's mediated music have intervened and carried her off into an adolescent musical world. At ten years old, she is already singing and dancing the music of rap, rock, and pop and is authoritative in her descriptions of several of its stars. As Lateesha is indirectly "taught" this music by her sister and sister's friends, she is also a "teacher" herself, transmitting the dance styles belonging to the music to her own friends on the playground and at "sleepovers." Having an older sister can be a clear advantage (the older, the better, perhaps, as in the case of friend Charmina's sister), and may well be a status symbol among fourth-grade girls.

Lateesha's choice of Coolio and Whitney Houston as her favorite music is striking, if only due to the distance between their musical styles and the cultures they represent. Coolio raps on recognizable 1970s oldies, delivering intricate, syncopated rhymes as if they were conversations. He tells the tales of a gangster living in the ghetto, of the ubiquitous violence around him, and of the love-hate relationship he has with the life it brings him. Whitney Houston, on the other hand, sings in the large, powerful, yet versatile voice she developed through her longtime membership in gospel choirs. Anything goes in the instrumental tracks that accompany her, from a standard pop-rock ensemble to the orchestral style of a synthesized "sound-block," and she weaves her mostly romantic ballads—often with accents of affluence and glamour—in and around them. How is it that Lateesha is attracted to these distinctive stars and styles? They are "yin and yang," musical images of rough-and-tough vs. softer, safer ways of life. Each may be dramatically different from Lateesha's own life—fantasies, even, and yet each may have a toehold in the realities she has sampled in her young life.

An indication of a ten-year-old's perception of musical form and texture was embedded in Lateesha's description of Coolio and his group. She noted the leader-follower interaction she has sensed between them: She had discerned the "main part" from the "background" music and described the group as sounding "*after* Coolio" rather than with him. Through implication, it seems that Lateesha is well aware of call-and-response form, the roles performed by the soloist and his chorus, and the phenomenon of background/foreground as it is portrayed musically. She may have developed these understandings by listening, but I wonder how much of her musical description is governed by the MTV images she has seen.

It is intriguing to consider the dichotomous roles that rap music plays in Lateesha's school. There is a ruling against its presence, yet its style has surfaced in the music class. The system by which the ruling is maintained is rather intricate, too, such that Walkmans are confiscated and returned only after consultation with parents. Yet rhythmic chant is one of the chief components of an Orff-styled pedagogy of music, so a modified style of rap is presented in music class even when it is outlawed elsewhere. Children like Lateesha know the difference, however, describing the music class rendition as just "kinda rap," without a rhythmically complex underlay of sound and with a text that is innocuous, "safe," and remote from the subjects and language of commercial rap. The rhythm and text distinguish real rap and the rhythmic speech "rap" of music class, which emanate from two different worlds.

Music is strongly appealing to Lateesha. She spoke of stars, styles, songs, and dance steps with the wisdom of a cultural insider—adolescent culture (and this, despite several years until she reaches the age that will qualify her). She clearly enjoys singing in the "honor choir" at school, and choir in combination with her music class gives her four thirty-minute periods of music instruction weekly. Yet it appears that it is Lateesha's outside-school musical experiences that beckons her; the music of her sister's preferences is rapidly becoming her own.

♫ ♫

Alan
I sing in my mind—not out loud—but my inside-singing is my guide to playing.

Alan is in his second year at Rivercrest School, having transferred from a parochial school in which he had been enrolled before his family moved from across the state. Rivercrest School consists of one class per grade level, from kindergarten through the fifth grade, with class sizes ranging from eleven to twenty-one students. It is situated in a small town forty miles from the city, many of its residents employed on the many dairy and berry farms for which the region is known, or in the service sector. Alan's family lives in a double-wide mobile home on the town's main street of motels and restaurants; the town is laid out much like so many other small towns that lie just off the interstate highway. His mother is a waitress in a family restaurant, and his father is a service station mechanic. His sister is eleven months younger than Alan; they share a partitioned bedroom. The family claims Native American roots, as his maternal grandmother is three-quarters Cree and his grandparents are, in Alan's words, "a good part Nez Perce." By his calculations, "that makes my sister and I maybe, almost, half and half," which I presumed to be his reference to an ethnic balance of European and Native American ancestry.

We sat on the floor in the "all-purpose room" at Rivercrest for our talk, our backs leaning against the low stage. Alan is wearing a green plaid flannel shirt, black jeans, a red water-repellent zipper jacket, low leather boots, and a bright red baseball cap that sits sideways over his red-brown hair. His shirttail hangs out, a ten-year-old's likely statement of what's in vogue among fifth graders. Earlier, the principal had ticked off to me some of the room's multiple uses: cafeteria, physical education classes, on-stage band and choir rehearsals, parents' meetings, school fairs and exhibits, and even evening basketball and volleyball activities. The cafeteria workers were cleaning away the lunch foods, and as Alan and I began our talk, the scent of pizza still hung in the air. At one point, we moved ourselves so as to clear the way for the vacuum's sweep of lunch crumbs; when the first physical education class arrived, the teacher invited us to use her office. Despite the low level of ambient sound and the interferences, Alan managed to be thoughtful in his conversation.

Q: Who's in your family?

A: I've got two dogs, my sister, my mom, and my dad. My sister's my age, but I'm older by eleven months and two days. Arnold is a tiny Yorkshire terrier, and Angus is a mutt. We've had Arnold ever since he was a little tiny baby, and we got Angus at the pound. He's medium, about this big. *He lifted his arms about three feet high by three feet wide.* And he's black, with fur that's a little wavy, and he has a special ability: he can smile. Angus is my favorite. He sleeps with me every night, under my blankets. He's a warm thing.

Q: Besides the music class, do you study any other kind of music in school?

A: No, not really. I do music at home. We have a keyboard, a clarinet, and a guitar at home. My dad plays the guitar. *He paused to reconsider what he had said and then proceeded to differentiate between* playing with *and* playing. He doesn't really play it, because he's not really very good at it. He knows a few chords. My sister plays her clarinet, or will as soon as she gets a reed. Me, I make up songs on the piano. It's really a keyboard, and it sits on a table.

Q: So this keyboard is yours?

A: Yes, I got it for my birthday, when I turned nine. I always wanted to play it. When I was younger, at my other school? *He raised his voice in question, perhaps to ascertain whether I was still with him, listening to what he had to say.* We had a piano in every classroom—first grade, second grade, third grade. We weren't allowed to play it just any old time, but during free time, when other kids would read or draw or play with some of the little-kid toys, I would ask to play the piano. The teachers would usually let me, because I didn't play it too loud.

Q: How does your keyboard work?

A: Well, it has a recorder, kind of like this. *He pointed to my tape recorder.* I can push a button and record songs. And other buttons are there, and I can push it so that my music can make the sound of an organ or trumpet or clarinet or flute or guitar. So I pick one of these instruments, and then I play along with it. There are other buttons, too, for playing "Beethoven" or "Happy Birthday" or whatever. I play with both of my hands. With my right hand, I can play the high tones, and with my left hand I can play the lower tones. *He pretended to play.* Either hand for the middle tones. *He referred to his system for sharing responsibilities for the middle area of the keyboard. As he had had no formal lessons, this system made perfect sense to him.*

Q: How does the keyboard play "Happy Birthday"?

A: Oh, you just press a button and the melody comes out. I can also do other songs, and just store them in the memory.

Q: What other songs do you like to play?

A: Well, there's no button to help me on that, just the keys. I try to figure out certain songs. Last night I played "The Star Spangled Banner." My friend was kind of doing it. The music sounded right to me, so after about ten minutes, I worked it out. You see, I was at his house, watching him, and then I came home to my own keyboard and figured it out. He was going: *(he sang the opening two phrases on* da, *his voice pinching out the highest tones).* I just remembered it and did it at home. A lot of my friends come over and just start playing on my keyboard, so I just sort of learn that way, too, watching, listening, doing what they do, adding to what I know.

Q: Do you ever make mistakes when you're figuring it out?

A: Oh yeah. *He shook his head vigorously, laughing as if to recall some of the unpleasant results of some of his errors.* Sometimes I mean to hit this one key and then hit another one instead. I know that it's wrong, and so I just sort of "self-correct." I can do the first part, and just sort of the middle, but I can play the last part really well. I sing in my mind—not out loud—but my inside-singing is my guide to playing.

Q: Do you sing in your mind very often?

A: Yeah, a lot. I sing in my mind when I'm trying to think of songs. I listen to the radio a lot, and I try to memorize the songs by singing along with them, inside. People can't really hear me singing, but I'm there, doing it. It's kind of like Beethoven. He couldn't really hear, so why should he sing out loud? He sang in his mind, and he could hear what he was singing. The difference is that I'm not deaf like he was. *He shrugged his shoulders and laughed aloud at his comparison.* Here in school, we can only do music in music class, so I find myself singing in my mind a lot during math, or spelling, or social studies.

Q: What do you sing inside?

A: "The Star-Spangled Banner." And "Happy Birthday." And humming music.

Q: Humming music?

A: Yeah, like this. *Again he sang on* da, *energetically, while he patted a pulse on his leg.*

Da...

And here's another one.

Da...

I like this one, too.

Da...

I hear that tune a lot. This is something that I'm making up. Lots of the humming music is my own music, not something I learned somewhere.

Q: So do you make up a lot of music?

A: I do. Ever since I got my keyboard, I've been making up my own songs. And I remember them later, and can do them again. I push a harp sound with one of the songs I make up, and have a "slow-rock" rhythm going with it. Some of my melodies are kind of sweet, and some are a little wild—you know, all over the keyboard, skipping around. There are no words to the harp song, or to any of the songs I make up, but somehow I still remember them.

Q: Have you played your music for anyone?

A: Just one person. I brought my keyboard over to my mom's friend's house, where we go when my parents have to work late, about a year ago. But I didn't get to play too much for her, because she wanted to play. My parents are too busy to listen very much, and they're tired when they get home. *He was nonchalant and matter-of-fact in his statement.*

Q: Is there any music playing in your house besides yours?

A: My sister's clarinet—when she has a reed. There's some Christian, slow rock, country on the radio. I personally like Garth Brooks, especially "Thunder Rolls." You know. *He sang the song more loudly than previously but started so low that the bottom dropped out at the end, so that he was speaking rather than singing the last few words.*

Thun-der rolls __ and light-ning strikes,   now the love grows cold __ on sleep-less nights. _

I can't play it on the keyboard yet. It's too hard. This is one of the songs that I sing inside. But I also sing it out loud, when I'm by myself, when no one's around. I make up songs to sing. I have a stump where I go. It's an old tree that was cut down, in the fields behind our home, way back. I ride my bike back to that spot, or sometimes I go when I'm walking Angus. There's no houses, no people, it's just way back in the fields. There are sticker bushes all around it, kind of to keep people away. No one goes there. The stump is about this high and this wide. *He gestured a height of about two feet and a width of four feet.* I just get up on the stump, and think there. And I sing, as loud as I can. No one can ever hear me. It feels pretty good.

Q: Do you listen to music in your bedroom?

Q: Yes. I've got a tape player, CD player, radio, and headphones. So that's how I usually go to sleep, with my headphones on. I get ideas for the music that I want to make.

Q: What if you had no music in your life?

A: Awful. I like music. It makes me feel good. If I'm sad, some music makes me happy. That's how it goes. If I'm OK and happy, some music makes me even happier. It gives me energy. When I'm on my bike, listening to music on my headphones, it makes me pedal fast, or to a beat. I feel like I'm flying.

Q: What might you be when you grow up?

A: Hard to tell. Maybe a doctor or a dog trainer. Not a mechanic. Maybe a musician or a sound engineer. I would record musicians, and help them to sound better.

Q: What do you think of this music class here in school?

A: The teacher's good. She knows a lot, and understands kids. She plays good, too. I wish we had more music time, that's all.

Commentary

The last statement has reverberated in me since its pronouncement by Alan many months ago. Here is one of the strongest statements in support of music in a school program, proffered by a boy who had also earlier noted that "here in school, we can only do music in music class." He inferred that at Rivercrest School, there is no music to be had beyond the music room walls, despite the many ways that music could be infused to motivate, enhance, emphasize, and clarify the learning of other subject matters. If Alan's observation is accurate, it is somewhat stunning that there should be no use of music through the school day for social, recreational, or therapeutic purposes: no singing of familiar songs for giving a sense of community and solidarity, no playing of recorded music to evoke a particular mood, no study of music for its reflection of cultural patterns. Perhaps his teachers are unaware of music's power and multiple purposes or uncertain about how to channel it into their classes. For this, both classroom and music teachers are to blame, as they have not taken the time to yet figure how they might support one another, enriching and enhancing the lives of their children through education.

On the other hand, if Alan finds himself singing in his mind during the study of other classes, he may already have found his own extended uses of music. Indeed, he sings inside himself for several reasons: to recall songs he knows or formulate those he will create, and to find a place of peace and calm in his school-day world of activity. Clearly, he relishes his "inside-singing," and his "humming music" visits upon him various melodies that he will later try on his keyboard. Alan calls attention to Beethoven, who once "sang in his mind," too—a point worth pondering.

It seems a pity when a school and its community cannot see their way to fulfilling young people's craving for knowledge in and stimulation by a particular subject. Alan pines for music instruction that is beyond the typical once-weekly music classes. Alan would greatly profit from piano lessons, perhaps through a keyboard lab, all too rarely found in schools. His "self-correct" trial-and-error style of learning to play is clever, although time-consuming; he would be greatly aided by a teacher who had the time in her schedule to listen, discuss, demonstrate, and direct his thoughts and skill development. His evident interest in song-writing and composition could be captured and developed through instruction in the creation of poems, rhythms, melodies, and harmonies. The pathway toward becoming a musician should be as available to Alan as are those courses leading to later careers in communications, accounting, engineering, and computers; children should not have to blaze their own trails in learning music and the arts. Even while Alan sings in his mind, there ought to be more occasions for him to make music aloud under the direction of a trained specialist.

Alan's interest in keyboard began early, perhaps in no small part due to the presence of pianos in the classrooms of his first few grades, as well as the willingness of his teachers to allow him to explore and experiment at these pianos. His explorations continue as he develops a fingering system that works for him, playing the middle territory of the keyboard with whatever hand is available. He has figured out a way of learning familiar songs like "The Star-Spangled Banner," explaining it as a combination of "watching, listening, doing" what his friends have done. Since he does not mention notation, Alan is most likely not musically literate. His ears are his guide; they are becoming stronger through his efforts at listening. Still, an opportunity to study piano would bring him a better balance of orality and literacy through the notational skills he needs to learn any composed music with ease and efficiency.

Children like Alan take comfort in music and are drawn to it for the positive psychological effects it offers them. Alan explains that "it feels good" to make music and to hear it. He is conscious of the uplifting feeling and the energy that music generates in him; music speeds his own body rhythms so that on his bicycle, it makes him feel "like I'm flying." The image of Alan with his dog, standing in isolation and at a great distance from a more frenetic world of home and school, is a memorable one. There on a stump among the sticker bushes, Alan can sing aloud the songs that are inside, releasing at once all of his energies, emotions, and ideas. In this image of Alan singing his heart out all alone in a field, the statement of music's power and attraction to a young boy is a strong and lasting one.

♫ ♫

Anna
I think, out of all the music I do, I still like dancing at weddings the most.

Anna is eleven years old, and a fifth-grade student in one of the oldest public schools in the city. The houses in the district show the wear and tear of almost a century's use, many with the three wooden stories, gables, and rambling porches of the large family homes of the 1910s and 1920s. A large Catholic church with two spires is perched on a hill, overlooking the spread of houses, shops, and small groceries. Anna's grandparents emigrated from Croatia just after World War II, and her mother was raised in the same house that she now lives in with her grandfather, mother, and two younger brothers. She remembers her father only vaguely but speaks of her stepfather (who also left the family several years ago) with fondness.

Her teacher described Anna as a good student, well-liked by her classmates, and with a particular interest in reading "every last one of the Molly stories" by author Valerie Tripp. She keeps her long, dark hair clipped back away from her face, and her dark brown eyes shine as she tells her stories to me. Her typical attire included black knee-length shorts, a loose-fitting T-shirt, multicolored socks, and Nike tennis shoes. In all, we spent about three hours together, spaced over two visits. Anna was on time to our meetings and talked easily.

We met at the back of her classroom, in an area framed by two long tables with computers on them, a corkboard wall with photographs of U.S. cities and essays about them stapled to it, and a window to the street. She characteristically straddled a chair backward as we talked, her folded arms resting on the back of the chair, often with her chin resting on top of them.

Q: Do you know why we're meeting?
A: Yeah. I volunteered to talk with you about music. That sounded easy enough. *She smiled, revealing a certain spunk and an eager anticipation of the topics we might touch upon.*
Q: Can you tell me something about yourself? Who are you?
A: My name is Anna. I live just a block from school, and I have two brothers,

ages five and six and a half. I finish this school in a month, and then go on to Adams *(a middle school).* Yesss! I'm ready for it. *At these last words, she punched the air with her fist.*

Q: Do you have any special interests in music?

A: Music is my main interest. I guess I'm cut out to make music. I'm in the band and I sing in the youth choir at Redeemer—Holy Redeemer, you know. And I just generally do a lot of music. It gets me going, and gives me . . . well, strength, I guess, sometimes.

Q: Do your friends make music with you?

A: My best friends Lisa and Joey—she's a girl—are in band with me. Lisa sings in the choir with me. At school, Lisa and I play clarinet together, and Joey plays flute. We usually share the same music stand, and watch Mr. Simmons wave his arms and beat the stand. *She demonstrated, counting "1–2–3–4" and slapping her hand on the back of the chair for each "1."* Actually, I usually know the band songs by heart, we do them so many times, but I can read notes for new music anytime he gives it to us. Which isn't often. He can be boring. *She stopped, and put her hand over her mouth.* You're not going to tell him that, are you?

Q: No. This is not for him. Do you and your friends ever play your instruments together outside of band?

A: Oh, yeah. We take our instruments over to Lisa's house, and play our own stuff in her bedroom. We might start with band songs, and then take off. You know, variations on them. Or sometimes we try out the songs we usually sing on our instruments. You know, stuff like "Frere Jacques" or "Simple Gifts," or songs from our tapes.

Q: Tapes?

A: Yeah. We might play along with Mariah Carey, or even toot some of the sax melodies from the old Bruce Springsteen tunes. They're good. Lisa's mom has all the Mary-Chapin Carpenter tapes, and I love those songs. I sing them, and I'm going to learn how to play them, too.

Q: Do you have these musical get-togethers very often?

A: Every Saturday, without fail! But Lisa and I also sing in the youth choir, and that means that Thursday nights and Sunday mornings, we sort of have this outside-school get-together, just us. We sing at choir, and we sing all the way over there and back. Lisa plays clarinet better than I do, really, but I'm probably the better singer. She practices more than I do, because at home, my brothers give me no peace. Plus, my mom needs my help with them, and around the house. *She wrinkled her nose, and then shrugged her shoulders.* So singing, that I can do even when I'm doing dishes or taking out garbage.

Q: Is your mom a musician?

A: No way. *She laughed.* But my stepdad is—he plays guitar, and good. And he had a tamburitza band, which you've probably never heard of. It's a Croatian group of instruments like guitars, and they play at all of the church parties, and at weddings. I think, out of all the music I do, I still like dancing at weddings the most. They're always fun—lots of food, sodas, sometimes slippery floors, too, and really good, peppy music, to make the dancing go so-o-o smooth.

Q: So it's dancing, singing, and then playing the clarinet—in that order?

A: Yeah. And don't forget listening, if you count that. That's in there, too, because when I put my headphones on at night, it's the one chance that I get peace, and privacy. The only chance, in my house. I just tune everyone out and listen to my tapes, or even to what comes on KUBA *(a radio station that programs mellow rock and country-folk).*

Q: You said that "music gets me going and gives me strength." How so?

A: It picks me up. You know, when you're depressed because your mom gets mad at you for no real reason, like you left your socks in the bathroom or something trivial, and you just *have* to have something that takes you away from all of it. *She folded her hands into fists and, like an old-time country church preacher, struck the top of her chair as if it were the head of the pulpit, periodically accenting words and syllables.* Sorry to say this, but she can drive me crazy. Just pick-pick-picking. She drove my stepdad right out of our house! So then I just retreat to my music. In my room, I close my door and on go the headphones. I might play my clarinet, or I might sing, or I might just close my eyes and listen. It puts me in a better mood, and perks me up.

Q: What songs do you know, that you could sing?

A: Lots. You don't want me to sing now, do you? I'd really rather not. But I know a bunch. Um, of the school songs, there's "This Land Is Your Land," "Shalom Chaverim"—we do that in a round—"Every Time I Feel the Spirit," "Cotton-Eyed Joe," "I Gave My Love a Cherry," some Mexican songs like "De Colores" and "La Raspa," "Simple Gifts," "Abraham, Martin, and John"—that one we sang in a program this year—songs like that. I know some of the Mary Chapin-Carpenter songs to sing them, and I *could* sing my favorite ones like "Stones in the Road" and "The Last Word." *I later asked her to sing all the songs she had listed, and while she sang with a breathy quality and slightly out of tune, in every case she was able to manage at least one verse.*

Q: What about church music?

A: Oh, yes. We do about three songs at mass every week, but we might rehearse a lot more than that. We did five songs at Easter, but that was a special event. Mrs. Brezina has us mostly singing the melody, but some of the songs have a separate melody that the high voices sing above the lower melody. Those are pretty. There are some old songs in Latin, and we sometimes do the "Pater Noster" after the consecration. You know, the "song-that-barely-moves." *In a half-mocking tone, she demonstrated the static quality of the melody.*

Pat - er nos - ter   qui es   in cae- lis,   san - ti - fi - ce - tur no - men tu - um.

Most of the rest is stuff Mrs. Brezina gets when she goes to choir directors' meetings. She's got a good voice, and she's always reminding us to stand up straight and take a deep breath. She'll make me be a better singer, I think.

Q: What's the music like at the Croatian weddings you've been to?

A: The best. *Anna stood up.* If you want, I can show you some of the dance steps we do. And I'll sing you one of the melodies. *She stood and moved to an open space beyond our conversation area and began to move in the small sideways steps of the* kolo, *a popular Croatian dance performed in a circle without partners. She sang a melody on* doo.

She sat down, flushed and breathing hard. But you have to hear the tamburitza band play it to know what it really sounds like. How can I do it justice for you? *She sat back down.*

Q: Do your friends know how to dance these wedding dances?

A: No. I think you have to be brought up with it. I've been doing these dances since I was three years old. We even have my first costume, with puffed lacy sleeves and a velvet vest. But I like the colored ribbons that literally fly around me when I dance fast. I guess I started dancing because my grandmother did it. She thought I was cute. Now I do it because it feels good, and I'm good at it. People that aren't Croatian? That don't go to these weddings? They don't know what they're missing.

Q: Do you study this music in school?

A: No. It wouldn't be right there. Each music belongs somewhere: the songs in music class, band room music, tambouritza music, church songs, and the tapes and radio songs. For me, they are all right—in the right place, at the right time. They're all right for me. You know what I mean?

Commentary

On the edge of adolescence, Anna fills her splintered young life with music. Perhaps music is her means for staying buoyant—even feisty—in a somewhat unstable home environment. She described music as her means of strength, her channel for peace, and her way to a better mood. At home, school, and church, and within her ethnic-cultural community, music is a powerful source of Anna's solace and happiness. She appeared to thrive on "doing music" and believes that she is "cut out" to make it.

Despite the boredom Anna may know with the slow pace and limited repertoire of her band class, a true testimony of her interest in clarinet-playing, and in music at large, is in her description of the weekly music-gatherings with her friends. Allotting Saturday playtime for school music, along other familiar musical favorites, is a straightforward declaration of Anna's musical values. It is intriguing to imagine a group of fifth graders intent on figuring out Springsteen tunes on wind-band instruments and to consider how rock, folk, and country music are modified by timbres atypical of these genres. Likewise, the girls' activity at varying and transforming band music into, perhaps, something more to their liking would be worthy of further investigation. Do their variations retain pitches but vary the rhythm? Retain the rhythm but vary the pitches? A little of both? A careful look at permutations children make to the music they know might shed light on their preferences for discrete musical components and also help to illustrate the processes of children's musical play.

Anna's home environment seemed not to be conducive to musical study. She admitted practicing less than her friend and complained of interference from her brothers, of chores that usurp her practice time, and of her mother's constant reminders to pick up after herself. Yet Anna sings when she cannot play, and although her sound is slightly off pitch, she has a repertoire of folk songs she learns at school and popular songs from tapes and the radio that she performs even while she is engaged in her chores.

The church and ethnic-cultural community feed Anna's musical appetite. She sings two-part songs in the church choir and recognizes that her commitment to the weekly choir rehearsals will pay off in improving her singing posture and breath support. Her links to her Croatian culture are strong, chiefly through the family's membership in the largely Croatian church parish. Beginning with her grandmother's encouragement of her dancing from an early age, and more recently with her stepdad's peformance in a tambouritza band, Anna is provided with frequent opportunities at church parties and weddings to "do" the musical activity she most favors—dancing. For Anna (as for Lateesha, George, Lisa, Carrie, and Ramona), dancing is as much the making of music as is singing or playing her clarinet. In interesting ways, children's physical responses to live or recorded music may be a type of musical involvement that is widely enjoyed but rarely viewed as musicking by musicians themselves. Yet the visceral nature of music cannot be ignored, and movement may be one of children's main means of participation in it. Anna's last statement shows reason well beyond her years: that music knows many contexts and functions. She viewed many musical styles as important, depending on their "fit" within particular environments and occasions. Her musical palette may be more varied than that of some children her age who have already closed in on their preferred styles and songs, but her enthusiasm is contagious, nonetheless. That she believes that "each music belongs somewhere" is heartening and worthy of contemplation by those who desire a broader and deeper musical experience for children.

♫ ♫

Tuyen

*My mom and dad have parties—once with eleven cars out front. That's when
I sing the Vietnamese songs, and everyone—my aunts, uncles, my parents'
friends—seems to like me.*

Tuyen is a slender girl of eleven years, one of the top students in the sixth grade
at Glendale Elementary School. She is president of the school's music club that
meets on Tuesday afternoons and has shown her musical inclinations since her
arrival to Glendale three years ago. Her music teacher described her as "a quick
reader, with a keen ear and an excellent memory," and is aware and encouraging
of her further musical involvement "on the outside." Tuyen's long, dark brown
hair is fixed in a high ponytail that bobs as she talks in her animated manner. She
wears round wire-rimmed glasses. She is articulate, friendly, and with a good
sense of humor, smiling and giggling easily. Her gold and green knit tunic sweater
hangs neatly over her green leggings, and she wears low black boots and a small
black shoulder purse.

Tuyen recalled a bit of her family's history, all the way back to her birth in a
small town in southern Vietnam. Her earliest memory, she said, was of being
carried by her father "across a bridge where the water was very deep, and he had
no shoes on, and he held onto a stick to steady himself." She described her family's flight to boats that took them to camps in the Philippines, where a younger
sister was born, and finally to the United States, where her youngest sister was
born. Tuyen sees herself and and her two older sisters as more strongly linked to
Vietnam than her younger sisters, since they acquired the language and traditional
customs in their earliest days. Both of Tuyen's parents are employed by the school
district as cafeteria workers at the high school two blocks from their home.

The school's neighborhood is an older working-class district of post–World
War II bungalows. Glendale's cornerstone shows its year of construction as 1949,
about the time that the last batch of bungalows went up in the neighborhood. The
community is integrated; newcomers from Southeast Asia and Central America
mix with African Americans and those of European heritage. The strips of shops
and restaurants on either side of the street on which the school is located display
their names and advertise their services in Cambodian, Vietnamese, Filipino (Taga-
log), Spanish, Russian, and English. Twenty-two flags fly on the school's front
lawn, representing the multicultural composite of the children enrolled there. This
theme is continued down the halls, where posters are hung to portray seasonal
festivals from around the world. Tuyen and I were meeting in the library at the
end of the hall, sitting behind a rack of books, where we had been warned to
speak quietly. Her congenial nature brought an easy flow to the conversation.

Q: Why do you think Mr. Ryan selected you to speak to me?
A: *She shrugged her shoulders and shyly smiled.* I don't know. He probably
thinks I like music more than most of the kids, and that's true.

Q: How did you get to be president of the music club?

A: They voted for me. I guess my friends like me. Or else they think I'm a reasonably good musician.

Q: What do you do as president?

A: Well, I help Mr. Ryan pass out candy at the music club meetings. *Once this was said, she seemed embarrassed of the menial tasks that were the president's responsibility, and she hastened to add:* But we'll also be involved in putting the spring program together.

Q: How so?

A: Well, we're going to be choosing some of the music, writing the narration, and advertising the concert.

Q: What kind of music do you make?

A: That depends on who's listening. *She giggled, and then looked both ways, pretending that what she had to say would indeed be dependent on who was in earshot.* As for here in school, I play the clarinet, since last year, with Mrs. Jackson. She's the instrumental teacher, and Mr. Ryan teaches recorder and singing in the music class.

Q: Why did you choose the clarinet?

A: I wanted to try it because people said it was fun. I went to a program at Kennedy *(the high school)* once, and the clarinets just sounded so good. Like honey. Smooth. There's a bunch of us studying clarinet: Tiffany, Kim, Shannelle, Cheryl, and Ian. *One by one, she ticked their names off on her fingers.* It's the most popular instrument to choose. Peter plays trumpet, and Justin and Aaron play trombone. Jackie plays cello. She's the only string player in my class.

Q: So clarinet is your first instrument?

A: No, we've studied recorder beginning in the fourth grade. We learn to read music then, and how to produce a wind sound. We develop our breath control and the coordination of our fingers by playing the recorder; then we're more ready for clarinet, trumpet, trombone. *Her explanation was familiar, like that of a professional educator, and I wondered whether she learned it from her time spent in class and club meetings with Mr. Ryan.*

Q: What do you think of the recorder as an instrument to play?

A: I like it. It's not a toy. *She paused to allow the comment to register with me.* I guess that's how I really started getting into music. It was easy to learn. I know lots of songs on it, including music in a variety of keys: C, G, D, and F major. *She jumped from one subtopic to another, eager to paint a picture of her study of the instrument.* We don't have our own recorder to take home. Mr. Ryan likes to keep them in the music room, and kids in every class use the same recorder. But he cleans them, so it's safe. But unlike most kids, I have my own recorder at home, which I got for Christmas last year. It's wooden and pretty expensive. That way I can play more. I can play my clarinet songs on recorder, and my recorder songs on my clarinet. You know, you can transfer the music—is that the word, "transfer"?

Q: Maybe "transpose"?

A: Yeah. But I do it by ear. I can do "Jolly Old St. Nick," "Go Tell Aunt Rhody," "Merrily We Roll Along," "Mozart Minuet," and that sort of thing without notes. *Although I neglected to ask, I was curious as to whether she had learned these melodies by note on one instrument and then transferred them aurally to the other instrument—or whether she had indeed learned them without notation from the start.*

Q: Which do you prefer: playing by note or by ear?

A: I like both. I do both. But I like to challenge myself to play different music on the recorder, stuff that I hear on the radio, TV, tapes. I want to be able to pick songs up like that on the clarinet, too, but it's too soon.

Q: Do your sisters play music?

A: Not really, except that my older sisters played recorder when they were younger, and my nine-year-old sister plays it in Mr. Ryan's class. But she's not very serious.

Q: Does your family do any singing together?

A: I once had a karaoke machine. We used to all sing to that. I know some Vietnamese songs, too, and so do my big sisters. After school, I go home and turn on my Vietnamese tapes and sing to them. Some of my favorites are about the way things used to be when my mother and father were growing up there. My older sisters know some of these songs, but I know them better.

Q: What Vietnamese songs do you know?

A: You really want to know? *For a moment, she stared as if not believing that I could be interested. I wondered whether the hesitation was also due to her thinking about how she could explain her family music to an outsider like me.* Well, there's one about a boy who gives gifts to his girlfriend, like a ring, but then he tells his mother that it was the wind that took it away from him when he was walking over a bridge. Another one is about a man on a date with this lady, and he gets upset because she doesn't really like him. Lots of songs about love, and water, boats, and stuff. We have tapes of these songs.

Q: Where do you get them?

A: There's some stores where you can get Vietnamese food, and books, and videotapes, and music.

Q: Why do you sing these songs?

A: Because it's fun. They're pretty songs. *She emphasized the next word, and paused grandly for dramatic effect.* Besides, my mom wants me to sing them, and she says that when we go to Vietnam, I may be asked to sing these songs. Maybe someday I'll go on stage there and sing for lots of people. My mom's a good singer, and she even taught me a few of the songs.

Q: Do you want to sing one of these songs?

A: No! *She backed away, and held up her hands to her face in a protective posture, and giggled.* Me and my friend Kim—she's Vietnamese, too—we sing some of these songs together sometimes. But not now.

Q: That's fine. When do you sing?

A: My mom and dad have parties—once with eleven cars out front. That's when I sing the Vietnamese songs, and everyone—my aunts, uncles, my parents' friends—seems to like me and says I'm a good singer.

Q: I'm sure you are. So you and Kim sing together, too?

A: Yeah. Kim and I sleep overnight at each other's houses; we're pretty close. Together, we probably sing more American than Vietnamese songs, but we know pretty many of each. The Vietnamese songs have violins, guitars, keyboard that play, and a long stringed instrument. *Dan tranh.* There's about thirteen strings, and you can play with long fingernails or finger picks.

Q: What sort of American songs do you and Kim like to sing?

A: You really want to know? *Again she hesitated, perhaps wondering whether she should talk about popular music with a music teacher.* Well, some school songs and choir songs. But also, Boyz II Men and So For Real do great songs. They sing "Candy Rain" and "Every Little Thing I Do." "Candy Rain" goes *(she sang in a light, soft voice, her eyes closed):*

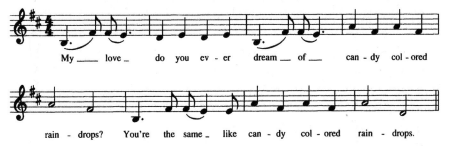

And then the verses come in between this part. That was the chorus that I sang. The group is all boys, and the guy who sings is Jason, but they call him "Chase." There's a 19-, 20-, 21-, 18-, and 14-year-old. The youngest is Chase. They're all brothers. They're pretty popular. My older sister likes Boyz II Men better, but if I had to choose, I'd go for So For Real.

Q: Could you ever play their music on your clarinet?

A: No. It would never fit their style. I think they sing in a way that would be hard to transfer to a clarinet, anyway. They, like, decorate their music.

Q: Is music pretty important to you?

A: Well, half and half. I wouldn't want to be without it, but I guess I could. It's not like food; you wouldn't starve without music. But it makes my life worth more?

Q: Is music ever boring?

A: Where's Mr. Ryan? *She laughed and put her hand over her eyes, pretending to search for him.* Is that a trick question? No, not really. Well, opera is boring, and slow music can be, too. Excuse me, but when the fat lady sings in a high voice, and you can't understand her? *She raised her voice as if to ask whether I was following her.* It's not so interesting. It gets on my nerves. But on the other hand, I don't like music that is purely instrumental. Voices that sing words I can understand, that are accompanied by instruments, that's more interesting music.

Q: Do you know any operas?

A: *As if responding to a quiz question, she spoke immediately, and seemed pleased with her knowledge.* Mozart wrote a bunch like *The Magic Flute,* and Beethoven wrote one. And I do like the story to *Carmen,* but still I can't understand the words.

Q: You said opera is boring to you. What music do you find exciting?

A: So For Real is exciting. And Mariah Carey, and Ace of Base. With any of these groups, there are voices and instruments. Ace of Base uses trumpet, and lots of them use keyboard, guitars, drums and all. Janet Jackson's a good singer, and so's Paula Abdul. I must say that I really like Mariah Carey.

Q: Why?

A: I like her high voice. But it's light, and not heavy. *Because of what she may have perceived as my musical interest, and maybe to reconcile her own dislike for opera, she offered me the next bit of information.* You know that I heard that Mariah Carey's mother was an opera singer. That's what I heard.

Q: But this isn't the music you hear in music class?

A: No. We get a pretty good balance of styles, but he doesn't play stuff that we could hear anywhere else. In music class, we get to hear the unusual, hard-to-find music.

Q: Such as?

A: Well, Beethoven, Strauss, Chopin, Bach, Mendelssohn. You can't find that music as much as you can So For Real.

Commentary

If there were music majors in elementary school, Tuyen would certainly qualify. She is broadly and deeply engaged in knowing music, weaving into her musical life the experiences of her school classes and lessons, her family's heritage, and the popular media to which she is so drawn in her preadolescence. By her teacher's account, her considerable musical ability is already clearly evident. Her election to music club officer is a tribute to her, as her classmates accept and distinguish her for the talents, commitment, and enthusiasm she demonstrates. Along with her independent practice and musical play at home, these qualities are the early makings of a solid musical career.

There are vocal/general and instrumental tracks at Glendale, a band, and an auditioned choir. The music club is yet another activity that complements the scholastic music program, designed to continue the education of interested children. It is a volunteer group, open to fourth, fifth, and sixth graders, many of whom are already involved in band or choir. Currently, there are twenty-eight members and a parent volunteer who coordinates the transportation for field trips, the snacks, and the PTA program. It was established by the music teacher six years ago, and he has received a small budget, an extracurricular fee, and a boost in his salary for his efforts in each of the last two years. The principal, parents, and teachers are supportive of this club effort. Tuyen is happily entangled in the activities of the club and her clarinet lessons (and the band) and is a member of the choir as well.

Tuyen's interest in the study of clarinet springs from several sources. Its reputation among older children was strongly positive, and it may be for this reason that it is the most popular instrument among her cohorts. She admitted having been inspired by her attendance at a high school concert, where advanced players impressed her with their "honey" and "smooth" quality. The introduction of the recorder in the music class is also related to the continued pursuit of instrumental study by Tuyen and her friends, as they have since fourth grade been developing the breath control and finger facility so vital to playing a wind instrument. (The recorder experience Glendale students have is not merely "tooting" on three pitches, either; I have heard fourth graders play impressively the themes from works by Mozart, Beethoven, and Dvorak. According to Mr. Ryan, the music teacher, the children can play "everything from pavanes to Pachelbel" in six keys and three parts by the end of sixth grade. He is rightly proud that in two classes weekly, he can accomplish this while still having time for singing and listening lessons.) Tuyen's description of the "transfer" (or transposition) of songs from her own wooden recorder to clarinet shows her ingenuity in setting challenges for herself. Her interest in clarinet is thus beyond the mere practice of exercises and is one that may well continue as she learns "to pick up songs" on her clarinet.

Mr. Ryan knows Tuyen's family and observed that her parents value a good education for their girls and encourage their efforts to accomplish themselves in their studies. Tuyen knows they support her musical interests, too, from the "pretty expensive" recorder they gave her at Christmas to the tapes of Vietnamese music her mother supplies to her. She described her mother's wish to return to Vietnam and to have her singing these songs, perhaps for friends and members of the extended family they left behind. Tuyen is called on to sing these songs at social gatherings in their home and clearly enjoys the feedback (and that "everyone seems to like" her). Her other sisters know some of these songs, yet Tuyen seems to be the one her parents have selected to carry on something of their musical heritage, aspects of their culture through music. Tuyen stands in two worlds, floating between the land of her birth and the land in which she now makes her home.

With her Vietnamese American friend, Tuyen is growing into the musical world of adolescence. They sing the songs as they are aired on the radio, likely late into the nights they spend at each other's home. She is learning the vital details of some of the popular artists, down to their ages and nicknames. When she sings their song, she is transfixed, her eyes closed, and may be living in her imagined world of these artists. Despite her interest in playing songs by ear, however, she does not think to "transfer" So For Real to her clarinet. Possibly, she hears that there are vocal and melodic nuances which she cannot now (or may never) completely realize. As she explained, they "decorate their music." She will no doubt join adolescent culture with a substantial backlog of popular music and culture which she knows and about which she has opinions.

As Tuyen has amassed her knowledge, she has also developed her taste. She can name a Mozart opera, and she can explain why opera is "boring" (she cannot understand the words "when the fat lady sings in a high voice"). Of course, further study may allow her a better window into the genres she knows less well, although she is clearly leaning toward instrumental music. Tuyen seems to value the styles to which she is exposed in music class and has come to terms with one reason for the listening lessons in these classes: "We get to hear the unusual, hard-to-find music"—a noble reason for music's purpose in the curriculum.

♫ ♫

Jonathan

Our teachers say that we have to make up the work we miss when we're at our lesson, so we do. Violin is a commitment, they say, but so is our other work.

Jonathan is a well-groomed sixth grader, dressed neatly in a navy blue polo shirt, tan-colored denim pants, and low brown suede shoes. His blue ski jacket hangs open, revealing its fleecy inside. At twelve, Jonathan is the middle of three boys in a middle-class home in this midsized community; his brothers are fourteen and nine years old. His parents are recently divorced, and he and his brothers spend their time in each of their parents' homes, just a few blocks from one another. His teacher described Jonathan as "cranky," contrary, and "a real pill since the divorce was finalized on Valentine's Day—can you believe it?" The neighborhood in which Lancaster Public School is situated is an amalgam of suburban homes and condominiums, most of them built in the last fifteen years when the city spilled out of its boundaries to this eastern suburb. Many of the residents are a part of the exodus of families from what they perceive as urban erosion, a second generation of "white-flighters."

One week in late winter, we spent two late afternoons in the corner of the music room. We looked out at music stands scattered randomly, and a large bulletin board brimming with composers' portraits and bordered with giant-sized eighth and sixteenth notes. During much of our talks together, Jonathan fiddled with his watch, a sportsman's special with large Roman numerals, pulling the time pin in and out and flicking the metal clasp at the back while we talked. He was slumped down in his chair. Occasionally, he swung his head back to sweep his light brown hair away from his eyes. He was generally alert and well-spoken, if somewhat edgy. In both of our meetings, he held his violin case in his lap.

Q: Are you ready to talk about music?

A: Yeah, I guess so. Mrs. Phillips said I should, but I wanted to, anyway.

Q: OK. Mrs. Phillips mentioned that you're a member of the school choir?

A: Yeah. I didn't particularly have a choice. *Given his aggravated tone of voice, it seemed that I was already coming to terms with the cranky disposition of which his teacher had spoken.*

Q: What kind of music are you singing?

A: *He shifted his weight, slumping further in his chair. He stretched his legs out in front of himself and folded his arms across his chest and above his violin case.* Well, we're doing "To Music," "Si me dan Pasteles," "Ca' the Ewes," "Siyahamba." She picks the songs. *By "she," I think he is referring to his music teacher.* My older brother knows some of them, because the sixth-grade choir sang them two years ago. So he had these songs stuck in his head, and I would hear him sing them, and now they're stuck in my head. *His hair swung back as he shook his head, as if to clear the song from it.*

Q: What do you mean, stuck?

A: I mean, every time I turn around, I hear this song or that song, kind of inside. It's catchy.

Q: Will you perform soon?

A: Probably. We've got to get the instrumental parts polished first, though. She picked a couple of people to play the drum part, but we all learned the rhythm.

Q: What does the drum part sound like?

A: Well, for one song—something about peace, freedom, and that kind of thing, it goes, you know, like this.

He lightly rapped the rhythm with his knuckles on his violin case, chanting, raising his voice on b and lowering on doom and bee. She sort of taught everyone the rhythm, but she only picked some people to actually play it. She usually picks the people that are doing the best, being the most quiet and paying attention. Like if you don't move except for singing—those are the ones that get picked to play. *He began to flick the clasp of his sportsman's watch.*

Q: Have you played?

A: No.

Q: Would you like to play?

A: Sure. But I can't sit still that long. Nobody should have to sit still when there's music. It moves, and makes you move. *He took an audible breath and swung his head back as if to claim some distance from what he obviously considered a poor selection process.* It doesn't matter, because the drums we have here at school are pretty lame. I've heard lots of congas and *djembes (a Ghanian drum)* that sound better.

Q: How do you know about djembes?

A: My uncle is a percussionist. He shows me lots of his drums, and I get to play them. The one in school is bogus, anyway; it's not the real thing. But anyway, no big deal. I like the choir allright. Sometimes. *He shook his head again and grimaced.* But today, when she was playing the piano part, the girl who was supposed to play the drum part just couldn't get in sync. Some of us were playing the rhythm on our laps while we sang, but this girl just couldn't play—even without singing. I don't get it. She just doesn't know the ones that know the rhythm. She's wasting our time, giving the drum to a girl who can't play. *He shifted his slumping position, and appeared more defiant than before.*

Q: This piece, did you learn it by listening to it, or by reading the notes?

A: A little of both. Mrs. Phillips sings parts to us, and we mimic her. But she also gives us the music. *He grabbed at the chair, using the arms as a brace. Meanwhile, I braced myself for a rain of complaints.* It's important to be able to read music, OK? But the choir music is confusing. There are so many words and so much music that we can't read as fast as the music goes. I spend so much time flipping through pages that I don't even sing all my parts on time. But when I go home, the song pops into my head, it gets stuck, and I'm singing it with no trouble at all. *He looked at me, then away, as he challenged me with his next question.* Don't you music people ever decide that too many notes might get in the way of the music?

Q: I think so. In some styles, we don't use notes to make music.

A: *He continued in an effort to defend his position.* I know. Rock musicians don't read music. Most of them don't. And they play some complicated stuff. I don't think jazz players read notes much either. Yeah, notes are good for writing down music you don't want to forget, or that you want someone else to play later on. But too many notes in these choir pieces—my part, your part, the piano part— they can choke you when they come too thick and fast.

Q: I think I know what you mean. But you basically like the choir?

A: Yeah. You can tell Mrs. Phillips that I do.

Q: What about the music class?

A: Yeah. I like it. Getting to go to music is something different.

Q: You mean you like music because you get to leave the classroom?

A: *He laughed, his voice breaking for the first time in a way typical of voices in the process of change.* How'd you guess? More than that, but yeah, that's part of it. Some people just like music class because they like music. I do. I have music and choir, and also violin lessons—three kinds of music here at school. I've been playing for two years.

Q: Why did you pick the violin?

A: Well, I like the looks and the sound of it. My mom didn't want me to play it. She thought it'd be too hard—maybe that's why I picked it. It's harder than a lot of instruments, because the violinist's two hands are doing two different things. *He produced a quick imitation of bowing with his right hand and fingering a melody with his left hand.* The bowing is tough.

Q: What can you play?

A: "Gavotte" by Bach, a minuet by him, and "Melody" by Vivaldi. I'm pushing ahead. Mrs. Franklin is helping me out on an individual basis when I need it. *He had returned to nervously clicking the clasp on his watch.*

Q: So are you challenged by the music you're playing on violin?

A: Some of the stuff is pretty easy, but some takes practice. It's the speed, mostly, that makes it tough. And playing evenly.

Q: Does anyone else in your family play musical instruments?

A: My brother in eighth grade plays piano and trumpet. He started trumpet four years ago. But now he's playing the guitar. He's going to buy his own, but he's playing my dad's until then. He went to a garage sale, bought four big speakers for fourteen dollars, and figured out how to hook the guitar up to the speakers instead of an amp. It's awesome.

Q: But you'd rather play violin?

A: Why does everyone sound so surprised? *He shook his head and clucked his tongue to sound a tsk. I had not intended my question to provoke him so, to bring his look of exasperation. He raised his voice.* Yes, I would rather play violin. *He softened his tone again.* We rented this violin, but I'm gonna get my grandmother's, she said, if I keep practicing. I'm thinking about how a violin would sound hooked up to my brother's speakers. Pretty awesome.

Q: So do you practice every day?

A: Yeah. The teacher says to practice an hour a week—ten minutes a day—but that's too little. So I go for about thirty minutes a day, every day. My mom can hardly believe it. *He rolled his eyes, as if to indicate that he could barely believe her.* Sometimes on the weekends I forget, but then I make it up by doing an hour. My mom and dad are divorced, but they still live close. Sometimes if I forget my violin at my mom's house when I'm staying at my dad's house, I just have to play longer the next time.

Q: When is your lesson?

A: Twice a week. It's every Monday and Thursday, during the last forty-five minutes of the day. There are five of us from the two sixth grades who take this group lesson. Our teachers say that we have to make up the work we miss when we're at our lesson, so we do. Violin is a commitment, they say, but so is our other work. I basically stay in at recess to finish up or get ahead of myself.

Q: What does your family think of your playing?

A: My one brother sometimes makes fun of me. He thinks the violin . . . he thinks any instrument is inferior to the guitar. The guitar is king to him. But we might play violin and guitar together sometime, and see what it sounds like. Some kids in this school laugh at the violin players. *He smirked, as if to pass off their comments as inconsequential.* They're the ones to laugh at.

Q: Why do they laugh?

A: Well, the cool kids play trumpet or sax. But I've wanted to play violin for a long time. I used to listen to tapes of Mozart and Beethoven, and Vivaldi's *The Four Seasons* when I was little. Lots. So now I hope I can finally begin to play some of that stuff.

Q: Where do you listen?

A: At my dad's, we just have one stereo. Whatever we put on, everyone hears. And my dad's collection leaves a lot to be desired: the Rolling Stones, Pink Floyd, *Bye Bye Birdie,* and some orchestra music. Opera, too. Yuk. At my mom's, I've got my own CD player and headphones in my room. I listen to Mozart, Chopin, and Sting there. I like Sting. My stepdad has a lot of jazz CDs, and sometimes I listen to that. My little brother listens to little-kid music, and my older brother mostly listens to Nirvana and the Presidents of the United States.

Q: That last one's a group?

A: Yeah. *He sat smugly, "in the know," but did not describe the group, leaving me wondering whether he knew (or cared to know) much beyond the group's name.*

Q: Do you think that jazz and rock are different?

A: Yeah. Jazz is more mellow. Rock is pretty rowdy. I don't like the style. I'd prefer jazz to rock, especially jazz piano and jazz violin. But I like classical more.

Q: What do you feel like when you hear jazz and rock?

A: Jazz relaxes me. Rock makes me want to go someplace else. I don't like it. Mozart is relaxing to me, like jazz. Last birthday, I got some Chopin from my mom—she's always giving me tapes; I wouldn't have any of my own without her. Now he doesn't do violin music, but the piano music is really fine. Some of it reminds me of jazz; it kind of sounds ripply, like water.

Q: What are some of your favorite songs?

A: To sing? *He seemed to cower a little, then tipped his chair away from me on its back legs.* I'm out of here, if that's what you want. Mostly, I like to listen and play.

Q: How many songs do you know, that you could sing all the way through?

A: I never thought of it. Hmmm. I could probably do about eighty songs, counting rhymes. But they don't really have tones. Like "Peter, Peter, Pumpkin Eater" and Mother Goose rhymes. We're learning a lot of songs in music class and choir. Much more than when I was in kindergarten through the third grade. We had a different music teacher then, and no one liked her. For two weeks or more, we would have to do "Twinkle, Twinkle, Little Star" or some other bogus baby song. And she would read us stories, and some of them had nothing to do with music. Then we would sing a really short and really easy song that went with it. She was boring, and I heard that some of the kids in one of the older classes started laughing at her all the time, and she was crying, and finally she left. Then we didn't have a music teacher for a year.

Q: Did you miss not having a music class?

A: Not after that last teacher. *He laughed rather scornfully, once again with a break in his changing voice.* But I would miss music now, because Mrs. Phillips is so much better. We sing good songs, we learn to read music, we play some instruments, we listen to good stuff, and she can play piano really well and sing well, too.

Q: Are there musical "things" you'd like to collect?

A: Yeah. No question. I'd get some more CDs, probably Bach: He's got some great violin music. But I'd also like to buy tickets to some concerts of the symphony. And some African music concerts. To get back to what we were talking about earlier, I'd like to hear some good percussion music—conga and djembe music.

Q: Do you like to dance?

A: No way. *His expression was adamant, as if it pained him to think about the very act.* My brother likes to head-bang.

Q: What's that?

A: You just move your head back and forth, and around, kind of hard. He does this while he plays the guitar, or pretends to play. No thanks. It gives me a headache, just like his music does.

Commentary

Despite the occasional sour remarks and somewhat defensive nature of some of his responses, Jonathan had much to say about the music he knows and would like to know. His tendency to criticize and complain could well be evidence of a newfound personality shaped through his reaction to his parents' divorce; he did indeed prove to be somewhat cranky, guarded, and once even downright scornful. Even his body posture displayed some of the distrust and discouragement that he was harboring, as he slumped in his chair, folded his arms across his chest, and rarely made eye contact with me. This behavior could be attributed to the on-slaught of an early adolescence that was simmering beneath his skin; a difficult divorce could also have amplified it.

Jonathan is both stimulated and provoked by several people who command a strong presence in his life; there are signs of love-hate relationships he has developed with them. He describes Mrs. Phillips's knowledge of music, while at the same time he complains of her furious pace of moving the choir through a choral score (and is completely bewildered by her selection of arhythmic drummers to accompany them). He dislikes his brother's rock music, does not appreciate his taste in music or his "head-banging" style of dance, yet he appears enamoured of the amps his brother has acquired and is curious and willing to explore the possibility of playing violin-guitar duets with him. His mother's doubt may be part of his challenge to play violin, proof of the contrary nature that has taken seed within him; yet later he acknowledged his mother's gifts of musical tapes over the years.

Of all his critical comments, Jonathan's description of his previous music class teacher is perhaps the most vivid. He ridiculed her use of "baby songs"—songs that to him, even as a young child, were too short and too easy. He found her stories irrelevant: "They had nothing to do with music." When the school did not hire a replacement in the year following her departure, he claimed no teacher as preferable to the one he had found so boring. Such a description of a poor teacher can be taken as an advisory of features to avoid. He later listed the qualities of his current teacher: someone who can play piano and sing (well, in his estimation), who is able to select "good songs" and "good stuff" for listening lessons, and who is teaching useful reading and instrumental skills. While he did not define "good" relative to the repertoire his current teacher selects for instruction, it is nonetheless appealing to his twelve-year-old sensibilities. Underlying all of his comments is the manner and style of a teacher's delivery of information and the teacher's awareness of students' interests. He seemed somewhat satisfied with her sensitivity.

As with George, it is again a sorry instructional situation when essential equipment is scarce; a single drum to share among members of a large group seems a poor practice. Jonathan's description of the criterion by which students are selected to play this drum ("being the most quiet and paying attention") seems, at first glance, a fair way to reinforce appropriate social behaviors. On the other hand, it is a poor determinant of who will play musically, particularly when some of the most musical children may never merit the opportunity to play. If time is limited and a "best drummer" is to be selected to accompany the eventual performance of the choir, some consideration should be given to musical accuracy—even if that drummer may not have been among those who, according to Jonathan, sit perfectly still. Jonathan's point that "music moves, and it makes you move," is well taken. For some children, minding the music through one's bodily response to it could well be a way of "paying attention." Perhaps Jonathan will find better outlets (his uncle's djembes) on the outside for practicing Mrs. Phillips's rhythm pattern, but most children will not have such an affiliation. In this case, the selection of a child who will play accurately may benefit all children, who can then sing to the sound of an appropriately rendered rhythmic accompaniment.

Jonathan's observations on learning to read music, and of notation's function, are worthy of contemplation. He claimed that the pace of music-reading is too rapid and confusing in his choir rehearsal. As a reader of just single-line melodies, two-part scores with piano accompaniments are a big leap for him! The pace at which instruction is given (and received) is certainly an issue close to the heart of teachers, who strive to deliver, observe, and then to adjust the pace at which they deliver information, based on their students' retrieval of it. Perhaps Mrs. Phillips has employed the sink-or-swim tactic, fully immersing her students in musical notation for the sake of the experience in order to stimulate those who are ready; still, some modification may be necessary so that she will not lose and frustrate students like Jonathan. Mrs. Phillips also appears to be employing listening and mimesis in her instruction, blending rote with note techniques in drawing her choir into a piece. Whatever her techniques, the children are acquiring songs that are now "stuck" in their heads, some of them internalized for life.

Jonathan called attention to musical styles that are transmitted orally, and he wondered whether "notes can get in the way of music." Indeed, some traditions and pieces may be best learned without notation, particularly traditional and popular music and the music of oral cultures. Even multipart songs can be learned sans notation, with the teacher modeling one and then another part, and layering parts when it is evident that each has found its strength among the singers. Some blend of note and rote approaches may benefit goals of both notational literacy and keen aural skills, an appealing outcome of any music instruction.

Despite whatever obstacles he may face, Jonathan seems keen on learning to play the violin. He claimed to have had an interest for "a long time," no doubt due to his earlier listening experiences. He is remarkably (and unusually) committed to his daily practice and seems nonplussed about taking his recess time to complete classwork he missed during his lesson. His violin teacher is encouraging of his independent striving to further his skills at a more rapid pace. It is striking, however, that she would suggest a practice schedule that amounts to less than ten minutes a day (an hour a week), which for many beginners is barely enough time to tune the instrument; the development of motor skills cannot occur without the essential element of continuous repetition. Thus, the amount of time spent at practice is directly related to the extent to which a student will become skillful. Jonathan's development will easily surpass his classmates if he adheres to his self-set schedule.

Jonathan's sensitivity to musical styles and the moods they create are notable. He calls jazz "mellow" and rock "rowdy," and he prefers the former. Jazz, like Mozart, relaxes him, while rock is currently so irritating to him as to send him elsewhere just to avoid it. He compares "some" of Chopin's music to jazz, in that they both sound "ripply, like water." However, the true tale of the music that affects him deeply, or that minimally piques his curiosity, is found in his description of musical things he'd like: CDs for his own private listening, and tickets to public musical performances.

Reflections

Fifteen slices of fifteen children's lives, these conversations ran the gamut of children in a wide array of communities and schools. Through these glances—single snapshots of children at moments in their childhoods—came impressions of the nature of children and their musical involvement. They spanned a spectrum of musical experience, from the musically exposed to the musically trained, and from those with informal musical encounters to those with formal training via lessons. These children defined, dissected, and defended music in individual ways as they described their preferred styles and unique experiences. They offered an earful of their musical thoughts and desires, channels for an outsider's understanding of their musical needs.

The Spectrum of Children and Their Ideas

The fifteen represented a wide cross section of children. They ranged in age from four through twelve and were (with the exception of the preschooler) enrolled in public school classes from kindergarten through the sixth grade. There were seven girls and eight boys living within the limits of a large metropolitan area, including its center, peripheral neighborhoods, and suburbs, and in separate cities and towns all still within an hour's driving distance from the city center. Some children lived in upscale communities, others in lower-income neighborhoods, and a few more in working- and middle-class suburban homes. Their family units varied, too, with nine living in intact families and six others in families of divorced or separated parents, several without fathers but with grandparents at home instead. The cultural diversity of the children was considerable: Several were bicultural and bilingual; six were of European ancestry, four African Americans, two Chicanos, two of Asian parentage, and one declared himself about "half" Native American. Even religious diversity was apparent: references were made to Roman Catholic, Hindu, Jewish, and Christian tenets and practices. Given the spread of sociocultural characteristics of the fifteen children, no collective, unified image of them can be easily drawn. Rather, these distinctive individuals form a collage of who children musically are, their thoughts and practices occasionally but not so predictably coalescing on matters of their musical interests, uses, and needs.

In conversation with children, I sat with them at desks, on floors, on wooden chairs, on benches. We faced each other or, because of the available space or conversational style of the child, looked at the tape recorder, the pad on which I recorded my hasty jottings, around the room, or even out the window. Some sat comfortably and appeared quite relaxed, others were eager to talk and were thus poised expectantly at the edges of their chairs, and a few more bounced, swayed, rocked, and swung their legs in perpetual motion. In elementary schools and early childhood centers, where there are few soundproof places, it was no less than amazing to me that the children could concentrate as thoroughly as they did while the sounds of talk, laughter, song, and instrumental music bled through walls or sailed down corridors. My sense was that children *wanted* to talk with me about their music, what they favored and what they found unpleasant about it—by itself and as it was fit into curricular plans within the school day; thus, they were able to block out most of these potential distractions.

While I opened most of the conversations, the children were soon off and running in a variety of directions. A few held their own on a single topic for a considerable while (Beth's discussion of Nelson Eddy and Jeannette McDonald, George's comparison of music and sound, Manuel's narrative of his family band). Others, especially the younger children, tended to switch topics in a single breath. It had not occurred to me that we would fall into discussions of music at basketball games, *Jurassic Park,* whistles, songs with "cuss words," Barney, or Croatian weddings, but the children led me there. They spoke of music's meaning to them by way of how they used it in their lives: as emotional expression, entertainment, or communication, or for social and religious purposes. Because I sought to understand their musical thoughts and values rather than impose my own, I found myself stumbling into territories unfamiliar to me. Yet as the conversations flowed, so too did the insights they gave to me of their musical selves.

Music and Not Music

Few children directly defined music, and I did not probe for an exacting definition of it.[13] Some inferred their definitions of music, however, although few chose to analyze and then technically describe music for its sonic components and functions. At age six, George was intent on defining music for what it is and what it is not. He explained whistling and singing as "close music," as opposed to "instrument music," which "is kind of far from yourself." He referred to single-tone whistles and bird sounds as "just sound" and spoke to what he perceived to be the truly musical sound of the more melodic slide whistle. As well, George clarified that "drums that just bang on and on" sound more like loud clocks ticking than musical rhythms, which must "change from just all shorts to longs and shorts"— just as melodic music "change[s] tones once in a while."

James was also puzzling out what figured as music, and he reflected his own experiences in naming criteria; to him music required sound, ritual, and group participation. He referred to the Pledge of Allegiance as "the flag song" but then retracted, uncertain of its "fit" with other music. The parallels between singing and pledging were considerable to him, however, as he explained the importance of speaking together (perhaps with rising and falling inflections typical of school-children), at the same speed, and following the teacher-conductor. He waffled between music and not-music in his description of the "wave," the rippling visual phenonemon produced when fans in a ballpark rise from their chairs and sit again.

He described the group cheers of stadium fans as a "scream-sing" type of music, thus coining a new musical genre of his own.

As children named songs, performers, and styles and talked of their engagement as singers and players, it became clear that while music they knew varied considerably, there were boundaries they inherently drew between music and mere sound. They conceptualized music as rhythm alone (as in rhythmic chants and percussive sounds) or rhythm with pitch, in vocally or instrumentally generated melodies. Many named or referred to specific musical genres as examples of their image of "music": orchestral, piano, rock, jazz, church, dance, and country, among them. Yet even the youngest children rejected mere "sound" in their discussion of music, inferring that the everyday aural phenomena of people talking, horns honking, and motors growling did not "count" in their minds as music.

All in the Family

Among the merging of their experiences and articulations, perhaps none presents so great a unifier of this disparate group of children than the extent of their family's pervasive influence on their musical thoughts and choices. Direct or indirect involvement in music by either parent, by siblings, or by members of their extended families steered these children to many of their musical reckonings. Several children were particularly impressive on this count. Manuel was a clear-cut case of "the family that plays together stays together." No doubt, he was spending many hours in rehearsal with his musical parents, siblings, and uncle, learning the repertoire of their family band. In a somewhat similar vein, Lisa regarded her home and family as a haven of sorts, and she happily anticipated their coming together in the evenings to sing the songs that were "saved up" for such family time. These were circumstances where the music appeared to stabilize children within their family units and where family relationships were developed partly through or as a result of the music.

Parents figured prominently in the musical lives of these children. Michael, Darryl, and Carrie recalled their mother's lullabies, no doubt because they still are (or were until recently) sung to sleep by them. Ramona acknowledged the unmistakable presence of her mother's voice at church; James told of his mother's frequent singing of Elton John's "Crocodile Rock," a likely influence of his attraction to the star's music; and Tuyen credited her mother with the Vietnamese songs that she knows. A number of children described their father's musical choices and alluded to their interest in them as well: Michael sang Willie Nelson with his father, and Ramnad was intrigued by his father's Indian songs. James noted his father's past experience as a trumpet player, a likely catalyst for both his brother's and his own interest in playing. Anna was enamoured of her stepfather's involvement in the tambouritza bands. As for George's father, a weekend musician, both the presence of his bass guitar and the shop of music instrument–making were enticements for George.

Siblings played no small part in children's musical encounters in the home. Darryl excitedly described his sisters' instruments, Carrie admitted that she was discreetly learning her older brother's songs, and Lateesha indicated that she was recipient of both songs and dances through the modeling by her teenage sister and friends. While Jonathan rejected rock music, I wondered whether his brother's keen interest in it would eventually draw him to the style. Similarly, although Ramona claimed to dislike rap, I could imagine that the frequent occasions she had for hearing her brother's music might be enough to influence her future musical taste.

Sometimes, other family members can serve to musically enculturate children. There were two musical uncles that figured importantly: Manuel's guitarist-uncle, who may well have been the leader of his family's band, and Jonathan's uncle, a djembe-playing percussionist who provided him with opportunities to explore his instruments. For Beth, even while her parents patronized the arts and provided her piano (and her brother's violin) lessons, it was her grandmother's music that sparked her greatest interest. Ramona's description of her cousins was indicative of their importance to her as channels of musical information and enthusiasm.

Children's friends sometimes can seem like an extended family; these peers, often intimate friends from the neighborhood or school, are powerful influences on their thinking and valuing. The drum-playing of Manuel's twelve-year-old friend no doubt enticed Manuel to learn to play drums himself; other "band-fan" boys living nearby were also potential influences on Manuel. Alan described his friend's attempts at songs on the keyboard and explained that his observations of these attempts inspired him to later begin to figure them out himself. From Anna's description, the Saturday sessions spent playing music with her friends were richly rewarding to her. Tuyen's sleepovers with her girlfriend brought them both opportunities to listen, sing, and talk about music they like, with one girl influencing the other on this two-way path of musical discovery.

Music in School

Aside from the children's musical involvement at home and at play, two questions on music at school arose in these conversations: What were the children learning in music class (in their *own* views)? And, importantly, were they enthusiastic about music at school as they were about music outside of school?

From a positive stance, several children commented about "good" music teachers who performed well and who were kind to them and understanding of them. As Carrie noted, her music teacher seemed "like a mama or a brother" to her, familiar and comfortable. Tuyen applauded her music teacher, his goals, and his class strategies. Manuel praised the expansive nature of his music classes and seemed pleased to be learning to sing, move, play, and read music. James claimed to like music class "a lot" and explained his positive outlook as due to a combination of singing "upbeat songs," moving, playing instruments, and providing "lighting effects" for some of the songs they were learning. For Lateesha, her acceptance into an honor choir at school was a source of pride to her, as it had reinforced her own belief in herself as a singer. Alan's comments were positive, to the point of wishing aloud for "more time" in music class in order to learn more. Solid teachers and a varied curriculum were apparently important to children for forming their favorable views of school music.

A few voiced their critical comments. George found music "long sometimes," without enough instruments to be shared among his classmates. Likewise, Ramnad found his music class lengthy, adding that there were "too many songs" and not enough time to play instruments. Anna's comment, that there was "no new music," indicated that the pace of her band class was not sufficiently motivating to her and that she would need more frequent supplements to her repertoire to be truly challenged. It was the scenario which Jonathan painted that was perhaps the most riveting, of the teacher who taught "baby songs" that were too short and too easy and who told stories that had little to do with music; so poor was her teaching that he had decided he and his classmates were better off with no music than with music as he remembered it with her. Jonathan was also troubled with his teacher's acceptance of inaccurate renderings of a musical rhythm and was critical of the selection process by which children in the sixth grade would play the single drum available to them. For these children, a lack of musical or instructional variety, a slow instructional pace (with too much repetition), music or instructional approaches that were not developmentally appropriate, and even the teacher's willingness to honor less musical performances marred their impressions of school music.

If one could tally children's remarks on their school music experiences, the sum total of positive comments would probably outweigh the negative ones. Yet I could not help but wonder whether I had tipped the scales in favor of more favorable comments on school music, either through the informal selection process by which teachers may have chosen the more musically interested childen for conversations with me or through children's own wariness of offending me, a music teacher, on school music issues. It is clearly possible that some children might have felt a need to please me with "the right answers." Certainly, they may have been more reserved in their views on this topic of teachers and their lessons than on others that were more directed toward their own personal interests in music. Yet I sensed that the children were mostly at ease and comfortable in our conversations, thus inducing their rather frank commentaries. Indeed, some of the children's negative comments were straightforward and of sufficient sting to leave no doubt in my mind that these children felt no need to step lightly around the subject. But the positive comments were the stuff that teachers dream to hear, while the more critical ones give one pause in choosing a wise path in the further provision of music in the schools.

In the Long Run

It is intriguing to project what might happen to the fifteen children of these conversations; I could not help but wish to trace their musical lives clear through to their adolescent and adult years. As I listened to their ruminations, I wondered whether music might become more or less important to them in time and how schooling and training as well as future experiences on the outside could further shape their musical values. It is likely that some of the children will become more attuned to singing, playing particular instruments, dancing, or creatively composing their own musical expressions; some will undoubtedly lose interest. Which ones, I wondered, showed signs of continued participation in musical experience? Which ones will turn more passive in their musical involvement, and what will trigger this passivity as they mature?

Michael may well become the "clonductor" of his current fascination; Beth may find true happiness in musical theater; Jonathan may turn toward chamber music; Lateesha may take the stage singing in a "Whitney Houston way"; Tuyen may choose to teach music in an elementary school. Or they may, each and every one of them, find a place for their musical pleasures while making their livings in ways unrelated and removed from music. Yet in the long run, these children will each follow a musical pathway made for them by the experiences and instruction they have had in their childhoods. If they find that, as Carrie predicted, "music would be just for fun," how much greater pleasure and more profound experiences could they find through education that is relevant to their needs and interests? This is a question for which music teachers have a certain response: that music instruction can enhance and further the musical thinking and practices of children.

3
For Children:
Prospects for Their
Musical Education

This third section reflects on the dialogues and descriptions of children's musical repertoire, practices, and thoughts and looks ahead to possible interventions: school music practices, training through lessons, and parent-guided musical enrichment for children. It considers who the children musically are au naturel—in their natural state—and suggests possibilities for all that they can musically become. Thus, this is prescriptive as well as descriptive, in that it acknowledges the voices of children and recommends channels for their development in and through music. It is important for me to reiterate that my thoughts here emanate not only from experiences of the children whose tales have been recounted here but also from a conglomerate of my experiences as a longtime teacher of children, and to emphasize my belief in the great benefits to be had from making moments to talk with children, to watch them at musical play, and to listen to their songs.

　　The type of investigation from which these scenarios have proceeded does not provide the same type of evidence as that provided by a statistical analysis of a properly sampled large body of individuals (Gall, Borg, and Gall, 1996). Instead, their stories (and my stances) arise from a combination of unobstrusive observations of children and from interviews—conversations with children—reflective of an "idiographic" approach that borders on those used by phenomenologists. I wanted to accept the notion suggested by Jean-Paul Sartre that an individual fittingly can be called a "universal singular" (1981) and that scrutiny of a handful of individual children and groups of children could bring me greater understanding of children at large. Thus, while there are variations among the children as to music's role and importance in their lives, there are also notable patterns and commonalities among them.

This section recalls the individual snapshots presented earlier but is intended to examine the collage that they form together. The reflections herein also extend beyond the children of my fieldwork, too, all the way to broad views of children as a whole. All told, this section is a conversion of what I have heard and seen regarding the nature of children's musical selves into prospects for their education in and through music.

Who They Musically Are

Music emerges from children, and those of us privileged to have spent time in their company have heard it often. Music is on their minds and in their bodies. It is evident in their conscious musicking alone and together, and in the various musical expressions they produce. It is present in their discourse about music, too, as their voices rise and fall to explain music's importance to them, incorporating as they do melodies and rhythms in their speech to say what they mean to say. Music appears to be everywhere in the lives of children, and they love the musical parts of their lives.

Music serves children in many ways. They group together to socialize through music, but they also take music into themselves at their most private of times. They receive it from many sources, and they learn to sing it, play it, and dance to it. They interpret it for its messages to them and absorb and rework it in new configurations as their very own music. They "have music" and "do music" for its visceral appeal, for its calming or stimulating properties, and for the associations it has with nearly anyone or anything they can name. Music seeps into their play, their social activities, their work, and their worship and is with them as they do what they do and as they think aloud or in silence about the various experiences they know.

Music, then, is a childhood constant, patterns of rhythmic and pitched sound that may or may not be fully intended by children as music. Yet intended or not by them, these patterns often *are* music. Teacher that I am, listening to children for who they musically are, I would wager that the frequency of their musical utterances is certain evidence of their extensive engagement in music. With this proposition in mind, we might also marvel at the unknown: How much more music may be stored inside them, awaiting stimulation and development? What could become of children were we to pay greater attention to their ideas about music and to figure further ways to work them into their enrichment and training? There are structures to the sounds and movements children emit, many in the recurring rhythms and repeated melodies that they themselves organize. To the ear of this beholder, children have many musical moments—whether they know it or not. Their daily musicking is true testimony that children do indeed have songs in their heads, music to reveal to others and to revel in themselves. It is one of the tasks of teachers to listen for the music children manifest and to gauge their musical interests and needs accordingly.

The Music in Them

All children, to a greater or lesser degree, are musical. In fact, I would venture to say that children probably have more music inside than we tend to credit them with. As John Blacking defined it, music is "humanly organized sound" (1973, p. 10), and it exists in children's lives because of their biological abilities to discern it, feel it, and express it. They have the mental and physical equipment to perceptually organize the sounds they receive and to logically and inventively organize the sounds they produce. On countless occasions, children show themselves to be perceptive listeners (as in George's listening to drums and whistles to "figure them out"), sensitive performers (as in James's self-assessment of his own ability to sing "on pitch"), and thoughtful creators of music (as in Alan's humming of his original internalized melodies). They possess the capacity to become more fully (and perhaps more outwardly) musical through opportunities to engage in music, to study it, and to experience it with guidance to its many facets. Their biological selves gravitate naturally and readily to full participation in music, and they are captivated by it.

Of all of the phrases that have gelled into a kind of common usage, few have been as devastating to children's development as that of "talent." This Eurocentric concept of musical talent evokes thoughts of Mozart, the wunderkind, composing at five and performing in the grand European courts as a schoolchild. It creates images of musical participation for the very few: richly endowed geniuses who manifest enormous musical memories while still in the nursery, virtuosic performers with their pyrotechnic displays of athletic agility in top-speed passages, and composers who think profound and "universal" musical thoughts and structures to commit to notes on paper. These images of musical prodigies bring to mind the rare and enormously gifted individuals and set them up as freaklike and marginal to society; these prodigies may be seen as so distinguished as to possess superhuman abilities that separate them from the "norm," the mainstream.[1]

In such a conception of talent, education and hard work have little place, and environment counts for naught. It is as if to say that children are either born with enormous musical talent, or they are not, and that there is neither a spectrum of musical gifts nor the chance to stimulate through training their musical growth. I find this view difficult to accept and am instead prone to see those who succeed and distinguish themselves in any field as products of hard work. If a society accepts music as a valued professional channel, then a child's effort can make much of a widespread human capacity to listen, perform, and create. Thus, if

Jonathan's family were to value and encourage his musical accomplishments, perhaps he would be likely to attain greater musical heights in his violin-playing. Likewise, were the musical moments of the young Zebras to be acknowledged and deemed important by their teachers, perhaps their structured daily activities would include a plan for the development of their basic listening and performance skills. The danger comes when people perceive talent as a rare genetic endowment and then question the use of instruction for the untalented masses. This position has been responsible for music's position as an afterthought, left out of the education of too many children. What then happens to the musical spontaneity, interests, and joys reflected in Lisa's songs? In Alan's self-discovery at the keyboard? In the raps, rhythms, and musical games of children at play? Unless we seize opportunities to develop what is natural through training and education, the musical impulse is likely to wither and fade.

Sadly, it is fashionable in most Western cultures to pay tribute to the musically elite minority who are tagged early on as "talented" and then tracked and provided with the training that others cannot have. Children who at the outset of their training do not fit the mold of what a gifted musician should possess are then given minimal stimulation in the schools, often not a great deal more than this thing called "exposure" (the result of a half hour's worth of group music instruction given once weekly—about twenty hours of music in an average school year). Thus are many children musically inhibited by a society's absence of an arrangement for their education, while the talented few are given an imbalance of full and continuous attention. The great majority of children are educationally disadvantaged by the very societies that claim to bring them a full development of their abilities through the schools they have created. The words of John Blacking surface again, striking at the plain and logical truth: "Must the majority be made 'unmusical' so that a few may become more 'musical'?" (1995, p. 130). The real-life response within our educational systems to this rhetorical question is telling of how musical ability is conceived within a society.

Some cultures do not accept this concept of musical talent or believe that there are unmusical people living among them. The Venda of South Africa consider all members of their society musical, although some may be better performers than others (Blacking, 1967). In Bulgaria, virtuosic instrumentalists are seen as the products of the time and patience required to hone a skill, rather than as a result of some mysterious endowment (Rice, 1994). Music saturates the homes of Mexican Americans, so that Chicano children are musically enculturated from earliest childhood and develop a propensity to sing traditional and popular songs of their culture (Loza, 1996). Balinese children absorb the music of the gamelan gradually and naturally, listening as they play near their elders who practice and perform (J. Becker, 1980). In the Tshokwe society of central Africa, babies participate in communal dancing with their mothers, who sway, rock, and shake rhythms into their bodies such that all develop a basic musicianship even in infancy

(Schmidt-Wrenger, 1985). Among the Suya of the Amazon River basin, singing and dancing are not an option but an obligation—events in which everyone participates; children later play with the music that they have performed with adults (Seeger, 1996). In these cultures, some are seen as "good at" making music, but all normally endowed persons are as capable of doing music as they are of breathing. If they talk, they can sing; if they walk, they can dance; and if they can hear or feel the vibrations of musical sound, they can respond to them. Music belongs to many, and they engage in it because they can and because it is a cultural expectation to do so.

If we were able to accept that there may be a certain biological bent that all persons have for music, whether by way of engaged listening or active production, we might then be able to conceive of musical talent in a new light.[2] As we recognize that many of the world's societies continue to advocate the full participation of its members in musical performance and invention, we may alter our own expectations of children's musicking potential. While it is likely that the mass media has been the cause in the Western world for much of the move from active musical involvement to passive reception, for most children this media is but a channel for musical information, a pause in their more active musical lives. Children still require active musicking by evidence of their conscious and subconscious musical behaviors. In the midst of an energetic and expressive performance by children, we may also realize the power music has to transform thinking and feeling. We may even come to grips with the extent to which children's individual capacities can be developed through education for even greater potency. Children, every one of them musical, deserve to be taken as far as their many "talents" can carry them. We teachers and parents are key players in this challenge.

What Music Means to Children

Children find music a meaningful part of their daily life, and they derive meaning from the music they experience. This may seem a straightforward "fact" at first, yet on second thought, musical meaning is a complex issue. Many writers have sunk their teeth into the topic, seasoning it with a personal perspective and then digesting it according to their given subdiscipline. Getting a grasp on what music means to children is coming to understand what they know and value. This leads naturally to considering what children need to know to become more fully musical—and more fully human. Thus comes this excursion across disciplines in an attempt to sort out what makes music meaningful, including its emblematic uses, its surface and deep structures, its parallels to language.

Musical meaning has been of interest across cultures and through the ages. Its acoustical and formal properties have been viewed as "vessels" of meaning, carriers of thoughts and sentiments. The ancient Greeks determined that modes contained acoustic messages that brought joy or melancholy to its listeners (Sachs,

1943). Indians have adhered to the tenet that particular ragas are appropriate for particular times of day (Wade, 1979), just as the choice of the Persian *dastgah* is also loaded with meaning and is fit for certain seasons, times of the day or night, and moods (Zonis, 1973). As well, the Chinese have applied cosmological interpretations to music through their Yellow Bell Theory (Han and Mark, 1980), in which each pitch is symbolic and richly connotative. Many have puzzled over the dimensions of music's cultural and personal meanings, but principally as it is conceived by adults who bring long periods of enculturation or education to given experiences and repertoires; children are either ignored or viewed as so early in the process of discovering its meaning as to be of little consequence for study. Yet if children possess music—and they do—they embrace it for what it already symbolizes and does *for* them and *to* them.

Some have philosophically addressed the issue of music's having either "absolute" or contextual meanings, and their thoughts have been influential among teachers of music to children. In midcentury, Leonard Meyer posed his thesis of emotion and meaning in music and distinguished three types of listeners (1956). He asserted that formalists value the abstract patterning of music in and of itself, so that musical meaning is regarded by them as absolute and unchanging in its meaning regardless of what experience the individual may bring to it. This view he contrasted with that of the expressionists, who accept music as a vehicle for expressing emotions, and referentialists, who find musical meaning through the extramusical images that music may bring. Meyer himself advocated the position of "absolute expressionists," who maintain that musical meaning is intrinsic in the music and who derive emotional meaning from an understanding of the interplay of music's component parts. Bennett Reimer's philosophy of music education (1970) was launched partly from Meyer's explanation of absolute expressionism and has been influential for several decades in supporting school music instruction for children for its power to mesh thought and feeling.[3] Yet all of this seems distant from recognizing which music *moves* children before, aside from, and as a result of a musical education.

Thoughts about what music means to people have been carried so far as to make comparisons of music with language, and attempts have been aimed at understanding not only the phenomenon and structure of sounds but also their designative and connotative meanings. Linguist Noam Chomsky (1957; 1975) posited that every sentence consists of both a surface and a deep structure. He claimed that the surface structure of language is related to the string of words—even phonemes, individual syllables—we hear, while the deep structure is related to the underlying meaning behind the sounds and symbols. Leonard Bernstein (1976) offered a compelling comparison of music with language, suggesting that meaning was not to be found in individual tones and durations but in the musical phrases that conveyed not only pitch and rhythm but also expressive information through the manner in which the sounds were connected. The maestro maintained that the essence of music was to be "read between the lines" and to be found around and within the notes and phrases. Fred Lehrdahl and Raymond Jackendoff (1983) elaborated on music/language parallels in their analysis of musical forms as grammatical structures and thoughts. Music, including music that children produce and prefer, is replete with phonemes and structures (and repeated melodic and rhythmic patterns) that convey to them, even without words, a sense of familiarity, safety, and stability. Embedded within the melodies and rhythms are messages that are as explicit as they are implicit—in expressions of ideas that are both concrete and abstract.

While instrumental music owes its meaning to its structures, Simon Frith contended that for vocal music, the meaning of a song may not even be conveyed so much through the melodies or even words that singers sing as through the way they sing it (1988). The pauses, sighs, elongations, changes of inflection and volume that the singer controls all convey tremendous meaning (p. 120). For Lateesha, it was not just what songs Whitney Houston sang but how she sang them, just as the nuances of So For Real's "Candy-Colored Raindrops" were very much a part of how Tuyen sang it. The vocal inflections and expressions are the essence of a singer's personalization of a song and are often what make (or break) their careers, endearing them to their listeners. As both the words and the singer's expressive performance give songs their meaning, children, too, carry and communicate their ideas and feelings through the manner in which they sing.

Semiotics, the study of a sign (or a text) for its concept rather than merely its name and "thing," has been applied to an understanding of what meaning music may hold for people. In 1990, Jean-Jaques Nattiez clarified his view of "the musical work [as] not merely text but also structures; how it is composed, interpreted, perceived" (p. 116). He claimed that the meaning of a musical work will vary among persons and cultures and that music-as-object can only take on meaning when the individual perceiver or producer places it into his or her own lived experience. From a semiotics stance, music is not only the component sonorities which the composer thought and weaved together but also the result of how it was expressed in performance and what personal and cultural perceptions the listener brought to it. Music's meaning is contained in the experience of it rather than in the sound alone and is colored by life and times of the individual. A song is then both personal and cultural baggage, and every singer of every age conveys far more than the rise and fall of pitches in a melody when he or she sings.

Ethnomusicological questions of music's meaning have arisen in the study of musical cultures, and many have come to terms with it semiotically. Mark Slobin (1993) offered the essence of semiotics as allied to music with his statement that "It isn't how the music sounds, but how it can be thought that counts: outsiders—even if certified by doctorates in music—all have tin ears" (p. ix). The meaning of a song, musical work, or event is thus seen as affected by the identity of each individual who interacts with it. Thus, Darryl sang Barney songs, while Michael warned me not even to ask him for one. Steven Feld's angle on identity was a somewhat reversed yet not opposing view: he claimed that some individuals find something of their identity *through* the music they experience (Keil and Feld, 1994, p. 93). A single musical work can be perceived in many ways, and each experience with it (even by the same individual) can vary considerably. Charles Keil described the individual's unique perception of a musical work or event and certified that, like personal moods, "Nobody has the same music"; musical choices vary because each work speaks uniquely to each individual (Keil and Feld, 1994; p. 163).

Musical meaning is found within the disposition of the individual while he or she is in the act of the musical experience—as listener, performer, or composer— and it is flavored by the culture in which the individual was reared or resides. Lucy Green's philosophical thesis (1988) on the duality of inherent and delineated meanings projects a somewhat similar stance, in which she explained that the former (meaning embedded within music's internal components) is connected to the latter (music's contextualization, and its subjective values to the individual). Music is meaningful, she claimed, because of what it is of itself and for how it is personally and socially situated. Meaning may be found not in a scientific analysis of its elements (alone) but by looking, as John Blacking did, to the "constructions which people put on it" (1995, p. 46). Thus, each child brings her unique perspective to a song or instrumental piece, so that its meaning is based on who she is and what her experience has been.

From a cognitive standpoint, music may affect several thinking and feeling domains within the mind and thus may hold manifold meanings for children. Music may "leak" from the location at which it is processed in the mind to other realms of experience and thought about it. The playground songs of the Horace Mann children, for example, may permeate clear through the musical domain to the realm of social relationships (as in the case of the "power ranger" rap), of language forms and expressions (as in "My Sailor"), and of forecasts of their future occupations (as in "Jump In"). John Sloboda (1985) first posed the possibility of music's having no semantics and being psychologically self-contained. He then refuted this claim, arguing that "music is not a closed sub-system. . . . There is some 'leakage.' Musical experience is translated into other representational modes" (p. 59). It seems that as listeners receive music, they often associate it with beliefs, sentiments, and images. They may characterize a musical work somewhat programmatically, such as linking its sound with a deep and lasting friendship, a heroic struggle, or the calm after a storm (p. 59). Likewise, Howard Gardner (1983) asserted that "music and language may have arisen from a common expressive medium" (p. 98) but stated that "there is still utility in recognizing different mental organizations associated with different levels of understanding" (p. 315). Music's meaning may thus be found in its association with, or as a symbol of, some extramusical event. The mind may be compartmentalized, but it also operates to blend what it musically perceives into a fuller and more integrated experience.

So how do children find music meaningful? And what sorts of meaning are to be found within their music? No doubt, music offers children powerful aural images by which they come to understand themselves symbolically and emotionally. Music is the repository for their varied moods, a means by which they can relate to who they are (or are in the process of becoming) at particular times and places. Through music, they reflect upon themselves, their experiences, and the relationships they have with their friends and members of their family. As they listen to a musical work, children may conjure up associative meanings, sentiments they "hear" conveyed through the musical sonorities and structures, or even stories they imagine the music to be telling them. As children sing or play, they are revealing not just mere skills but also thoughts and feelings that they can convey in no other way. When they improvise spontaneously, they are expressing what they are musically thinking in that instant (although it may be the end product of years of musical experience), and their compositions are the results of working out and preserving for future performances what they have come to think and feel about music or a host of other matters that are important to them. Music in general has meaning because no other avenue allows quite these occasions for children's thinking and feeling aloud. Meanwhile, separate songs and styles hold unique meanings based upon who they are—personally, culturally, and as the result of musical experience and training.

Music: Good for What?

For children, musical meaning is deeply related to function. "Good music," we say, should be the stuff of children's experience; "good for what?," they want to know.[4] They use music in its every guise and function and find that as they think and do music, they are buoyed by it, comforted in it, reflective through it, and exuberant as a result of it. Their uses of music range from the playful to the serious, and from the solitary to the social. These uses or functions fit categories raised by Merriam (1964) and Gaston (1968); I use Merriam's list as an organizer here. Importantly, music contributes in positive ways to children's lives, and many recognize—even in their youth and inexperience—that they could not live without it.

Emotional expression. Music's power to express raw emotions is not lost on children. For Alan, one of his chief reasons for singing on the stump so far removed from everyone and everything was as a means of releasing his emotions, expressing his feelings, and trialing his musical thoughts without interference. With no one within earshot, his wailing may have been as much for the sheer release of tension as for the opportunity to hear himself at full volume. The six-year-old girl's outcry ("Alive, I'm alive!") was indicative of the joy she knew while swinging freely through the air. Lisa's patchwork songs had been emotive, too, and a channel for letting go—particularly on the neutral syllables, when words no longer interfered with the melodies she was thinking.

Aesthetic enjoyment. Contrary to popular belief, the deep emotional and intellectual enjoyment of music is not an exclusive "adults-only" experience. Children are drawn to music for its power to bring fuller enjoyment to their lives. Of those with whom I conversed who studied an instrument, a few had been motivated by their peers or by other musicians they had heard, yet I detected that some were drawn by the sense that lay deep within them of the great pleasure they could know in becoming musically proficient on an instrument. This deep fulfillment was also evident in the words of Darryl, who had claimed that he sang when he was happy; I wondered whether he became "happier" as a *result* of his singing, and in Anna's declaration that music "gave her strength" as she tuned into a musical world that could bring her benefits that she could know in no other way. Particularly revealing to me of children's aesthetic enjoyment were their gestures during Mrs. Bedford's listening lessons; they bounced, patted rhythms,and pretended to play imaginary instruments, clearly delighted to be riding the music's energy and flow.

Entertainment. Children might not call music "entertaining" to them, but on many occasions that is precisely how it functions. It was clear through numerous conversations that children are entertained by their tapes and CDs, by radio music, and by the music on TV, films, and their favorite videos. From what they said, music appears to be at the forefront of their amusement, as in the case of those who fall to sleep with their favorite tapes playing. Some inferred music's way of hovering just behind the animated and dramatic stories on the TV programs and films which they watch. Visitors to the toy store were in several instances visibly entertained by the musical parts of a selection of toys and sound machines. Music also played an integral to the games that entertained them; the hand-clapping and jump-rope games they played were rarely without the rhythmic chants or sung melodies of the rhyming verses.

Communication. Important sentiments are conveyed through music and can be understood as well by children as by adults within the same society. Numerous times, children allowed their speech to turn rhythmic and even melodic in its inflections; Darryl's rhythmic resopnse to one of my remarks ("The table's not an instrument. Don't you know?") and the preschool children's chant ("If you drop it, pick it up") are two such examples of their verbal communications turned musical. But in addition, they receive messages intended to be communicated by the music—from the romantic images conveyed by popular songs to the solidarity and strength expressed by a family's singing of a funeral song.

Physical response. To many children, music and movement are inseparable. Besides their consistent kinesthetic involvement as singers, players, and listeners, some acknowledged their attraction to music for "dancing to"; George, Carrie,

Ramona, Manuel, Lateesha, and Anna had spoken enthusiastically of music's function in inciting dance. James went so far as to explain adult music as "sit-there-and-not-move" music that challenged (if not deterred) his listening to it, and Jonathan articulated the kinethestic reality of music for children: "It moves, and it makes you move." Children danced as they played and worked (for example, in their tasks as members of the cafeteria cleanup crew); they jumped, clapped hands, patted legs, conducted, swung towels, and tapped brooms and dustpans in time to the music they heard. Whether choreographed and stylized, or free and spontaneous, movement is a principal means of children's musical engagement.

Enforcement of conforming to social norms. Two illustrations clarify music's use to provide instructions or warnings; both are adult-initiated but clearly received by children. Parody is a fairly common instructional technique by which new words are added to a familiar melody in order to introduce concepts and information to children. Carrie's first-grade teacher had parodied "Up on the Housetop," laying the spider verse atop the popular Christmas song's melody; the catchy melody worked well to deliver the informational "goods" to Carrie and her classmates. As for music's function in providing a "warning," perhaps James's reference to the Dragons theme as a "signal tune" is appropriate. This melody's function was not only to energize and unite fans but also to give them notice that a game was about to begin or a particular play was on the verge of happening.

Validation of religious rituals. Children are aware of music's presence in their prayer and religious practices. Ramnad had confided that when he heard Indian music, he felt like praying; the sound was reminiscent of his weekly visits to the temple with his family. Ramona referred to the gospel music of her church services, Beth mentioned the music of the bar mitzvah, and Anna and James described their participation in the children's choirs of their churches. Their families and communities had directed them toward worship that was well seasoned with music.

Continuity and stability of culture.   Music functions in children's lives as a means of linking them to their cultural heritage and reflecting the values of their ethnic culture. Ramnad's description of Divali, Ramona's participation in gospel-style singing, Manuel's performance of mariachi music, Anna's dancing to tambouritza music, and Tuyen's intent to learn the songs of her first country—all are illustrations of musical cultures that are kept alive and well for children (and by them) in their families and communities. These are cases in which music's use is to preserve in children the cultural expressions that are deemed important enough to be transmitted to them by their elders—by us.

Integration of society.   Music brings children together and unites and integrates them within a society. Their "society" is their family, their school group, their neighborhood. Whether they sing together, as in Darryl's family, "bang" together rhythmically on pots and pans, as in Ramona's family, or play in a family band like Manuel's, they coalesce and draw closer to one another. Certainly, their singing games and the polyrhythmic activities in which they engage (for example, in Mrs. Bedford's class) bring them closer to the friends with whom they play. Their membership in social groups that sing and play music at home and on the school ground is also a means of their greater unity through music.

Thus are children drawn to music for its personal and social uses, verbally explained or demonstrated by them through their musicking behaviors. Music's meaning is its function to them, and it may hold its own center stage or may enhance another activity in which they are engaged. For each musical experience a child may have, its meaning will be related to its use to them and will be wrapped around the experiences which the individual brings to bear upon it.

Learning, Enculturation, and the Schools

Children develop in similar ways across the human species. Without denying the individual identities of each child on C-bus or in Mrs. Bedford's music class, nor of Lisa, Lateesha, and all of the other children with whom I conversed, there are biological universals among them. Children are wired for sensory experiences, and these senses feed them information on their surroundings. Intuitively, they explore their worlds and develop through trial-and-error experimentation a sense of who they are and how they can satisfy themselves. They seek to feed their appetites, to quench their thirsts, and to stay safe and warm. They come to understand their relationships with people and learn how to effectively communicate with significant people in their lives. They progress through stages of language and conceptual understanding that unite and define them as children regardless of the environment in which they live. In short, like all young animals, children make use of their senses in understanding their world.

Yet even though children are biogenetically configured in much the same ways (Sloboda, 1985), their social and cultural environments lend some variety to their neurobiological development. While certain information is perceived and understood by children at large as a result of their membership in the human family, other knowledge is shaped by the cultures in which they live. They are who they are as a result of growing up within families, neighborhoods, and religious, social, and ethnic-culture communities, each of which has particular information to impart. As a result of their individual family circumstances, six-year-olds George and Carrie and eleven-year-olds Tuyen and Anna hold four quite separate worldviews. Children are socialized within these groups and are products of their perspectives. The nature/nurture issues arise, as children's natural selves are nurtured by the many and varied influences of the social units to which they belong.

In their ongoing use of their senses to adapt to their environment, children are learning. I see this learning as falling into three categories: (1) *Enculturative,* natural and without formal instruction; (2) Partly *guided* by informal and nonconsecutive directives; and (3) Highly *structured* and sequential in process. The first learning type occurs more often outside school than within, the third more likely within school than on the outside, and the second both in and out of school settings.[5]

The enculturative learning of children quite occurs naturally and without the direct attention of adults. This intuitive learning proceeds informally through children's immersion within and exploration of a culture. Children are enculturated prior to schooling as they experience, evolve theories, and learn symbols based on what they see, hear, taste, smell, and touch. They learn the values and expressions of their culture, including language and music. Yet even as their schooling begins, this natural learning continues. As their more sophisticated needs are addressed at ever higher stages of cognitive processing within the school curriculum, children continue to be enculturated by parents, teachers, siblings, extended-family members, friends, and the media. Through these channels, the tenets of the culture, including musical culture, are passed on to them (including what Charles Seeger calls "the music from below"—their musical roots). Enculturation is the primary means by which young children receive information and remains an important source for their acquisition of knowledge and values even as they mature.[6]

Guided learning occurs when experts describe, explain, and model ideas and behaviors to novices; a typical scenario is adults guiding children. As children mature, they increasingly are guided by the adults who teach them the ways of the world informally and in a nonconsecutive manner. They watch and listen to their parents, mentors, teachers, and elders, and while the information may not be passed on in a sequential and orderly fashion, children learn nonetheless. Guided learning typically involves the intent of the transmitter to teach and of the receiver to learn, but it may occur at home, in the backyard, or in their grandmother's kitchen. Learning to stir-fry vegetables, to repair the flat tire of a bicycle, to sing a "grace-before-meals" song, or to play a boogie-woogie bass line on the piano can all be accomplished by way of guided learning. It is not "happenstance" or coincidental learning but is purposeful and aimed at a particular learning outcome.

Highly structured learning is the stuff of schooling and the school curriculum. It is, as it sounds, a carefully laid out instructional plan that proceeds sequentially from one step to the next to ensure learning. The order of presentation is thoughtfully designed according to the age and experience of children, but the logical progression of information toward the goal is evident. Multiplication tables, grammatical structures, and the reading of music are typically accomplished through a sequential process, with teachers intent on delivering strategies that result in their students' learning. This tradition is didactic and nonconstructivist in nature.

Schools exist to pass on to children the principal heritage of a society, large-scale cultural knowledge that is deemed important for all, not only for children's own survival but also for the continued enlightenment of members of that society in generations to come. Schools are the sites where education transpires, where teachers are entrusted with the responsibility of imparting the substance of subjects to their children. A school's educational goals are embedded within its curriculum, and each subject is included on the basis of its perceived importance for children to know, along with the realization that it may be too difficult to learn elsewhere. From ages five through eighteen, or thereabouts, children are expected to master the concepts and literacies of these school subjects.

Learning happens to children as a result of schooling, yet much of their natural ability requires the assistance of teachers. The instruction children receive requires structure and a well-tailored sequence fit especially to them by those who are knowledgeable in both the subject and its pedagogy. Learning also happens in spite of schooling, because children do not always learn what the schools articulate as their goals. Many become "good citizens," but some do not. Many become more humane and more greatly enlightened of their societal heritage, while others choose instead to ignore the school material in favor of what they can acquire at home, through the media, and on the street. Since children are influenced by their own personal and cultural worlds, they typically will examine information they receive from their teachers, match it to their needs and interests, and discard the parts they do not find relevant. Children can be persuaded of the relevance of certain knowledge through their teachers' explanation and illustration of its application to their lives, however, although this is all too rare an occurrence. The standard school curriculum and its manner of delivery are appropriate for the prototypical "normal" student, but many children's interests and needs are not well served by a middle-of-the-road, standard, or sometimes even elitist curriculum. Thus, rather than acquiring and retaining much of their societal heritage, some children allow only the relevant, intuitive, and environmentally influenced knowledge into their lives—knowledge embedded within their communities.

The education children receive in school can support some of their "outside" enculturative learning, however. In fact, it must. Schools that divorce themselves from the challenges of the real world of everyday children, that scale back and simplify beyond recognition the meaning of a subject, and that give little opportunity for children to apply what they have mastered to new contexts cannot accomplish the noble goals of transmitting and preserving heritage. Bright and well-informed young people are the result of schools that *honor* children's earlier and concurrent pathways of enculturative knowledge. Their teachers do not assume this knowledge to be inferior but find ways to associate what children know with what they need to know. Intuitive and informal learning beyond the school can be the launch and the motivation to a more thorough and lasting understanding of the concepts and literacies that schools profess to teach.

The Mission of School Music

There is responsibility that comes along with the privilege of knowing well children's musical interests and values and of recognizing that structured learning through schooling can take them beyond their natural, intuitive, and enculturated musical selves. Within the plans that schools have for educating children in the primary and intermediate grades, there is usually some articulation of the importance of developing children's expressive and artistic capacities. The expressive can stretch as far as creative writing and inflective and dramatic reading, but the artistic typically refers to education in the visual arts, music, dance, and drama. If we laid aside the last two because of their rarity (or their occasional subsumption within physical education and language arts lessons), art and music are the most commonly found expressive and creative subjects within a school curriculum. They are long-standing fixtures within school programs. They may stand firmly on their traditions within a school, district, and community, and sometimes they flourish. Occasionally, they are relics of a bygone era when the arts were well funded, but in financially unstable periods they are viewed sideways and skeptically as "frills." Too often, they limp along on their encounter-class "exposures" of music in thirty minutes or less or are integrated in trite, unthinking, and haphazard ways into the general curriculum to enhance the learning of other subject matter. In some settings, art and music face extinction from the curriculum, or they are already gone.

Consider the varied perceptions and disparate values of music study—by musicians, teachers, and the public at large. From the standpoint of musicians and music educators, music is important to the education of children. The purposes of school music instruction have been variously offered. The *National Standards for Arts Education* declared the benefits of arts education, including music, to be the cultivation of the whole child and the provision of "bridges to things we can scarcely describe, but respond to deeply" (1994, p. 7). Bennett Reimer's stance of music education as aesthetic education has long been grounded in leading students through training to a fuller aesthetic enjoyment of music for its intrinsic power to cause feelingful responses to it (1970). While he recognizes music's nonmusical functions, Reimer holds firmly to the value of its musical-artistic nature. For Keith Swanwick, music and the arts are "unique activities where mastery, imitation, and imagination can be sustained and amplified through and beyond childhood, unlike overt play which tends to disappear" (1988, p. 50). He noted that teachers "pick and mix" their curriculum from several options, including the continuation of traditional values of the cultural mainstream, the nurturance of children's individuality and creativity, and the enlightenment of children in the cultural roots of popular media music (pp. 10–17). David Elliott pronounced singing and playing instruments as the heart of what music is and emphatically proclaimed that music education ought to be centrally concerned with teaching and learning musicianship, with "music making as a matter of musical knowledge-in-action" (1995, p. 72). Each of these positions is centered on well-reasoned logic and is persuasively presented—at least, it appears so to those within the field of music education.

Beyond the world of the music professionals, music often falls in stature among the subjects of a school curriculum. Classroom teachers at large (and their administrators) often accept in principle that music is a fundamental facet of a common cultural core of knowledge, yet they may feel uncertain by a sense of their musical inadequacy (however unfounded and untrue it may be) or confused in the selection of music materials and methods to use, or anxious as to how they can fit music of any sort into a chock-full schedule. Some uphold children's right to know the music of Mozart and Beethoven, Bernstein and Sondheim, as well as work songs, spirituals, and play-party songs, and they hope for the inclusion of the music "somewhere" along the way. A few advocate a study of the origins and texts of certain songs and musical works as a means of knowing the people for whom these cultural expressions and events were meaningful, at particular times and places, and a few more may even integrate music into their lessons in the social studies and language arts. The greatest number of classroom teachers will pass the responsibility of musically educating children to the specialist-teachers whom they regard as the trained performers, more musical than themselves.

Even farther afield from the music professionals' stance are community members at large, including parents. They, too, hold opinions on the status of music and the arts in the curriculum, some of which are sadly negative (or neutral at best). Since music is a pervasive force in our society and available twenty-four hours a day at the press of a button, some question the reason of adding it to a school menu loaded to capacity with the bread-and-butter subjects. They pose questions on the necessity of the arts for children's survival and future success in the world, for finding their roles in society, for enlightening them about their world. "Kids know what music they like," they argue, when in fact they may more accurately "like [only] what they know" (or are taught to know). Some may see the value of music—usually of the instrumental variety—for the talented few but may argue that tax monies are better spent elsewhere than on singing and "general music" classes. Across-the-board music instruction for all children is simply not wise spending to many folks, and the return is unclear or questionable. The elitist concept of musical talent again rears its ugly head and threatens to sweep music out of the mainstream of education.

Yet when it comes to the issue of music's necessary place in the curriculum, the public may have a point worth pondering. For music is easily accessible for multiple uses. Music does attract children among its avid fans, including the very young, who require little to no guidance to cherish their choices. No one adult needed to lead the children of the Horace Mann schoolyard in their musicking, nor was there adult intervention in determining what songs should be sung on the C-bus. Children are still able to engage in music beyond the schools, in their own way and at a speed that is comfortable for them. They choose music for which they have a special affinity and which suits their own particular personality and mood. They sing songs by modeling their favorite singers, and they play keyboards, guitars, and drums by listening, watching, and exploring their possibilities.

Many children "do" plenty of music on the outside, relevant to their interests (more relevant to real life, they may think, than marching bands or Orff xylophones). Music is there for children to enjoy, and they do enjoy it. Thus, as Keith Swanwick observed, "Music is not a problem until it's institutionalized" (1996). Brought into the scope of their schooling, curricular music presents challenges to teachers, taxpayers, and even students.

Like the old Indian parable of the five blind men who feel five different parts of the elephant, there are many views of music's mission and its place (or lack of one) in the schooling of children. The eloquent philosophical statements of leading music educators on music's purpose in the curriculum are level-headed and impressive, so it is unfortunate that their impact is not often known or perhaps understood beyond the membership of this comparatively small professional group. The supportive views of friendly teaching colleagues for music as part of the core of subjects are appreciated—as well as those who hold music to be an important part of a heritage to be passed on to the progeny. The views of those farther afield, the public at large, are troubling and made more distressing because they are the most widely known; they are thus the most dangerous to children's prospects for structured means for the development of their musical potential. The disparity of positions is dizzying, and the last position requires a thoughtful (if seemingly defensive) response.

In the array of wordy expressions and staunch perspectives, a child's view may at first seem the least eloquent and somehow insignificant. Yet the mission of music in the schools may be reduced to its bare-bones reality through the words of an eleven-year-old. In all of her young wisdom, Tuyen had groped for a way to explain why music was important to her. Her tone was determined, and the questioning inflection at the end was more a matter of ascertaining whether I had understood her than of doubting her own position. She announced: "You wouldn't starve without music. But" (with every little thing she learns about it, she sees that) "it makes my life worth more?" There it was in a nutshell, the clear purpose of musically educating children, *to make life*—their lives—*worth living.* [7]

Many of the school's subjects—mathematics, the language arts, and the social studies—hone the skills vital for succeeding in society, for earning an eventual independent living. But the arts give living its joy and passion and magnify children's life events as they also allows occasions for its contemplation. The more we learn about music, the deeper and richer our lives. The challenge of schooling—and the task of teachers—is to draw out the best of each child's potential as a thinking, acting, and feeling being. We owe the Tuyens of the world a chance to know enough music well to select it out for their many moods and uses outside of school. Every child, regardless of family resources (or lack thereof), deserves a chance to participate in music as skillful singers and players and to enjoy it as a unique outlet for their expression.

Children's Big and Little Cultures

Children constitute their own "big" culture, united by the experiences of their brief lives and the knowledge they have acquired and stored within them. In their early phases of learning, children's acquisition of conceptual knowledge is rapidly developing, and this knowledge is still in various formative stages. Their worldviews are different from those of adults and adolescents with longer life experiences, and while their perceptions are colored by their sociocultural surroundings, they share with each other similar extents of knowledge, as well as play preferences and interests that are associated with their similar intellectual, social, and physical development.

But children's culture is large and multifarious and decidedly pluralistic. The children in the toy store, on the playground, on the bus, and in the preschool displayed a wide variety of play preferences, vocabulary and expressive styles, and musical uses. From four-year-old Michael to twelve-year-old Jonathan, the disparate musical interests of children were telling of the enormous variety that constitutes children's culture. Among the factors most likely to break the larger culture into subcultures (or "little" cultures) of children, age and stage of learning are prominent.[8] Jean Piaget divided childhood into four developmental stages from infancy through age twelve (1951), and Bruner noted three age-based phases of learning (1966). Children's culture can also be divided by types of care and schooling provided to them: nursery or daycare, preschool, elementary school (and middle or junior high and high school); they are further distinguished by primary and intermediate grades, and even more so by grade levels. Distinctive children's groups are also based on factors such as gender, ethnicity, socioeconomic status, and ability level.

It may thus be difficult to conceive of a single children's culture and to "lump" children into one musical culture. As with flowers, there are many varieties, or subcultures, among them. Like snowflakes, each one is unique and not easily homogenized into a single entity. Perhaps, as Mark Slobin (1993) suggested, big music cultures like "children" are best conceived in smaller units (p. 11). His claim that people live at the intersection of three cultures suits children well. They can be conceived of as members of the "super-culture" (the large and overarching category, children), several subcultures (embedded units, e.g., preschoolers or fourth graders, girls or boys, African American or Chicano children), and "inter-cultures" (units resulting from shared experiences and widespread influences that cut across the subcultures, such as players of various ball games, or listeners of mass-mediated popular music) (p. 12). (To this can be added each child's idioculture, or culture of the self, to which Charles Keil has given considerable thought [1994].) Children have their idiosyncratic thoughts and behaviors and can take their place as members of multiple cultures, each with its own musical affiliations.

All children start out in the nuclear culture of their family and then graduate to others (Slobin, 1993, p. 55). Their musical knowledge spins out from this primary source in ever widening concentric circles, first within and then beyond the family. These circles are the result of developmental changes, so that with increasing age they graduate from one progressive layer of age-culture to the next. Children's first live musical experiences are often the lullabies sung to them by their parents, particularly their mothers, during infancy and throughout their first year as "lap babies" (Whiting and Edwards, 1988, p. 5). While these lullabies may vary in pitch and rhythmic information from one family to the next, their soft and slow qualities nonetheless are universally intended to lull little ones to sleep. Remarkably, some of this early music is remembered and recalled even into adulthood, so integrated are they within their young and impressionable minds.

With toddlerhood comes the play songs of the "knee children," which continue to be sung through their later preschool years as "yard children" (Whiting and Edwards, 1988, p. 198). These songs are sung as children play in yards and parks, on swings and in sandboxes (and certainly indoors as well). Play songs—like those of the children in the toy store—are not always consciously rendered but nonetheless trickle out of children as they are playfully engaged. Their musical content is taken from songs they have heard, some of it beamed out to them from their TVs and car radios. Yard children rarely play in silence; they talk, make sounds, and often sing to themselves and others with whom they play.

A shift to the next age-based musical culture occurs as children enter school. At five, six, and beyond, they may still hear lullabies at bedtime, and they will probably continue to semiconsciously sing as they play or work on their projects. Yet when they graduate to the level of "schoolchildren," they have entered into the realm of singing games, clapping chants, and regular and purposeful rhythms. These musical genres depend on the interaction of children with other children, in patterns of socialization that were previously unimportant to them. In partners and circles, with or without props (jump ropes, balls, scarves), most girls and a few boys—like those on the playground or in the cafeteria—learn and preserve traditional and contemporary melodies, rhythms, and choreographed forms given them by other children. As in the cases of lap babies and knee and yard children, the particulars of music and text may vary from one cultural subset (i.e., neighborhood, religious or ethnic group) to the next, but the engagement of children in these musical genres is a natural result of their entry into this age-based culture.

A particularly intriguing facet of children's cultures is the manner in which their songs can be distinguished by the ethnicity of its singers. Carol Merrill-Mirsky observed that Euro-American and Asian children were likely to sing pitched melodies while at play, while African American children performed more nonpitched rhythmic chants (1988). She described African American children's singing games as more numerous, more syncopated, and more likely to make use of formulaic introductions than those of Euro-American, Asian, or Latino children. She found not only musical but also gestural distinctions among the songs belonging to children of the four broad ethnic cultures. Some of these distinctive qualities were born out among the children of the conversations: recall the songs of Ramona and Lateesha, for example, and compare them with those of Michael and Anna.

Meanwhile, as children become embedded in the living musical cultures of their families, neighborhoods, and schoolyards, the mediated mass music rains on them as well. It blares at them in the background of their favorite TV shows and through the jingles that advertise the toys, food, and drink they hope to have. It undergirds or outwardly carries the messages and morals of the videos they watch. The mediated popular music appears as ambient sound or as a provocative experience, and neither children nor their families need to produce it to "have" it. But while children receive the media's music already packaged for their passive consumption, they also continue to want to actively participate in it. From Darryl's fondness for Barney and his songs to Anna's fixation on the music of Mary-Chapin Carpenter, children sing, move, and groove to mediated, commercial music. They are receiving the musical grammar and idiomatic expressions of popular music, the orally transmitted urban folk music of their time.

Just as popular music constitutes a musical interculture that is widely shared by children across many subcultures, so does the phenomenon called "school music" provide them with a common repertoire. James shared "Zudio" as he had learned it in the classroom, Ramona remembered "Bluebird," and Anna ticked off a list of school songs that ranged from a Woody Guthrie classic ("This Land Is Your Land") to Mexican or Chicano songs featured in school music textbooks. The music that teachers select for their lessons and programs varies from teacher to teacher, of course, but there are also standard sources to which teachers refer in planning lessons and a common canon of songs and musical works that they pass among themselves at workshops and professional meetings. For over a century, patriotic songs like "America," "America, the Beautiful," and "The Star-Spangled Banner" have been appearing in school programs and assemblies; added to this are favorites like "This Land Is Your Land," "This Is My Country," and the more contemporary "God Bless the U.S.A." While Stephen Foster songs are rarely sung anymore, basal series textbooks like *The Music Connection* (Silver Burdett & Ginn, 1995) and *Share the Music* (Macmillan, 1995) offer a varied fare of traditional and composed songs for singing and listening. Under the rubric of "multicultural music," songs like "Sakura" from Japan and "Sorida" from Zimbabwe recently have been added to old standbys like "Shenandoah" and "Swing Low, Sweet Chariot"; state-mandated policy for cultural pluralism has governed selections that now rest securely under the umbrella of "school music," The campaign for "Get America Singing . . . Again!," a project initiated in 1996 by the Music

Educators National Conference, is also likely to fix in place some of its recommended list of songs as part of a school music interculture.[9]

Children of all ages constitute the larger superculture and are grouped together and said to be recipients and processors of similar musical knowledge through similar experiences. Yet it is absurd for us to conceive of children as a single musical culture extending from infancy through pubescence, all united by the same experience. The concept of children fitting into multiple cultural units is far more logical. Indeed, the microcultures and micromusics defined by Mark Slobin suit the many musical realities of children, for their musical worlds are indeed many-splendored, a true conglomerate of styles and influences far too complex to pin down or generalize.

A Diversity of Musicking

As intensive as their musical involvement can be, so too do children demonstrate a diversity of participatory interests. "Musicking" is a fitting term for the spectrum of their engagement because unlike "making music," which denotes performance only, "musicking" encompasses all manner of participation—listening, composing, dancing, and even "taking tickets at the door" (Small, 1994). Children are involved musically when they are the producers, when it is performed live by others, and when it is mediated to them. Moreover, they are musicking even as they hear the music within them, singing and playing the songs in their heads. "Our children" were no exception: they were "musickers" all.

Doing. The import of children doing music cannot be overstated. Their listening may be of a concentrated sort, but they are seldom "still" for music, preferring instead to pat, hum, sing, whistle, or "groove" to it in a physical way. Children learn by doing music as much as by thinking it, by entering the musical arena as active players rather than sitters in silence at the periphery. Darryl's description is apt: Music is "about stuff you do." For many, to "do" music is to come to understand it, in that their physical involvement brings them a fuller intellectual and emotional experience. Charles Keil (1994) offered a passionate plea for the physical side of the musical encounter: "Unless you physically do it, it's not really apprehensible, and you're not hearing all there is to hear inside the music. You're not entering it. Participation is crucial" (p. 30). Because the muscular and neural networks are so intricately interwoven (Gardner, 1983), what children physically do with music is what they will remember; it will become what they have truly learned. The mind-body connection is real for children, and the ultimate way to a deeper musical experience may well be through their active participation in singing, playing, dancing, and engaged listening.

Integrating. Children often deepen their musical involvement by combining more than a single means of experiencing it. They become entangled in multiple ways of performing and responding to music and of thinking and acting musically. Quite commonly, they move as they sing, or they sing as they play. To the children of the Horace Mann playground and the Rundale Cafeteria, the musical experience is an integrated one that may initiate in the ear but that then triggers responses in their voices and bodies. Integrated musicking is one which many cultures share, in which singing, dancing, and the playing of instruments happen all at once (sometimes by a single person!). Occasionally, music will even be combined with the dramatic arts, from staged plays to puppetry. The Javanese traditions of the *wayang wang* and *wayang kulit* are prime examples of the fusion of music, dance, and theater (J. Becker, 1980), as is the *Gesamtkunstwerke* concept of Richard Wagner's operas, where multisensory stimulation of the audience (by way of music, drama, stage sets, and costumes) is the goal. In the minds of many, music is not "only music" to receive passively through the aural channel, and children in particular seem to understand full well the benefits of the multiple musicking experience.

Singing. Certainly one of the most natural means of musical expression children have is singing. Carrie sings despite her belief that she cannot sing well, while Beth explained that she sings because "I *am* a singer." Lateesha, James, and Anna described singing as enjoyable to them, and Alan reported that his loud singing "feels pretty good" to him. Singing is intimate musicking, as the voice is the sound from within, the human source of musical sound. In his classic tome, *The Rise of Music in the Ancient World: East and West* (1943), noted musicologist Curt Sachs went so far as to posit that the world's music sprang from singing (p. 21). Certainly, the first "music" which children can claim is their vocal expressions. Newborn babies arrive with the capacity for vocalization, and in their third month they are given to producing "euphonic musical sounds approximating pure, harmoniously voiced tones" (Papousek, 1996; p. 48). By the time children enter school, they are typically able to match pitches as they sing and are often singing or humming melodies of their own invention. It may be that, because of its intimacy, some children find conscious singing too exposed an activity to perform in front of their classmates, yet under cover and in familiar surroundings, they sing as they play with toys and friends—for social purposes, to communicate an idea or feeling, and for the sheer emotional release that singing can bring. Children may choose to sing a different repertoire than they did a generation ago, and some may find singing alone or without the backup accompaniment of tapes too stark for them, but they do now as then still find power and meaning in the singing act.

Moving. As they rhythmically move to music, children show how it is that the human body ranks with the voice as a personal source of their musical expression. Jonathan's stance may well echo the sentiments of children at large, that "nobody should have to sit still when there's music." Children occasionally perform stylized dances (particularly older children who are learning the latest popular dance trends), and sometimes they may invent playful choreographies. Yet far more frequent are the movements they make without even their own awareness of it, as if this rhythmic performance was concretely linked to the music itself. They may rock, sway, nod, wave their arms or shuffle their feet, or emit any of a host of rhythmic behaviors in their bodies as they sing or play, and they may be compelled to move by live and mediated music that surrounds them. This affinity to move allies children to cultures where music and dance cannot be separated, where dance cannot be dismissed as an ornamental "other" or extramusical extension, as in Nigerian juju (Waterman, 1991) or the music and dance of the Khmer and Thai royal courts (Sam and Campbell, 1992). Children's rhythmic movement can be telling of what they hear, and even what they are thinking. Perhaps one of the principal purposes of their songs and instrumental pieces centers on their desire (if not need) to move.

Playing. Ramnad had intimated that school music might be more tantalizing if instruments were a part of the program. His is not a lone voice, either, for musical instruments fascinate children.The sound of *things*—these musical objects called "instruments"—is intriguing to them, and they are eager to learn the mechanics that will enable them to produce an appealing sound. Children seem to appreciate that they can see as well as hear their sound production while playing an instrument (as opposed to the more "covert," nonvisual activity of singing), and their active fingers, hands, and arms have them involved in more pronounced physical activity than does singing. Instruments are also viewed as less personal to children than their voices; as extensions of the children, instruments may be considered less likely to bring exposure and possible humiliation. There are certain sociocultural phenomena that also play into the gratification they receive from instrumental performance. In most schools, instrumental study is withheld until children are thought to well enough along in their physical and cognitive development to be able to handle the instrument and the instruction that is provided. Thus, playing an instrument is a rite of passage that usually occurs at age nine or ten (although outside school study may begin earlier). As well, instrumental performance may be linked to particular performers whose appearances and lifestyles children admire; the visual image as much as the sound of the instrument are often motivation for study. For many children, instruments are the tangible symbols of music, and instrumentalists rather than singers constitute the "real musicians."

Listening. Musical sounds surround children, and they hear music from dawn to dusk in the home, at school, in stores, and in other public places. Directly and indirectly, consciously and at the outer edges of consciousness, children are listening to music. Their listening engages them immediately to move, sing, or play, but may also affect them in more subtle ways as the sound style settles into their ears and minds for later retrieval or reconfiguration in performance and creative musical inventions. Often in children's lives, music functions as background for their images and fantasies, as in the case of popular music's backing up of the image of a star singer or serving as the undergirding for the lyrics' story. Much of the music children hear derives from TV and video, such that they rarely listen to music in the abstract. Children may well be the ultimate nonlinear viewing generation, and MTV's quick pace, flashy images, and bright colors appeals and provides experiences that may be far more visual than aural. Yet children also listen to other musical styles as it comes available to them, be it a Mozart tape for "dreaming beautiful dreams" (Michael), Dvorak at a children's concert (James), or the jazz music in their parents' collection (Jonathan). They also listen to themselves and others perform, often in very discriminating ways. Concentrated listening may be more rare for children in this era of visual images than in the past, but most can and do rise to the challenge.

Playing With. Children play with music, and they play through music. Incidents of musical play were scattered throughout the cases and conversations; Lisa had invented her own hybrid of hand-clapping songs for play with her friends and family, and the children in the toy store had expressed themselves in spontaneous musical ways in their interactions with toys, games, and playthings. Both Jean Piaget (1951) and Lev Vygotsky (1978) have explained play as a means of constructing an understanding of the world. It follows that musical play—by way of organized singing games, improvised humming, whistling, singing, and "rhythmicking" (rhythms they play on their bodies or on surfaces external to them), and even the more disciplined formulation of a musical idea into a composition— brings children a clarification of music's structures and meanings. Children take long-standing songs and singing games and vary them in whimsical ways or according to "grammatical" rules of the musical culture they are coming to know. They produce musical "doodlings" (Kartomi, 1991, pp. 55–56), melodic and rhythmic segments that are sounded on the spot while they are engaged in another activity. These doodlings reflect earlier musicking experiences and may surface later in more full-fledged and intentional songs and compositions. Their compositions, written or not, are marks of children's playing with and working out of the musical elements that please them and represent their thinking. Playing with music helps them work out tension and blow off steam, and it is also a means for their further cognitive understanding of music.

The diversity of children's participation in music is stunning. Single images of a child engaged in music—the choir child, the budding violinist, the headphoned listener, the dancer, the young composer—are but splinters of all that children musically do. None of these images alone do justice to the phenomenon of musical children, but together they present children as the various and integrated musicians they are.

Their Music

Myths abound about what constitutes "children's music." Importantly, their self-initiated music is characteristically vocal rather than instrumental, so that along with the rhythms they produce in their bodies, song is more precisely the point of much of their own musicking. Parents, teachers, and professional songwriters often establish that songs suited for children should be simple in rhythm, sparse in pitch information, and quaint in their texts about animals, friends, and modes of transportation (i.e., trains, boats, and planes). While many of the songs children sing—particularly those perpetuated by adults in their interactions with children—fit these criteria, many more do not. In fact, children's musical expressions do not fit always fit the adult conception of some universal progression of forms from simple to complex, either (Blacking, 1992). Songs, called "childsongs," that children invent or refashion from earlier music materials and that they preserve in their transmission to other children (Campbell, 1991a) may often consist of greater musical complexities and more diverse texts than those found in the numerous collections of songs that adults have prescribed for children. Their musical grammar arises without, and often prior to, formal instruction. Singing games, rhythmic chants, and purely rhythmic "pieces," as well as spontaneous musical utterances and the familiar songs from adult-oriented and commercial sources, flow continuously from children and are tributes to their musical thinking and doing.

Childsongs and Singing Games

Childsongs are given less attention by teachers than they deserve. Peter and Iona Opie (1985) have probably done more for the comprehensive collection and analysis of children's songs than any other scholar before them or since. In their seminal work, *The Singing Game,* they researched 133 singing games (and numerous clapping chants as well) for their origins, textual symbolism, manner of performance, and variants throughout the United Kingdom as well as in other English-speaking countries (and occasionally in Europe). They sought out songs that accompanied games, some stemming from practices in ancient Greece and Rome, and many more surviving from the Middle Ages. For them, singing games were those that "fulfilled a social function in days gone by" (p. 29). Yet also included within their collection were "parts of songs, or misrememberings of songs" (p. 29) believed to be tailored by children into singing games on the patterns of older games and their functions. Musical analysis was never intended to be the focus of the Opies' scholarship, which also explains the absence of song segments or children's performances of a rhythmic-only nature; their title clearly stipulates the genre of their particular interest. Yet several musical observations they offered serve as points for further discussion.

   In their prefatory remarks, the Opies remarked that "the tunes often revolve round a very few notes: the alternation between notes a third apart is very frequent. . . . Almost all employ major, diatonic keys. Most of them are in a lilting 6/8 or 12/8 rhythm" (p. vii). Of the music collected and noted within these pages, just three are truly singing games ("Little Sally Walker," "Jump In," and "Hey,

Little Walter"). One of the melodies was clearly set in a major tonality ("Little Sally Walker"), and another in minor ("Hey, Little Walter"). "Jump In" 's chant alternated between two sung pitches and spoken rhythms, and the more developed melody of "Little Sally Walker" eventually gave way to rhythmic chant. None of these singing games were in "lilting meters" of 6/8, 9/8, and 12/8; rather, they were sounded in a straightforward duple (or quadruple) meter.[10] The three songs do meet the Opies' description of relatively few pitches, although "Hey, Little Walter" ventures beyond the alternating notes of a third to a blues set that stretches an octave. Of other musical factors that emerge, particularly notable is the extent of syncopated rhythms that are present in all three singing games.

Beyond the singing games per se, there were also examples in this collection of hand-clapping chants ("My Sailor," "My Mama Told Me," "I Wish I Had a Dollar," "Apple on a Stick," "Three, Six, Nine," "Fudge, Fudge," and "Down, Down Baby"), jump-rope chants ("Miss, Miss," "Blue Bells"), and even a rhythmically rapped piece. These were playfully rendered as childsongs of their own invention, variation, or continued preservation. Like two of the singing games, the hand-clapping "Down Down Baby" blended both melodic and strictly rhythmic sections. Its melody consisted of three pitches that were repeatedly sung to a syncopated rhythm, and its clapping pattern placed three movements against the 4/4 meter. "My Sailor" was musically interesting for its chromatic melody (with raised sixth), as "My Mama Told Me" had its own chromaticism (a raised fourth). Four of the hand-clapping chants ("I Wish I Had a Dollar," "Apple on a Stick," "Three, Six, Nine," and "Fudge, Fudge") were rhythmic and inflected with the rise and fall of expressive speech but were not melodies to be sung. Two jump-rope chants, "Miss Miss" and "Blue Bells," consisted mostly of even quarter- and eighth-note rhythms for texts that were laid out in clear two- and four-measure phrases. Some of the same text appeared in "Blue Bells" as in "Down Down Baby" ("I like coffee. I like tea. I like the [colored] boy[s] and they [he] like[s] me"); it was chanted in a "straighter" and less syncopated manner in the jump-rope than in the hand-clapping version. One raplike rhythm, "Power to the People Rangers," is of considerable rhythmic interest: Not only was the soloist's chant syncopated, but the group's syncopated vocal ostinato produced a polyrhythmic texture as it was combined with the solo part.

Musical Utterances and Spontaneous Songs

Besides the formalized, structured, and sometimes long-standing songs of children's socializations together, there are also the spontaneously generated songs and chants that children call their own. As well, there are the musical utterances, the seemingly effortless flow of melodies and rhythms that exude from children as they play. These are their musical daydreams, their musical doodlings (Kartomi, 1991), their semi- or subconscious voices declaring themselves without their awareness. All these are melodies and fragments derived from their musical experiences, some of which may flow into finished musical products: songs.

The musical utterances were fascinating for their widespread presence in a variety of contexts (on the playground, in the toy store, inside and outside at the preschool, and in the cafeteria). They fluctuated melodically, from seconds and thirds to full octave leaps, while the spontaneous rhythms were often syncopated—and always pulsive. As exaggerated speech or reflections of the music that surrounded them in their daily lives, these musical utterances offered intriguing glimpses of children's musical thoughts.

Children's spontaneous songs are typically open-ended, with beginnings and endings unpredictably developing from and returning to their playful interactions with toys and other children. Some are intermediary forms, performances that sit somewhere between speaking and singing (Nattiez, 1990). They include from this collection "I'd Rather Have Fingers," the chant of the two second-grade children at Horace Mann school and the preschool children's taunt, "If You Drop It." Songs and singing games, on the other hand, are typically closed, with clear-cut beginnings and endings, and any variation children give to them will adhere to basic formal properties. The open musical forms that children produce may use a single rhythmic or melodic phrase repeatedly. One child's part may be joined to another, as in case of the two-part "jump down/huh-uh" pattern chanted by the two fifth-grade girls at Horace Mann, or the rhythmic eruption that occurred in Mrs. Bedford's music class, when a single clave pattern launched a group of four boys into their open-ended improvisation. These open forms may turn quite lengthy when given the occasion for doing so, becoming musical ramblings even as children are engaged in other ways.

One example of a clapping chant that was probably spontaneously invented (and, by Lisa's own admission, was in need of adjustment) was "Clap, Clap, Clap, I Like To." Unlike "Down Down Baby," "My Sailor," and "My Mama Told Me," there was not yet a notable storyline, nor was there melody, syncopated rhythm, or even a clear organization of the words or rhythm. Perhaps it would become an acceptable chant, but at least several of these features would need to appear as Lisa sang and refined the chant to qualify it as a musically and textually cohesive unit.

Children's musical expressions may appear spontaneous, but many of them are a blend of bits of songs, rhythms, and music they have known before. The rhythms they use in their chanted "mouth music" of semantically meaningless syllables and in their clapping, slapping, tapping, and stamping are combinations of quarter and eighth notes (or eighth and sixteenth notes), as Constantin Brailoiu (1954) suggested. Yet these rhythms are frequently peppered with the various dotted patterns found in their own childsongs and in the popular music they know. The melodies vary with the songs children inadvertently stitch together, and very few of them are stuck in a groove of the descending minor third. Indeed, children's melodic meanderings frequently consist of at least five tones, and they may vocalize two octaves or more. My observations corroborate those of John Blacking (1973), W. Jay Dowling (1984), and Helmut Moog (1976), all of whom could not find much evidence for the universality of an "ur-song" for children. Beyond the use of this minor third in calling chants, the music of children's musical play is far more varied melodically and rhythmically.

Familiar Songs

Children also sing songs taught to them by adults. They sing them intact or as parodies (for example, "We Three Kings"). In this collection, several songs are particularly notable as long-standing singing games that adults deemed important enough to preserve and transmit to children. "Bluebird" is an Anglo-American children's singing game at least a century old (Opie and Opie, 1985, p. 365); two children had learned it in different ways from mother, teacher, sibling, or friend or had either erroneously sung it or intentionally revised it. "The Noble Duke of York" is an old dancing game performed by children for at least a hundred years in England to the older hexatonic melody for "O! A-Hunting We Will Go." Its appearance in a music classroom was as it always had been, to accompany a double-line country dance (or contradance). The young boy's parody of it could be added to its many variants known in England, Scotland, Wales, and in the United States (Opie and Opie, 1985, p. 215). Another teacher-initiated singing game, the syncopated "Zudio," had been recycled from the playground to the classroom and may have been on the way back to the playground through one child's remembering and practicing it. Its relatives include "Willobee" or "Step Back, Sally," sung by African American children in the 1960s and 1970s (Kenney, 1974, p. 66; Opie and Opie, 1985, p. 404). Although once truly childsongs, emanating from children's musical play and practice, these three songs had been deemed by adults to be useful, amusing, or otherwise worthy for children's experience. Perhaps the sources of these songs were the adult transmitters' own childhood experiences (rather than one of the numerous printed collections in which these three songs are contained), in which case they *are* childsongs, a generation or more removed.

Segments of songs emerged here, incomplete performances which, for reasons of time, uncertainty, or lack or interest, were not performed "in full" by the children. Still, they were illustrations of children's musical thoughts, their knowledge and experience in music. Song segments consisted of one or two melodic phrases (or less), sometimes with words and sometimes wordless. "Mary Had a Little Lamb," "Rock-a-Bye, Baby," "The Barney Song" ("I Love You"), "Don Gato," "Step Back, Sally," "The Pocahontas Song" ("Colors of the Wind"), "The Indian Love Song," "The Star-Spangled Banner," and "The Thomas the Tank Engine Song" (the theme from *Shining Time Station*) were some of the songs that were begun but were abandoned by children. When these segments landed in conversations, they may have been intended by children only as efficient means for identifying them. Their curtailment by children at play, on the other hand, may have been to make way for other melodies they were thinking or to move into improvisations of melody and text based on their initiation of these phrases. Sometimes one verse of a multiple-verse song was sung, with no continuation coming forth, as in "My Mama Told Me" and "I Know an Old Woman." The tonal and rhythmic content of these segments contrasted greatly with one another, from the three-tone "Mary Had a Little Lamb" to the chromatic, "diatonic-plus" melody of "The Star-Spangled Banner." Some used a small range of pitches ("Mary Had a Little Lamb" and "The Barney Song"), while "The Pocahontas Song" and "The Star-Spangled Banner" stretched well over an octave. Most song segments, like the complete songs that surfaced, moved in duple meter (with the notable exceptions of the triple-metered "Rock-a-Bye, Baby" and "The Star-Spangled Banner"). Clearly, a variety of musical information is received, retained, and retrieved by children as they sing segments of these songs.

Children sang or described a selection of songs as "familiar" to them, songs they thought they could (but were usually not pressed to) sing. These songs fell into several categories. There were folk songs that have for centuries been part of an Anglo-American oral tradition of songs sung to children by adults: "Tideo," "Yankee Doodle," "Twinkle, Twinkle, Little Star," "Mary Had a Little Lamb," "I've Been Working on the Railroad," "Skip to My Lou," "This Old Man," "Oats, Peas, Beans," "Clap Your Hands" (from "Old Joe Clarke"), "Simple Gifts," "Bought Me a Cat," "Mulberry Bush," "Looby Loo," and "I Gave My Love a Cherry." There were traditional songs, some of which were composed and some of which are merely more recent additions to children's standard song repertoire. Most of these have fallen into an American (albeit multicultural) oral tradition of song-singing by virtue of the rote manner in which they are learned in school and in recreational settings. They included African American songs ("Ev'ry Time I Hear the Spirit," "Uncle Jessie"), the ever popular French nursery rhythm "Frere Jacques," and a host of others: "Over the Sea to Skye," "Mbube" (or "Wimoweh," "The Lion Sleeps Tonight"), "The Battle Hymn of the Republic," "Shalom Chaverim," "Don Gato," "Sorida," "Che Che Koolay," "De Colores," and "La Raspa." Several church and temple songs were also reported by children as songs they knew from home and family. More than a few recalled songs and melodies they knew from Disney and other popular movies, videos, TV programs, and tapes and CDs ("Can't You Feel the Love Tonight?," "I Just Can't Wait to Be King," "Colors of the Wind," "The Gypsy Song" (from *The Hunchback of Notre Dame*), "Who's Afraid of the Big Bad Wolf?," and "Puff, the Magic Dragon." Here again, the musical grammar of these songs varied, providing a wide array of musical structures for the children who listen to and perform these songs.

The popular songs children sang, or claimed to be able to sing, were of current or recent vintage but also included several classic "oldies." Segments of So

For Real's "Candy-Colored Raindrops" and Garth Brooks's "Thunder Rolls" were sung, and several other recent hits were recalled: Michael Jackson's "You Are Not Alone," Whitney Houston's "I Will Always Love You," and Mary-Chapin Carpenter's country-styled "Stones in the Road." As well, the songs of Coolio and Courtney Love were acknowledged, or even defended. Older rock songs also appeared as a result of children's exposure to them by adults: a physical education teacher's use of "Monster Mash" for a movement experience, a mother's frequent singing of "Crocodile Rock," and the conversion of a mid-1970s hit, Queen's "We Will Rock You," into a popular stadium "scream-song" cheer. Other artists and popular styles were described, but the songs that were sung or specifically named by children were comparative in their duple meters and diatonic scales and either driving in their high-energy rhythms or emotive in their reflections of love and life.

It is a revelation to explore children's own musical inventions, the songs they preserve, and their responses to popular music. The images we carry from our own childhood experiences, or accept from what the media conceives children's songs to be, is often in opposition to the realities of children's music today. An examination of children's music yields rich information to use in tailoring instruction relevant to their needs and interests.

All That They Can Musically Be

While children are musical without expert guidance, they become more musical as a result of it. Their lives are enhanced through instruction in and through music as they become all that they can musically be—and more human as a result of knowing music at many levels, in many guises. What children musically do and say is the launch for their further development; I am campaigning not to "de-school" music but, rather, to bring instruction in line with who the children musically are. It is a natural inclination among children to have music in their lives, but it is also their right to know *more* music *better* for its various uses by them and for its most profound meaning to them. As teachers, parents, and responsible adults, in charge of children's welfare and education, we have the responsibility of bringing children's natural musicking to full flowering. We should not be musically educating them, however, according to some outmoded theoretical concept of children or through lessons that are, in the words of Donald Pond, "faggoted together . . . out of moth-eaten formulae" (1981, p. 4). Children become more musical through the authentic interventions we provide for children at home, in the private studio lesson, and through the thoughtfully prepared program of music at school.

Authentic interventions are the ways and means of nurturing children's musical development. They can be highly structured instructional strategies, set sequentially or as part of a lengthy teaching sequence. They can also be an idea or a loosely conceived plan for children's nurturance through music experiences that are carefully selected but that are not in principle "lessons" or educational sequences. They become authentic when they are rooted in children's actual needs and interests, rather than a prescription that is without a base in the reality of children's own thoughts and doings. This having been said, authentic interventions vary according to the nature of individual children, in that not every intervention will apply to every child in every circumstance. These interventions are not intended as dogmatic or universal principles to abide by but are meant to be malleable and effective in the hands of the thoughtful teacher.

In fact, the thirty interventions that follow are more akin to musings than prescribed plans; they point out various practical issues and approaches for educating children in musical ways. The words of children are the launch to these ruminations and recommendations, but the ideas are derived as much from the field-based observations (Part I) as from the conversations (Part II). There is also the broader swath of experience from which I draw and from which rich insights on the nature of musical children were developed, including my own classes and choirs of children and my interactions as instructor of courses for prospective and practicing teachers of music to children. From a reflexive position, I cannot rule out any of these sources that inform the recommendations, for they are all part of the weblike, interactive hypermedia that have brought me to this understanding of children's musical selves.[11]

The personal, social-familial, and functional perspectives of their musicking are intended for initiating discussion and inciting action on the further development of children's knowledge, skills, and values. There are reflections on children's motivation for studying music on their own and comments on their musical choices (as well as those of adults for them), followed by suggestions for more relevant music and teaching strategies for children in the school music programs. These interventions spin from the words or deeds of children presented earlier in this tome yet are offered in the spirit of their broad use for children in a variety of settings.

The Personal Side of Music

Music gets me going and gives me strength.

As we observe the effects of music's force, flow, and energy on children, how can we help but to want to include more of it in their daily lives? Music is a powerful phenomenon, and we see how it it stimulates, relaxes, and inspires children, how it brings tremendous shifts of mood to those within its circle of influence—within earshot! It can calm the crying child and convert the high-energy "wild child" into a more thoughtful, reflective individual. It can perk the lethargic child, inspirit the unmotivated child, and draw the introverted child into a sociable circle of friends. It can serve the timid and the thick-skinned, the serious and the happy-go-lucky, and the restrained or repressed and the emotionally "unbridled." Our careful choice of music for play, work, and quiet times can do far more than simply provide an ambience; it can empower children, instill in them a strength of spirit, and prepare them to perform their waiting tasks with energy and even "good cheer."

Having acknowledged music's capacity to effect dispositions and behaviors, we can proceed to the myriad ways of bringing music into their home and school experiences. It would benefit us to tap into the knowledge of music therapists, who are trained in the application of music for the treatment of particular types of social behaviors, emotional conditions, and even moods. They have developed the sensibilities to employ music and musical activities to "get children going" or to "settle them down" and can recommend possibilities for musical uses within the family or in the classroom. The development of stronger relationships between music teachers and therapists may prove beneficial to children's well-being. For a description of music's therapeutic, healing potential, see John Diamond's *Life Energy in Music* (1981), Joachim-Ernst Berendt's *World Is Sound* (1983), and Pat Moffit Cook's *Shaman, Jhankri, and Néle* (1997). Suggestions for the use of music as therapy can be found in Jayne M. Standley's *Music Techniques in Therapy, Counseling, and Special Education* (1991).

I love the feeling of music.

No doubt, we are aware that music is more than an auditory sensation: It is a thoroughly and all-encompassing physical experience. Children tend to feel music in a visceral way and are compelled to respond to it kinesthetically. We may strive to provide them with chances to "listen with their bodies" to music, to dance and move to music in the ways that they find naturally appealing.

Children's propensity for movement can be used to its best advantage in instructional settings, for movement is a means of knowing music. When we carefully observe their movements, we begin to understand how it is linked to particular musical components. How do they move? To what are they responding: the pulse, the subdivisions, the meter, the rhythmic patterns, the melody's pitches or contours, the timbres, textures, or forms? With a few responses to go on, we can then design experiences to reinforce children's natural movements while also implementing plans to extend their music and movement repertoires. When we model for children certain gestures that illuminate the music's meter, a prominent rhythm, or music's repeated and contrasting sections, we are building musical understanding on the basis of children's natural propensity to move; we are also giving them the particular kinds of movements that "go with," or underscore, the musical properties of which children should be made aware.

Too often, children's musical experiences are harnessed into sit-and-listen events; even singers and players are directed to do what they do through the exclusive use of a few "performance muscles" (for example, the vocal cords or the fingers) rather than their fuller physical selves. For many children, music is at its most fulfilling extent when it has been kinesthetically felt, such that their ears, minds, bodies, and "hearts" function as a single entity. We would want not to deny children their physical access to music but to provide every opportunity for it. (For further thoughts on movement education, see *Nobody should have to sit still when there's music.*)

Whistling and singing are close music.

How many times have we heard children distinguish between singing and "music" (meaning instrumental music)? Such a quip can irritate singers, who do not consider themselves outside the sphere of music! Yet the distinction could be taken as an innocent reference to vocal music as the most personal of all types of musical expressions, as opposed to the somewhat more "distant" performance on instruments as extensions of the body. The "invisible" voice is so close as to be the natural musical personification of the individual. It is affected by the singer's physical self: When she feels good, her voice can sound "good"; when she has a cold, her voice may sound less healthy, too. The voice is influenced by the state of the singer's mind, too: Rarely can a troubled and unhappy singer sound genuinely joyful. The voice is conveniently situated, easily transportable, and able to perform a continuum of communication that stretches from speech to song. Undeniably, singing is part of person's inner and unseen self, yet while the vocal mechanism and production process may seem abstract, singing is very real.

Many children sing beautifully, spontaneously, and often. Yet there are those children, particularly from families and cultures where singing is not so highly valued, who may not appreciate singing for its physical, emotional, and social benefits. At school, some older children may vow not to sing, whether for reasons of anxiety (children who are uneasy about singing in front of their peers for fear of ridicule), peer pressure (children who would sing but for the fact that their friends do not), disinterest in or dislike of the repertoire or manner in which singing is taught. Several responses are worthy of our attention as teachers and parents: (1) Sing to children and with children often, so that singing can be perceived by them as a natural thing to do: (2) Choose songs with sensitivity to the subject matter of the texts as well as the musical challenges (for example, reserve the lullabies and animal songs for the younger children): (3) Offer children chances to plan a public performance of their selected songs, thus giving them more responsibility for the vocal music they have learned: (4) Lead children to an understanding of the physiological mechanisms relevant to singing, thus increasing their awareness of singing as a physical challenge (to the extent that it once was a physical feat of the ancient Greek Olympians!). We would do well to encourage children to share their music with others—at home, in school, at places of worship, and in the community at large. We can sing around the table after dinner, in lieu of a videotape, in the car and on the road to anywhere, and as a wake-up-and-go-to-bed ritual. Singing is close music, with the voice contained as it is physically within the body and close to the center of children's thinking and feeling.

I'd be like a museum, keeping the songs.

Children are preservers of music. They store inside themselves music from their family and community experiences, and many occasionally perform it aloud but will also rehearse it in silence. They retain and maintain their repertoire, keeping it for some future chance to share it. When family members, friends, and teachers show interest, they may open the doors to their "museums" and let their songs be heard. The music they preserve is telling of their worlds; when we listen, we come to know the folkways, mores, and values embedded within that music, as well as the musical structures and sonorities with which they are familiar.

In their sharing of their preserved music, children provide music for other children to know and learn; they are transmitters of music as well. Too often, teachers look elsewhere for the music children should learn, forgetting that they have their own to "exhibit," to "show and tell." Yet what one child gains from sharing his music, others may learn and be enriched by. Whenever children gather, the possibilities for calling up and sharing their stored musical repertoire are great. Children's melodies, rhythms, and songs are well worth teasing out of them and putting on display.

I know it, I made it, me and only me, mostly.

We might be accused of using the overworked "c" word in our descriptions of children—"creative"—and yet we know from our experiences with them that they have the capacity to invent and to express their thoughts in clever ways. Children are often adroit at solving problems, and they often pose intriguing and inventive questions. They produce drawings and paintings, clay figures, block buildings, and eventful stories that captivate our interest. We call their products "creative" when they are unique yet still within bounds of our own (and our culture's) standards for beauty and function thus reserving the "c" word for their extraordinary inventions and expressions.

Children are proud of their creations and eager to boast their ownership of them ("I made it, me and only me"). The outer two phrases ("I know it . . . mostly") are also illuminating, however, as they point to how something like a song can only be fashioned from materials that are within the creator's grasp, framed by his own experiences. Just as children build their ships and planes of red and white Lego blocks or shape a new monster from a canister of yellow Play-doh, they also make up their own songs and rhythms from the music they already know. The rhythms and tunes of their musical parts emerge in their made-up songs.

Beyond the endless enthusiasm that pours forth from adults on the importance of nurturing children's creative instincts, the procedures for how to teach for creativity remain somewhat amorphous and veiled in mystery. Yet what is known with some certainty is that children require affective support by way of persons that encourage and reinforce them in their efforts, and cognitive support through the knowledge and skills that persons can give them before and during the creative process in which they are engaged (Gardner, 1993). Parents can provide the affective support, while teachers can provide both the motivation and the "goods"— the knowledge and skills—for stimulating children's individual and inventive musical ideas. For however "naturally creative" some of children's musical utterances and spontaneous songs may be, these may be just the starting points for more creative expressions to come. For ideas on nurturing musical creativity, some of the most ingenious and inspiring approaches are still to be found in the classic works of composer R. Murray Schafer, including his *Composer in the Classroom* (1965) and *Creative Music Education* (1976). See also John Paynter's *Hear and Now* (1972) and Rene Upitis's *Can I Play You My Song?* (1992), both of which offer provocative approaches to the stimulation of children's creative impulse. Schafer's suggestions are appropriate for use at home, in scout groups and social clubs, and by general classroom and music teachers.

The Social-Familial Sides of Music

When I sing, everyone seems to like me.

It is hard to resist the social benefits of making music. There are the relationships that develop through the interactions while in the process of performing or creating music together. There is also the undeniable reality of respect, regard, and gratitude that one receives on performing to an appreciative audience. We may fondly recall the warm reception offered by listeners to a single simple song, or to a full recital we have offered them, and the warm-and-fuzzy feeling of acceptance we have received from friends, family, colleagues, and even "experts" who have enjoyed our performance. Music is a gift, and whether it be a song, a recorder melody, or a new trumpet etude that is rendered thoughtfully and sincerely by a child, it brings great joy to grateful listeners—joy that is turned back to her as reinforcement for a job well done. The results of children's concentrated study of music (performance techniques, the "know-how," and repertoire, the "know-what") should not be concealed but rather brought forward to all who are willing to listen. Those who give the gift of music will receive their "just desserts," not the least of which is the favorable responses their listeners will give them.

I think you have to be brought up with it.

We should not ignore the experiences of children's own particular "upbringings"— their family cultures; rather, our highlighting of them can prove enlightening to all. Children's own personal and social identities are often wrapped up in the music of their immediate and extended families, and of their religious and ethnic-cultural communities. They each have "heritage music," be it gospel, *ramvong*, *rondalla*, polka, R and B, mariachi, country, or some other of the myriad styles enjoyed by them and their parents, their grandparents, relatives, and friends. Because their family and close community music is so much a part of their young lives, children may take it for granted or even express surprise that someone like a teacher would be curious about it, or uninformed on it.

Children's heritage music may be a source of pride to them, as it is also enriching to their friends and classmates for what cultural understanding it can offer. Some children will be eager for opportunities to sing, play an instrument, perform a dance, share a recording; others might need a little coaxing. At school, we can design or encourage the scheduling of individual classroom events and schoolwide assemblies for children's performances of their heritage music, and for the guest appearances of family members with interest and expertise in the traditional and popular arts of their heritage. (Grandparents, in particular, have bundles of stories and songs to share, and often time enough to share them!) A study of traditional clothing, cuisine, fabric arts, and customs of different places and times gone by are valuable additions to children's understanding of themselves and others in the world; cooperative efforts among classroom teachers and teachers of music and art can culminate in a multidimensional study of heritage. As we are all "brought up with" particular folkways, including music, the potential for knowing the multicultural mosaic of our school and community populations is there within our children and their families.

I try to concentrate on what I'm doing and relate to the others.

We have seen children concentrate on things that fascinate them: a new book, a puzzle, a bead-design project. They also are intent as they play together: at soccer, with dolls and racing cars, at a computer game. Musical performance demands multiple levels of concentrated thought from children, too—all of which they are quite capable of giving. Young performers must center their attention on the mechanics of the instrument (or voice) and on the technical and expressive features of the music, blocking out distractions and focusing on the skills they need to make their music. When two or more young musicians gather, they are further challenged to perform not only technically well but also in synchrony with one another. Music then becomes both a personal and social challenge and hoped-for accomplishment through the necessary interdependence inherent in contributing one's part to an ensemble.

Indeed, the social merits of ensemble performance are not to be underestimated, for as children perform together, they build relationships with one another. School music—singing in choirs, playing in bands, xylophone ensembles, recorder consorts, percussion groups, and fledging orchestras—is often about such group musicking (and, as a result, the development of socially interactive relationships as well). Many principals, parents, and teachers advocate the presence of music ensembles for the social cohesion and sense of community they provide. Performing in groups requires children's cooperation and reliance on one another's parts in order to contribute together to the whole and finished musical product. It demands a heightened musical sensitivity, too, in order to remain true to (minimally) an agreed-upon tempo and a homogenized blend of instruments or voices. Individual, soloistic performance is usually inappropriate within the ensemble, whereas a team effort aimed at a collective product is very much the point.

Given the social as well as personal outcomes of musical performance, we cannot help but recognize and articulate the diverse merits of children's musical participation. For the sheer need to employ concentrated thought, but also for the tremendous opportunities to forge relationships—to say nothing of sharpening one's musicianship!—there are few experiences in school or out that can contribute so greatly to children's intellectual and social development. We have reasons to celebrate the organization of group musicking experiences for the many riches they offer.

My mom wants me to sing.

Children are enticed and fortified by our interests in them for what they can do and have done. We accept the logic of this, yet we may need to remind ourselves of the meaningfulness to them of every little reinforcement we can offer. With full knowledge of the multiple outcomes of their musical training, we can steer them toward piano lessons, membership in a choir, dance classes, and instruction on orchestral, band, and other (including folk) instruments. (We can also recognize children's self-initiated musical efforts as well: the tunes they produce as they play with their toys, their musical doodlings on recorders and keyboards, their camp songs and parodies of TV themes.) Children often choose to study or to make music in earnest because of the direct encouragement their parents and teachers give them, and also because of the cameraderie they have observed others having as they perform. Directly and indirectly, influenced by models, the media, and peers, children are inspired to study music, sing it, play it, create it.

Yet once "enrolled," children will come to recognize that performing, creating and composing, moving musically and artistically, and listening analytically are not as easy as they first appeared to be. Thus, the hard work of practice should have its regular payoffs, too, from the exclamatory remarks by parents and teachers (saying "good" with real meaning and specificity: "I thought your left-hand technique was lighter and so much better today, so that I could really hear the right-hand melody come out") to the hugs and the pats on the backs. Teachers have stars, badges, and musical "trinkets" (treble-clef pins, pencils designed with quarter-note motifs) for diligent children, and parents may provide the occasional nonmusic reward (a special snack, a favorite TV show, a sleepover) for a job well done. All of these function to let children know that we appreciate their efforts and recognize their progress. They need to know that we are pleased and proud of their musical accomplishments all along the way.

The Functional Side of Music

Music is about stuff you do.

If ever there is a message that children send to us through their behaviors, it is that they prefer action to passivity. Rather than listening and looking while others demonstrate or tell about a topic, children want to experience music for themselves. Can we blame them? Lectures and long-winded descriptions do little for the learning of most children, who must hear, see, and do to understand. While they also will need to learn onlooker-audience behavior as they mature, music allows a multitude of possibilities to fully satisfy children's incessant drive for doing.

Knowing how children define "doing" helps us to provide for their musicking needs. Singing counts as doing (although some children are compelled to combine it with playing or moving to truly qualify it as "stuff you do"). Movement and dance are means by which children engage themselves in the music, responding to music that's already been done—composed. Musical instruments are obvious avenues for children's active musical doing, whether by way of reproducing what they have heard before, exploring new territory, or even improvising from what skills and repertoire they have developed. Keyboards, a guitar, or an old hand-me-down clarinet from Aunt Mildred can initiate the kind of instrumental doing that tantalizes children. Toys may offer opportunities to make music, too, from violins that play themselves to electronic rap-and-drumming pads that respond with a spectrum of timbres. "Found sound" objects should not be discounted, either: spoons, pans, blocks of wood, wastebaskets, keys, boxes, empty tubes, PVC pipes, bottles, bowls, cups of water, rubber bands, and string are all useful by themselves or in combination for producing sounds that are potentially musical and that allow children the means for doing music. (Making instruments at home or in the class-room can enlighten children on music's scientific-acoustical properties. See *Making Musical Things* [1979], by Ann Wiseman, and *Kids Make Music* [1993], by Avery Hart and Paul Mantell.)

There are countless ways to do music, both by making it and by responding to it, with opportunities at home, in the community, and through a vast set of strategies for the classroom. For many (if not most) children, the more musically active they can be, the more profound and long-lasting their musical experience will be. Suggestions for children's active musicking can be found in a variety of sources, including *Music in Childhood* (Campbell and Scott-Kassner, 1995), *Music and Young Children* (Aronoff, 1979), and *Sound Choices* (Machover and Uszler, 1996).

Some music helps the stories along.

We need not look very far to recognize the extent to which music is linked with stories, plots, plays, and shows. Children are regular viewers of and listeners to these productions, yet they may not often perceive the role that music plays to enhance the drama and the development of the characters. Music communicates sentiment and ambience, as it also supplies motivic material to signal "the good guys" and "the bad guys," the terrifying and the timid. Music is an important player in the productions children have grown up with, yet they may need to be guided to a fuller awareness of music's function as a vehicle to communicate, express, and enhance stories.

With children, we can experiment by turning sound off on the TV or video-tape. What is Disney's *Lion King* without the music? Or *The Snowman? Star Wars? Jurassic Park? Raiders of the Lost Ark?* Or Rabbit Ears's productions of *The Velveteen Rabbit* or *The Steadfast Tin Soldier?* At least, these stories on film may have greater impact *because* of their music. Not until it's gone may children realize how integral music is to films and countless TV programs on nature, history, science (and even sitcoms). On the other hand, with children we can seek out the TV programs or audiotapes of stories that have no musical track: how dull and dry are they without music at key points to carry or at least perk them? With the visual image playing, children can invent dialogues, sounds, and music to fit the scenes. A thirty-second episode could be made the frame for composing music that is powerful enough to tell that segment of the story.

Storybooks can also be the launch to children's imaginative musical play. As one child narrates the story, others can dramatize, dance, sing, and play an instrumental accompaniment. We may suggest possibilities for its performance, but children can develop a plan, rehearse it, and perform it. Small groups of children may take on a story to perform to others, while older children can create the whole production and organize themselves for presentations to younger children. Xylophones, keyboards, recorders, and other percussion instruments can be combined to present leitmotifs (themes associated with particular characters, thoughts, or actions), dance music, and accompaniment for songs children may sing. MIDI (Musical Instrumental Digital Interface) technology also offers a treasureload of possibilities for producing a musical story.

Fitting music to stories is an endeavor that can involve music teachers with classroom teachers, who will be able to recommend books that children are currently reading. The following books are among my favorites for inviting children to create music to "help the stories along": *The Polar Express* (by Chris Van Allsburg), *How Raven Brought Light to People* (Tlingit tale, retold by Ann Dixon),

Jack's Fantastic Voyage (by Michael Forman), *Peach Boy* (Japanese tale, retold by William H. Hooks), *Follow the Drinking Gourd* (by Jeannette Winter), *The Girl Who Wanted a Song* (by Steve Sanfield), *The Dancing Dragon* (by Marcia Vaughn), *The Carousel* (by Liz Rosenburg), *Where the Wild Things Are* (by Maurice Sendak), *The Magic Moonberry Jump Ropes* (by Dakari Hru), *A Tale of Two Rice Birds* (Thai tale, adapted by Clare Hodgson Meeker), *The Rainbow Fish* (by Marcus Pfister), *Miss Spider's Tea Party* (by David Kirk), and *Tikki Tikki Tembo* (Chinese tale, retold by Arlene Mosel).

Nobody should have to sit still when there's music. It moves, and it makes you move.

From natural responses to choreographed dances, children move and groove to the music they hear. They are compelled to move to music; some are even "propelled" by it. (See *I love the feeling of music* for a discussion of movement as a visceral experience.) We may sometimes admonish children for not listening when we see them fidgeting. As we match what they are doing with what we are hearing, however, we may recognize that they are indeed listening and responding through their physical movement. Across a broad sweep of cultures, music and movement are fused into a single entity where it is simply against the forces of nature for people to be physically oblivious, silent and still, to the vibrations in the air. In fact, when they are permitted to respond kinesthetically, neither a Mozart string quartet nor a Malawiian polyrhythmic event are beyond the capacity of children to understand and enjoy.

Some children will be well served by the opportunity to study dance, through classes in creative movement, ballet, tap, or "ethnic" styles, and their physical and musical selves will benefit. Even gymnastics and ice skating require a certain blend of discipline and artistic expression, with movement that must correspond to the music. Dance education is unfortunately rare in most school programs, even where it may be acknowledged that dance is the sole discipline for developing children's sensitivity to space, time, and energy (as in the 1994 *National Standards for Arts Education*). In some cases, physical education and music teachers take up the slack, and attempts are made to educate children's awareness of their bodies' capacity for movement. The aesthetic element is usually absent from such efforts, however, as the goals of most PE and music teachers' employment of movement is more likely motor coordination and social skills than posture, position, grace, flow, and artistic expression.

A few children may be fortunate to acquire music through the movement-based approach to music learning called Dalcroze Eurhythmics. For nearly a century, this pedagogical method has used movement challenges and games to increase children's responsiveness to rhythm, pitch, dynamics, and other musical elements. I have elsewhere advocated the expansion of this training into school music programs (1991c), for I do not cease to be astounded at the musical sensitivity of children who have had eurhythmics experiences. Dalcroze Eurhythmics offers a thorough development of children's musicianship, due to its means of intermingling children's aural, intellectual, and physical selves in its activities. Its results also extend to improved attentiveness, concentration, and motor coordination at large. (See Virginia Mead's *Dalcroze Eurhythmics in Today's Classroom* [1994] and Julia Schnebly-Black and Stephen F. Moore's *The Rhythm Inside* [1997] for a description and examples of the Dalcroze approach.) Formal instruction in eurhythmics, movement, and dance builds upon children's natural kinesthetic sense and is well worthy of exploration for the benefits it can bring.

Music is all right—in the right place, at the right time.

Musical styles and functions vary widely, and it would be irresponsible of us to deny children exposure (minimally) and instruction (optimally) to a rich array of them. A musical diet of sweets but no starch is simply not balanced: Disney themes and MTV clips give pleasure, but they fulfill only a few of the facets and functions that music is capable of expressing. Along with music for entertainment, children deserve to experience music that is used for work and worship, for solitude and meditation, for bringing solidarity to a community, and for conveying emotions that range from elation to grief. Children are capable of understanding music of their own time and place as well as throughout history and in various other cultures, and they often gain tremendous insight through these musical explorations.

Not only through a broader swath of music for listening to at home or in school but also through their participation as singers, players, and dancers to the music of many Western and world cultures, children will develop a respect for diverse ways in which people musically express themselves. This they cannot do by themselves, but they can do it with our guidance and facilitation. Parents can offer their children musical options for listening, concert-going, private study, and community music involvement, just as teachers can ensure that the school music repertoire is representative of the larger world of styles and functions. A string of lessons on music for births (and birthdays), babies' lullabies, weddings, funerals, the new year, springtime, harvest, and the wintry season of "lights festivals" (for example, Christmas, Channukah, Divali) sends the message of musical functions that are widely valued yet diversely celebrated. Audio and video clips of music theater (opera, Broadway musicals, Chinese [Peking] opera, Japanese kabuki) and dance performances from Armenia to Zaire provide children with brief yet lasting images of music as it is linked to various functions. Music for solo, small, and large ensembles of voices and instruments in the West and the world are there awaiting our sampling of them with children.

If children are to accept that all "music is *all* right," they will need to know for themselves what music is out there beyond their immediate world, what it means to the musicians, how it is used, and why it is valued by the people. They may return to the music of their greatest familiarity, but at least through the experience and education we have facilitated for them, they will know something of the palette of musical expressions from which to choose.

Self-Study of Music

I listen and figure it out.

Few of us would argue that listening is the key avenue for learning and knowing music. We would probably agree that young musicians should develop notational literacy when the musical system provides it (as in the case of the Western art music that is the basis of traditional school band, choir, and orchestra programs). Yet even then, an understanding of notation cannot be expected of children until the symbols are matched to the sounds, and only then does the notational graph make sense. As music is first an aural phenomenon, not even the most pyrotechnical performer can survive and thrive in music without well-trained ears.

Listening to "figure out" music takes time, but it is time wisely spent. Careful listening enhances children's learning of a song, a rhythm, or a complete musical piece. We can provide children with opportunities for attentive listening to music by requiring their concentration to count the silences, conduct the meter, draw the rising and falling lines of the melody, or determine what purpose the music may serve the composer or performers. Children can be led to sing or play musical dialogues, imitating the rhythmic and melodic phrases that are delivered to them, and later devising answers to the musical questions. Certainly, we can also challenge yet guide children to take the major leap in listening so thoroughly as to learn a musical work by ear. (I have suggested an array of ear-training and larger listening strategies for children in *Lessons from the World* [1991b], and R. Murray Schafer's *Ear Cleaning* [1967] offers a treasureload of provocative activities.) Notation is a godsend, a remarkably useful time-saving technology for learning music quickly, but the ability to learn music by listening is not to be underrated or overlooked in developing our children's musicianship. (See *Do too many notes get in the way of the music?* for instructional approaches to the development of notational literacy.)

While we are on the subject of listening, it is fitting to note that musical training provides listening skills for applications far beyond the subject of music. Many children are strongly geared toward visual means of knowing their world, yet our society continues to value the acquisition of information by listening. Much of the manner in which parents and teachers present information to children is oral, thus necessitating children's ability to listen. By learning to listen to music, children develop their abilities to listen to speech and thus strengthen their concentration and communication skills for the academic tasks and social networks they are building. The keen listening required for music is clearly transferable to other domains.

I challenge myself to play.

We are always amazed with the children who not only meet the requirements of our assignments but who surpass our expectations for them. Children who are motivated to learn may indeed move themselves beyond the goals and objectives that teachers set for them to those that they themselves set. They have taken the leap from an extrinsic to an intrinsic motivation for learning, from other-directed to inner- or self-directed aims. It happens at various ages and stages of children's development, in music as well as in various other domains: Something "clicks" (a successful experience, a trusting relationship with the teacher, a healthy competition among peers, a desire to please parents, a moment of intellectual curiosity), and children are off and running on their own independent tracks to be the best that they can be. It is exciting to learn of children who are self-starters and who earnestly channel their energy toward what they wish to accomplish.

We should so challenge our children within their lessons and class sessions, and in their individual practices at home. Do we? Or do we expect too little of them, lowering our standards and reducing the degree of their accomplishments? Even worse, do we sometimes teach them what they already know? For example, it is common knowledge that most first graders understand the concept of soft-loud (and have since the age of three) (Moog, 1976), yet some teachers "teach" it and teach it again. If we teach children what they already know, or if we expect less from them than what they can do, we may well miss our chance to seize the energy and momentum toward their becoming more fully musically thinking and feeling beings. As we strive to know our students, their strengths and capabilities, their dreams and goals, we can be there for them—even those independent, self-motivated children—as references, trouble-shooters, and guides. We can also occasionally push the envelope, offering them greater skill development (including, sometimes, an accelerated rate), so as not to lose the best and the brightest from our programs. We can vary the complexity of what we teach: Some may be hungry for a quicker pace and a greater challenge.

I'm thinking about how a violin would sound hooked up to speakers.

We observe time and again children's curiosity with sound and how to make it, vary it, and "invent" it anew through the various technologies that are available to them. As children understand the mechanics of the equipment and the means of making instruments, electronic sound systems, and computers work, many will want to explore their uses and applications. A microphone attached to a tape recorder can be a fascination to some, who enjoy the increased intensity of hearing their voice as they sing (to say nothing of the chance to hear it played it back at them!). Others are captivated by the conversion of acoustic instruments through electricity to louder and fuller sounds, from electric guitars and keyboards to electrified flutes and fiddles; for them, a stereo speaker wired to their instrument is a first step into the world of fully amplified sound.

MIDI is a key development in music technology over the last decade, providing its users with the means for generating and sampling sounds, for controlling, recording, altering, or reproducing these sounds. Found in an increasing number of schools and home studios, MIDI is the armchair composer's dream, for her thoughts can be almost immediately realized for any assembly of instruments or voices. Well within their elementary school years, children are ready and able to take full advantage of all that MIDI can offer.

I've always believed that children of sufficient maturity should be allowed a space at the back of the toolshed, the garage, or the basement to tinker with mechanical things, to pull apart and put together toys, clocks, old motors, radios, record players, and speakers. In a related manner, they deserve opportunities to explore sources of musical sound and to try new twists on the traditional sources (i.e., instruments) they know. Indeed, in a round of Saturday garage sales we might collect a carton or more of potential sound producers and "old technologies" to sit on the back table in the classroom for the experimentation of budding inventors, mechanics, engineers, and composers. This is not to discount the need for MIDI and other high-tech (and still somewhat costly) musicking via synthesizers and computers; it is merely one more way of stimulating children's curiosity and inventiveness.

My inside-singing is my guide to playing.

Singing inside oneself may seem at first an illogical idea, or some image more romantic than real. Who sings inside for no one to hear? Plenty of people, most of all many thoughtful musicians who need to work out inside, intellectually, what they will perform aloud. For "inside-singing" is singing silently, hearing inside ourselves what we have heard before, what we have once performed or will again perform. It is a reasonable strategy: a tendency to rehearse, or a means for remembering music that is in some way meaningful to us. Singing on the inside happens to musicians at all stages of development, including children. Composer and educator Zoltan Kodaly was chief among those who advocated inner hearing, something akin to inside-singing, as one of the main goals of a musical education (1974). Even today, the training of teachers in the Hungarian or Kodaly method is fixed on the goal of inner hearing, the capacity to think the musical sounds without hearing them or externally voicing them. Likewise, Edwin E. Gordon (1994) supports inner hearing through his pronouncement of audiation as a chief accomplishment for children and adults; he argues that musically educated persons are those who "hear" the sound of the notation they are reading even when it is not physically audible. Both inside-singing and inner hearing are manifestations of aural skill development, a certain sign that the ear has undergone some training and has realized more of its capacity.

We can do much to encourage children to listen and sing what they will eventually play. The mindless "motoring" on an instrument that children can produce through the nervous emission of their kinesthetic energy is somewhat empty of purpose; it can be avoided when they think about what they will do. Young composers may also fare well by thoughtful inside-singing. Thinking *is* doing, as children fare well by listening to others perform it (including their teacher or peers) and then by singing it aloud and silently to themselves. In lessons and classroom sessions, teachers can make the necessary time for children to sing a phrase and then to hear it inside—once, twice, three times, or more. There is rock-solid reasoning to the Indian tradition of singing (sometimes for years) before taking up the study of a sitar or sarod, for example; this arrangement exercises the ear, mind, and voice to perceive and remember (and reproduce) aspects of the music that will later be transferred to the instrument (Neuman, 1980). Later, some of these same musicians are heard singing softly *while* they play. Likewise, children who listen, silently sing, and then play become "compleat musicians" who have more fully integrated the music than those who have not had the opportunity to sing inside themselves.

Musical Choices

Nobody knows my music but me.

The music that children call their own may emanate from a particular film or TV show, a favorite singer, or even a favorite composer. It may also be their original creation or a variant on something they have known but which they have personalized in their own ways. We can never know this personalized music precisely as they do. We can only hope to hear it, honor it, pay tribute to it, and perhaps, if the children are willing, figure ways of working it into lessons or activities. Hearing children's musical utterances, we can apply new words and extend them into tuneful phrases of conversation all united by the same pitch content and melodic twists and turns. We can observe the melodies of these jump-rope chants and songs and ask to join in with them, learning their repertoire and their means of teaching it. We can create with children accompaniments on xylophones, percussion instruments, and keyboards, and we can challenge children to notate the rhythms of their calls and chants and their table-top percussion pieces.

The possibilities are rich for exploring children's music, yet these extensions must be approached with sensitivity, our enthusiasm checked. For this is indeed *their* music, thus they should be principal players in its development, lest it turn into something to which they may no longer owe their allegiance or interest. We do not wish to deny children the privacy of their music or to tamper with it to the extent that we zap it of its character, and we should remind ourselves to seek their permission and their input in bringing it out of their playtime activities and into the classroom.

Some kids' music is pretty silly, like voices sounding like animals.

Why do adults manufacture music for children? Certainly for all the right reasons: for children's education and entertainment. Much of the music recorded for children is tasteful, treating subjects that are (or perhaps should be) of interest to them in carefully crafted texts and musically sensitive performances. The tapes and CDs feature children singing in natural or in trained voices, and adults singing in grown-up fine-tuned voices, with orchestras, bands, and folk instruments playing with masterful flair. But I am wary of manufactured children's music, so I issue this warning: Beware that brand of cute "kiddie music," for it can be trite, its high-gloss cover concealing its low musical value. The recording is packaged in a colorfully illustrated case, the song titles appear to be age-appropriate, and the citations from this expert and that organization appear impressive. But is the recording "safe" for use with children, and enriching to them? Or is it too much of the same silly thing, sung in contrived and mechanical voices, accompanied by bells and whistles and gizmos too numerous to mention?

If we ask to listen to children's recordings, many storekeepers and clerks will oblige. We become the judge as we critically listen and raise questions: What is its musical quality? Are all of the timbres the result of some low-grade synthesizer? Are the voices and instruments in tune? Are the vocal timbres natural or contrived? Are they appropriate for the style, from playground songs to seasonal carols to art songs? Is the music expressive, with occasional stylistically appropriate changes in dynamics or tempo? Some of my favorite recordings for children, due to their musical power and sensitivity, are *Heigh-Ho Mozart* (1995, Delos International), featuring Disney movie themes arranged for orchestral instruments in a variety of composers' styles; *Classics for Kids* (1993, RCA Victor), with Arthur Fiedler, James Galway, Eugene Ormandy, and others in selections from Ravel's *Mother Goose Suite,* Saint-Saens's *Carnival of the Animals,* and Tchaikovsky's *The Nutcracker; Sadako and the Thousand Paper Cranes* (1995, Dancing Cat Music), narrated by Liv Ullman with guitar by George Winston; *Nursery Days* (1992, Smithsonian Folkways), a collection of traditional and composed songs made by popular by Woody Guthrie (who performs them); *How the Rhinoceros Got His Skin* (1987, Rabbit Ears Productions), with music by Bobby McFerrin and narration by Jack Nicholson; and the musical stories of composers like *Beethoven Lives Upstairs* (1989, Classical Kids; see "Michael" for titles of other productions).

In our own selection of recordings to share with children, we should not ignore traditional songs, instrumental music, and musical stories of various ethnic cultures (for example, Anglo-American, African American, Caribbean, Chicano, and Native American). Nor should we withhold opportunities for children to know a Chopin piano etude, a recorder sonatine by Telemann, or a wind piece by Stravinsky. Complex music of any time or place can be understood by children, with different layers of their understanding developing with each hearing. Sometimes, indirect listening experiences (with children listening while working on a class project or eating a meal) can obliquely lead to interest in a piece or style, which is expressed by children in their discussion, their pursuit of further listening, and even their wish to study the instrument or piece. Finally, music for children need not exclude the music of adults, for what children enjoy may be far beyond the hypothetical category of "kids' music" as established by adults.

She just doesn't know the ones that I know.

No doubt, knowing our children will lead us to making their instructional experiences more relevant. While we may be musically knowledgable and skilled as a result of our long experience and training, many children have at an early age a surprising amount of their own music within them. They may covertly make their music beyond the listening radius of adults and may assume that adults would not be much interested in their music anyway. Some children may be disappointed or even frustrated with the extent to which adults lay their musical choices upon them, without so much as a nod to children's own music. Children's musical preferences deserve to be acknowledged, however, as this is the repertoire in which they are already steeped; it is a part of their selfhood, their own identity. Their music may warrant our inclusion in a class session, lesson, or program. As we plan for our lessons and learning experiences with them, we must understand something of our children's musical selves. We need to know them in order to teach them and to acknowledge and validate them through a recognition of who they musically are.

He can do "Hot Cross Buns," but the Dragons tune is much cooler.

As the intermediate schoolchild begins to learn to play an instrument, the music that motivates him may be less likely a nursery rhyme than the music he hears on a more regular basis. Typically, children learn to play tunes like "Hot Cross Buns," "Lightly Row," and "Go Tell Aunt Rhody" on their flutes, clarinets, violins, and trumpets. All have simple rhythms and limited pitch content, their melodies stepwise up and down and around the tonic. These tunes and others like them have become almost permanent fixtures in instruction manuals, partly due to the belief that they are songs with which children are familiar (and partly because they are technically easy to play). Yet many of these tunes are not familiar to today's children, as song collections, singing circles, teachers, and the media have long ago dropped them from the repertoire.

The choice of selecting familiar music for children to play is a sound one, for their internalization of melodies and rhythms guides them in their playing. (See *My inside-singing is my guide to playing* for a discussion of the importance of inner hearing.) If they've heard the tunes and sung them, a natural progression is for children to next play them. Yet we can hardly help but recognize that what was relevant to children's lives "then" is not necessarily so now. If we seek melodies with few pitches and basic rhythms that can be accessible to young instrumentalists, we can surely find them among the music that children are currently hearing. These tunes may be the jingles of TV commercials, the "signal music" (if not fanfares) of sporting events, and the catchy phrases of popular songs. The familiar melodies could certainly include, through our careful plan for direct and subliminal listening, segments from traditional music of the world's cultures and themes from quartets, operas, symphonies. They may also be the songs that children have sung in class or on the playground. If at least some of the music that children are learning to play in their first (and later) lessons should be familiar to them, then we must gauge the familiarity of this music to children so as to pique their musical interest and motivate their practice.

The only music you can listen to in school are classical and kids' music.

Children deserve broad but balanced musical listening experiences. Among the genres to be shared with them are children's traditional songs and the so-called classical music (which may to some children encompass all "serious" music of Europe from ancient to contemporary times, including the truly "classical period" music of Viennese composers like Mozart, Haydn, and early Beethoven). Yet this palette of genres should also not exclude the very music that many children find appealing: mass-mediated popular music. As in the case of choosing exemplary works to represent lullabies or singing games, the same careful choices must be made to represent swing, rock and roll, 60s rock, soul, heavy metal, grunge, rap, doo-wop, and techno. Not just any piece will do, though, and those that do not offer a hearty taste of the best of the batch (or genre) are probably not worthy of children's time and attention.

So who chooses this "other music," the popular and rock styles? Can we be expert at selecting from the styles we do not know? There are several approaches to selecting popular music for use at school. Sometimes, children (particularly in the intermediate grades) can identify pieces. They suggest titles for us to seek out in the record stores or bring their copies of the CD to us, and we can then listen and decide for ourselves whether the pieces are justified in our teaching. We can also go, unprompted by our children, to the music store, become informed by a sales clerk about current styles and artists, and listen to the samples that she may play for us before purchasing. We can read *Billboard* for the "rising star" songs, figuring that a song on its way up the charts stands a chance of having a few good months of air time and use in our classes. We can scan *Rolling Stone, Spin, Down Beat,* or *Guitar Player* for ideas and take in a few columns in news magazines and newspapers on trends in popular music and late-breaking releases. We can also strive, in our presentation of a balanced musical diet, to offer real rock music rather than the antiseptic and dejuiced "for school" pop music that seems a mere shadow of the real thing.

We may also wish to purposefully discard certain popular music selections. The lyrics of some songs might suggest images of sex and violence that we deem inappropriate in children's lives. Over the years, we have seen the censorship of particular styles, songs, and pieces of music in an attempt to protect young people from the emotions and meanings this music may convey. School officials may draw the line on which music belongs in school and which music is out of bounds and inappropriate for children's in-school listening time. Guidelines are frequently imposed on music in much the same way as dress codes are dictated, for the sake of steering children toward music and texts that are deemed to be intellectually, emotionally, and aesthetically substantive (if not morally uplifting)—and for steering them away from that music which is not. (Count Elvis Presley, Jerry Lee Lewis, Alice Cooper, Kiss, The Sex Pistols, and Snoop Doggy Dog among those whose music, rightly or wrongly, has been designated as "off limits" to students, in particular times and places.)

While the concept of music censorship is commonplace, the particular music to be disallowed in school is arguable. The question of *which* music stays or goes is a key issue, and this requires careful listening and discussion among teachers, parents, and children (at least, children who have reached the intermediate grades). For any music that is prohibited in school can be easily accessed outside of school, if not on the sly *in* school, which defeats the purpose of music censorship. If an important outcome of censorship is the development of children's own discrimination and understanding of why certain music might be less redeeming than others (although this decision will always, in the end, remain within the ear and mind of the beholder), then healthy discussions with children about popular music, its texts, and its performance contexts are vital. Mass-mediated popular music is a reality, and while it is not all "good," there are certainly representative samples of it which, when studied, may offer children a further understanding of both music and culture.

More of a Musical Education

Harmonicas sound thicker than whistles.

Children are perceptive listeners of music, sometimes keenly so. They begin to discern music's qualities from infancy onward: its pulse, accents, and patterns, its melodic shapes, pitch registers, and directions. (For a discussion of young children's perceptual and cognitive development, see Deliege and Sloboda, 1996). Their performance of music is dependent on their perception of it, in that what they hear can guide them in their singing and playing. The sharper their listening, the more accurate their performance is likely to be.

While children may accurately perceive musical sounds and their relationships, they must also be able to describe and communicate to others what they hear. Understanding the meaning of "melody," "rhythm," "meter," "texture," "choppy-smooth," and even "high/low" is the result of a musical education; these words must be taught and learned before they will be used with confidence and ease. When children have no vocabulary for describing their musical experiences, they will create their own: "thick music," "music for thinking," "close music," "football sound," for examples. Sometimes these descriptions can be refreshing, colorful, and geared to the individual's personal experience; they may be poetically laden with aural and visual images. Such descriptions are valuable to the children and worthy of note by adults, yet they are not usually sufficient for communicating precisely what children musically perceive and know. Imagine the confusion of using an idiosyncratic, personal language to convey mathematical principles or historical facts! In a similar fashion, discussions about music should proceed from the use of an established vocabulary if people are to be mutually understood. Along with the skills necessary for performing and creating music, the ability to describe it is an important goal for children to attain.

We all dream about making a music video.

To many children of the video age, music is not just an aural entity but a performance art that involves singing, the playing of instruments, dancing, props, sets and staging, costuming, and the dramatic arts. Children's fantasies are frequently the stuff of the music videos they know. Why not involve them in the making of one? The educational benefits are real, as children can gain tremendous knowledge of music's structures, its performance practice, and its technological production in the process.

In making a video, producers must first study its elements. Together, children can watch and analyze a classic video (Michael Jackson's *Thriller* comes to mind). Where are the changes of scene? (Often, at the end of musical phrases or sections) At what points do the dancers shift positions? (Often, at the harmonic accents, or on the first beats of measures.) Where is the greatest activity of the dancers? (Often, at the points of the greatest musical intensity—volume—and density—textures.) Children can choose a musical work they know (Mozart's *Magic Flute Overture*, Handel's *Hallelujah Chorus*, a favorite song, a successful rhythmic percussion piece), record it, analyze it, and then map a design for its visual reproduction. How long are the sections? What tonalities and textures beg for particular visual images? Where are the accents? What kind of movements match it? How does text define the choice of images? Once the analysis is completed, children will need a VCR, a monitor, a stopwatch, a blank tape, and a fair amount of imagination, cooperation, and patience. Their production will demonstrate their abilities to make music, perceive music, and produce it technologically. Their thoughtful plans can render their video dreams real.

Do too many notes get in the way of the music?

Too many notes too soon can be frustrating to children, thus pointing to the necessity of sound before symbol, of the musical experience before the musical "graph" (See *I listen and figure it out* for a rationale for educating children's aural skills prior to notation.) Children who have listened, sung, and played with music are better prepared to make sense of the notation than those with insufficient experience in a given musical style. If we recognize notation as a technologically efficient way of preserving and transmitting music, then we are obliged to offer children its benefits—at a moderate pace and through a stepwise progression.

A sequential program that develops notational literacy as a complement to listening and performing is a good bet. The Hungarian pedagogy of Zoltan Kodaly offers a comprehensive approach to reading and writing music so that children can grow into musically independent individuals, eventually able to decipher the notation for themselves. First two- and then three-pitch melodies lead eventually to tetrachords and pentatonic melodies, and within a few years, children are performing what they read and notating what they hear. A Kodaly curriculum begins with children's singing of folk songs and singing games in earliest childhood, and soon the pedagogy's ear training emphasis leads to inner hearing—hearing what one sees. The Kodaly sequence is described in Erzebet Szonyi's *Musical Reading and Writing,* pupil's book, vols. 1–8 (1979), Erzebet Hegyi's *Solfege according to the Kodaly Concept* (1975–79), and Lois Choksy's *Kodaly Method* (1974). It is also in play in Katalin Forrai's *Music in Preschool* (1988).

One of the most motivating ways for children to discover notation's importance is to apply it to the documentation of their own songs, singing games, and musical utterances. Within even an elementary training in rhythm and pitch notation, children can record their performances, listen and listen again to themselves singing, and puzzle out the notation that "stands for" what they have performed. It can be highly motivating for a child to be able to give their musical codes—

notation—to another child to sing or play. Likewise, there is great satisfaction to be gained from deciphering a friend's notated music and performing it. Since children's music can be somewhat sophisticated, it can be challenging, yet rewarding, to write and read the many nuances of their own music.

I could play if my teacher would let me.

In the time we spend with the intent of giving musical enrichment to our children, how often do we talk more than we "musick"? Adults are highly verbal in their descriptions and explanations, while children are generally less so. Throughout a school's daily curricular studies, both the nature of the subjects and our pedagogical approaches to them lend themselves to verbalizing about knowledge. Few subjects are devoted to nurturing children's expressive selves: Music offers the rare opportunity for children to "sound off" in nonverbal ways. Yet all too often we resort to verbalizing about music and thus stall, block, and prevent children from making the most of their music time.

I often find myself recording a class I teach and then checking the amount of time I have spent talking about music. I am always astounded by my lack of word economy, so my next move is to figure out ways to reduce the talk time. Children want to play, sing, and move to music. From their earliest years, they are eager to get their hands on the instruments they see sitting in corners or lined up on tables and shelves. They look forward to singing because it feels good. They want to listen to music they understand and can relate to, especially when it comes at them from a quality sound system. So why should we deny them (or delay) these experiences while we talk? Children can always talk about music later (or listen to others talk about it)—after music time, and when they themselves become the verbal adults that we are.

The violins sounded good when we were that close.

"Canned music" is an image that some of us may have from our own school music experiences, where the music to which we listened came from the recordings the teacher would spin on the stereo set. If the music teacher could play, we might never have known it, for she instead "facilitated" our listening, lecturing at us before, during, and after the many records she served up for us. We rarely heard "live" music at school, from her or anyone else.

Yet in every community, there are musicians. Some are amateurs, or students, teachers, or professionals. A few are associated with such organizations as Young Audiences, Inc., where school programs of performance, discussion, and student participation are their goal.[12] Many musicians have the time and the inclination to play in public, to convert their Tuesday morning rehearsals from a living room space to a classroom, and to test the waters for their next performance with a group of young (and sometimes quite critical) listeners. Have we tapped these musicians, inviting them to our schools? Some children have never seen or heard "live" a violin, a French horn, a Japanese koto, or a blues guitar, or they might be enthusiastic about the music these instruments play. To meet a real musician is to truly humanize it, to give it a three-dimensional human form. A good many performers have never considered a school as a possible performance or rehearsal venue, or they might recognize the potential of children as "sounding boards" and "test audiences" for their music. The occasions for the meeting of artists with young audiences are unrealized, but thus await our attention.

Nor do I see why we sometimes deny or diminish our own abilities as performing musicians. It seems reasonable for us to take every opportunity to sing and play for children—and with them. We are their musical models. We have access to instruments, some of which we can play proficiently and others which we can at the very least demonstrate. Recorded music has its place and function for the many musical styles and works that we cannot know, but the live musicking that we and our friendly community musicians can offer children are rare treasures. Children will know and grow in music and will certainly maintain a high motivation for learning music when its presence in the classroom is alive and well.

In school, we all sing and move and play together.

School music programs are typically geared toward instruction en masse. (For a discussion of music's social benefits, see *I try to concentrate on what I'm doing and relate to the others.*) Even as individualized and small group instruction are common to math and language arts classes, there is a tendency for children to be musically educated at school in traditional ensembles and in their large class group. While mass instruction may moderately benefit children, individual and small group projects are important means of developing children's musical knowledge and skills. For as children will continue to sing in choirs and play in bands, orchestras, and other large ensembles, they may also require opportunities for thinking and doing music apart from the crowd.

Individualized instruction and independent learning can happen in many ways. Occasionally, children may be assigned to listen to particular recordings at home (commercial or teacher-prepared tapes) or to view a music special on TV; these experiences can then lead to the preparation of individual oral or written reports on aspects of the music's style, function, and performance practice. There are other projects in which children can be involved individually beyond the school: taping their parents and grandparents as they sing the songs of their heydays (and then notating them); interviewing or developing oral histories of musicians who live in their communities (and then transcribing and writing them up); listening and writing about music that typically occurs in their homes, stores, and other everyday venues; recording and then notating the sounds of birds, or street traffic; constructing their own instruments from materials they find at home; composing music for "found sounds" from their kitchens, basements, and backyards.

At school, individual learning can happen, even in the presence of the full group. Children may listen to music together but then respond in individual, inventive ways through their own personal and creative movement, or verbally on paper. They can be turned loose to invent their own four-tone, eight-measure melodies on recorders, xylophones, and keyboards, or to explore ways of infusing a particular duration or rhythm into a four-bar percussion piece. Children can be asked to "solo" for their classmates, singing or playing individually a part that the class may be learning together. They can distinguish themselves musically, sitting one after the other around a circle as they sing or play in improvisatory fashion a four-beat phrase. Clearly, children need not be expected always and only to contribute to a "mass-class" sound.

Likewise, the possibilities for small group explorations and performances should not be neglected. Collaborative and cooperative learning works quite well in the music class, as children guide, stimulate, teach, and check each other on assignments in which they are engaged. The more expert musicians can lead the novices, as the less musically enriched children provide the more musically experienced with challenges for articulating and demonstrating what they know. This can happen through song-gathering and notation projects, in improvisation and composition assignments, and in a variety of chamber music contexts where children combine their sounds to form a coalescing musical whole. Large-group learning may have hailed from some automaton time when everyone was expected to function uniformly; such an arrangement is not always in the best interests of children's development as independent thinkers.

I wish we had more music time.

One of the highest compliments a teacher can receive is a child's wish for more of whatever learning experience has been offered her. "More music time" plays as a happy little tune in our ears, yet we also are inclined to move beyond its congratulatory nature to the essence of one of our scarcest commodities (and the plight of all teachers): the lack of time for teaching children what we think they ought to know. While curricular programs may officially pronounce that children receive up to several hours of music instruction per week, it is not unusual for a school music class to run for a thirty-minute time period once (or, for the more fortunate, twice) weekly. We can grieve and gripe about the minimal music time, but with our best foot forward we may be better off taking steps to determine how better to use the allotted time we have. However minimal it may be, we can figure out ways of maximizing that time and can also devise channels and circumstances for music's infusion into other segments of children's days and lives.

Making the most of minimal time necessitates running the class efficiently, with every moment jammed with musicking and directed listening experiences. A well-paced music class for children can provide far more music than what many classes average, particularly when we cut the long verbal discourses about music, clip back the extensive tirades on behavior that is/is not appropriate (and use facial expressions, gestures, and our movement toward "trouble spots" to curtail behaviors—without missing a musical beat), and channel our own and children's thoughts and actions toward musical matters. Young children have a tendency to talk on, if not channeled, about subjects remotely related (if related at all) to the focus of a class, while the thoughts of older children may drift to topics of other classes, their friends, and outside-school activities. One of our primary and ongoing tasks as teachers is thus to gain and maintain their attention; this requires our high energy, frequent vocal modulations, continuous eye contact, and meaningful gestures. A subsequent challenge is to fill the class time with the substance of the subject: more music to listen to, to sing, and to play.

As well, music can be linked to learning of other subjects. Again, the potential for partnerships among teachers beckons; through such partnerships, music specialists and classroom teachers may confer about ways of using music as transitions between classroom sessions and subjects, as recess and break-time activities, and as actual classwork. Songs, rhythms, and listening experiences can be integrated into lessons on the social studies, the language arts, mathematics, and the sciences. Music's infusion into other moments of the school day may happen in a variety of ways: by playing music as a backdrop to a science project (a low-impact channeling of music) or by setting a poem or a story to music (a high-impact channeling of music). Children learn language through song, culture through the study of the materials from which instruments are made, and mathematics through rhythm games. Since children enjoy music, they are motivated to learn by it and through it.

It is also no small mission to advocate that a greater portion of the school curriculum be relegated to children's musical training. In some schools, music is part of children's daily activities. There, children learn to read and write music as they develop their general literacy and numeracy skills. Singing is a constant, something that everyone is equipped to do and that gets better with each additional practice. Children (and their parents) in these settings are led to believe that music, as much as other parts of their curricular load, is essential to their development as knowledgeable and well-adjusted citizens of their society. They become competent musicians because it is a cultural expectation to do so, and a human achievement to be carefully sought and nurtured.

I would miss music now, because Mrs. Phillips is so much better.

What makes a good music teacher? To children, the teacher is the human factor in their quest to know music, the face that they attach to their musical training.

The teacher is one of the key motivating factors of their continued progress toward becoming performers, composers, and careful listeners; the teacher can also be the cause of children's waning interest in music as a subject to study. Performing musicians tend to be fairly introverted, independent, anxious, and lacking in conscientiousness (Kemp, 1996)—hardly traits that would seem to endear them to children. The Myers-Briggs assessment of personality types indicates that teachers of children in general tend to be extroverted, sensing, feeling, and judging people (Myers and McCaulley, 1985). Music teachers may need to develop a more balanced way of communicating with children than they might have had as performers, moving at least to the middle of the road with regard to dimensions of introversion-extroversion, dependence-independence, and anxious-calm traits.

As we might have suspected from talking with and observing children, good music teachers are dynamic individuals with high energy and enthusiasm for what they do (music) and who they teach (children). They are ready to do music for and with children, to sing, play, and move with them, and to honestly recognize children's strengths while also addressing their weaknesses. As children describe them, good teachers emerge as having skills to share, a sense of humor, an anchoring in the real world, flexibility in their plans, an awareness of what is developmentally appropriate (and what is not), fairness in the time and attention they devote to each child, and a willingness to take from children's own experiences while giving them what they need to become more fully educated. These essential elements of good music teachers challenge us all, and we become introspective as we consider how we can hone our skills in communicating to children the many ways in which they can follow our lead and reap the joys that come from developing their musical selves.

Musical Mosaics

A discussion of children's education and welfare must invariably sweeps across the many facets that comprise them. Each child is a mosaic of sorts, with colorful pieces contributing in complex ways to form the whole of his physical, social, intellectual, and emotional selfhood. In helping a child to achieve his integrated and holistic self, parents and teachers are wise to want to examine his "pieces," to check carefully on the conditions of each one and to help in polishing, restoring, and maintaining them. A child's "mosaic" includes his logical, verbal, kinesthetic, physical, social, and artistic parts and pieces. All deserve attention, as each adds its own lustre to the child's mosaic whole.

Children's musical enculturation is already well under way by the time they enter their school years. Although by no means completely set, their sensitivity to certain musical styles, their uses of music for particular occasions, and their musical vocabularies and grammars are already gelling. Their family and community experiences have influenced their perceptions of what music means to them, and they enjoy and value particular types of music as a result of these experiences. With schooling comes most children's first formal education in music, even as their informal learning continues at home. Lessons may follow, even as enculturation continues. In important ways, the home and school—and the efforts of parents and teachers—can take children from who they musically are to all that they can musically become.

As we intently listen to and watch children, as we talk to them and with them about music, we become aware of their musical interests. Through our observations and conversations, we gain the information we need about children and their music so that we can design a plan for their further education and training. We then no longer speak from some vague and neutral conception of children, music, and pedagogy, nor from too broad a curricular scope, but from what our own ears and eyes have taught us about them. We consider interventions for nurturing their capacities to perceive, perform, and create music, and we route our course with full knowledge of the music that our children have known in their pasts, that they want to know, and that we think they full well *should* know.

The design we draw of music for children is a balance, a give-and-take between children and us—the parents and teachers—whose responsibility they are. If our plan is carefully considered, founded on the music of their play and leisure, kindled by the music of their hopes and dreams, and shaped by the specialized skills we can deliver to them in lessons and class instruction, they will fully realize their capacities as musically expressive individuals. Music is for every child, after all: a god-given right to which they all have access. As they attain their wholeness of being, the musical pieces are some of the brightest, most shining parts of their mosaic selves.

Afterword

Like Nathan, whose remarks launched this endeavor, other children in these cases and conversations demonstrated to me the very real presence of songs in their heads. Perhaps these songs are akin go "music on the brain," musical impressions with staying power. Some of this music is of the "stuck-in-the-groove" variety, those unforgettable melodies that catch the ear from first hearing, enveloping young listeners and developing in them a need to hear it repeatedly, almost inexhaustibly, to sing it, and to move it. Yet these songs are those that only they can sing—their own music—fashioned by them from their individual experiences, music of the sort that seizes them and that has the potency to transform them even as they engage in creating and re-creating it. Children are touched and challenged by this music, and may engage in it deeply.

Many children released or shared some of their "head-music"—familiar melodies, rhythms, songs, and themes, or even their very own invented music, while others chose to keep their music to themselves, and to continue the more intimate and indeed "private" affairs they have had with it all their young lives. The relationships that children individually have with their music comes as a result of the type and extent of music that has entered their ears and minds, and the manner in which they rework and reconfigure this music within their cognitive structures. What music I did hear from children may have been just the tip of the iceberg, with much more from where that came from spinning within them. At least some of this music is awaiting stimulation and development, I am certain, through the training and enrichment that we can provide to children.

Some of the words and images of the children whom I came to know are lingering long after my visits with them. Alan, determined to play keyboard despite the lack of lessons to guide him, had described his "inside-singing" as a guide to figuring out the songs he liked; the "humming music" that played inside him were some of the melodies he sought to transfer to his keyboard. Jonathan, involved as he was in music ranging from violin and school choir to the sounds of his uncle's percussion instruments, referred to songs that had become "stuck in his head," their tunes sounding constantly inside him without his stimulation or effort; he half-complained yet was also in awe, I think, of music's staying power. The children in Mrs. Bedford's class had musical ideas that differed from her own; the music within them came leaping out with the stimulation she offered.

Children's inside-songs, chants, and rhythms sounded in a variety of circumstances, their music meshing with the tableaux I now hold of them musicking as they ate, rode the bus, jumped rope, made sand pies, hunted garden beans, swang on swings, cleaned tables, swept floors, and teased and taunted their friends. One of the most delightful images to me is that of the little girl who sang out the bus window to the wind one afternoon on her travels homeward from school. She had no title nor words for these songs and also claimed that she did not *know* the songs herself. Yet they were there, flowing as naturally from her as the wind that ruffled her hair. Her melodies were a constant stream of ideas, and they were intricate. They were in her head yet also making their way out to give pleasure to those who listened nearby.

This book was never intended as a "how-to" methods manual of strategy-by-strategy lessons, nor has it ended that way. It is more a collage of children in music and on music, of their actions and words, with ruminations and recommendations springing from them. It is testimony to the music as a human phenomenon, dwelling within even the very young and awaiting the call to expression. Perhaps the book will serve as prelude to the choices we make regarding children's musical education in school and on the outside. It may even trigger further explorations of an interdisciplinary sort by those whose interest in music and its meaning in children's lives, with collaborative efforts by specialists who can criss-cross the fields of education, ethnomusicology, anthropology, and folklore.

My hope is that the book may serve its primary purpose, to function as a means for teachers (and more than a few parents) to stand still and away from the day-to-day busy-ness of talking at—rather than listening to—children, in order to assess who they are, what they do, how they think. We require these moments of watching, listening, and contemplating in order to enrich the lives of children for whom we are responsible. This book is a result of these "moments" that beget other moments within the lives of musical children.

Appendix 1

Outline for the Observations

My observations of musical children follow a course I have developed through many years of observing student teachers, earlier experiences I have had in observing children in their natural environments, and descriptions in the literature of nonparticipant observation as a technique of ethnographic research. The following outline delineates the stepwise progression I took in observing children for the narrative tales of children at musical play, and is one that has been successfully employed by education majors, teachers, and graduate students engaged in research on children's musical involvement. There were preliminary actions *prior to the visit* that opened doors for me and prepared me for what I would need to do while "in the field" of the children's environment, an array of behaviors to watch and to listen for while there (*during the visit*) and a number of actions *following the visit* that I needed to take in order to bring closure to the observations while also proceeding onward to the writing of the tales. In gaining a response to the question "What (musically) is going on here?," we do indeed need to attend to the "imponderables," the minor matters, as well as to issues that are typically of greater relevance to those of us whose interest is children and their music.

Prior to the Visit

1. Select a setting, one to which there will likely be access for multiple visits. This accessibility can be confirmed by phone, often through questions to a secre-

tary as to the institution's policy on visitors for purposes of educational study or research. (For prospective teachers who will make observations, these settings may be preselected and arranged by the instructor of their methods or field experience course.)

2. Call the teacher or caregiver within the institution to request time with their children. Explain in some detail the purpose of the observations, what knowledge there is to be gained, and how it will be used. Confirm the intention not to disrupt the ongoing events but to maintain a decorum that is unobtrusive and beyond any direct interaction with participants. Guarantee also that the identities of those to be observed will be protected in any reports that may be produced.

3. Send a letter to and/or make an appointment to meet with the teacher or caregiver prior to the first observation so as to explain in greater detail the purpose of the observations. An in-person visit is helpful in addressing more fully any concerns that the teacher or caregiver may have about the intrusion of a stranger into the children's "space."

4. In the case of observations for the purpose of research, file all forms of permission and protection that may be required by the affected institutions (the observer's and the observed). In some instances, institutions geared to the education, care, and protection of children may require a letter of introduction, to be sent by the observer to each parent, and a parental permission form that will be returned and kept on record at the institution. These forms can take several weeks to complete, collect, and file, so advance planning may be necessary.

5. Collect equipment for the observation: a notebook (small notepads that fit easily in the pocket are convenient), a few pencils, a portable tape recorder, video camera, and a stock of blank cassette tapes and videocassettes. A video camera typically has its own case with strap for carrying, while the remainder of the material is usually easily transportable in a backpack or small duffel.

During the Visit

5. On arrival, begin to take notes. Never rely on mental notes; instead, develop a personal system of shorthand or speedwriting to record on paper what you see and hear.

6. Describe the classroom, playground, bus, home, or other "field" site of the observation. Note the physical features that comprise it. For example, is the school's exterior brick (what type?) or wood (what color?)? How old is it? What condition is it in? Is the classroom carpeted or tiled? How large is it? What and where are the instruments? What do the bulletin boards and walls display? How sound-proof is the space? What sounds leak through from the halls or even the outside? Jot down the visual and aural environment of the place in which the observations will occur. A video camera can freeze the scenes, too, for later repeated observations.

7. Describe the children who figure prominently in the scene of the observation. What physical features define them (for example, height, hair color, hair length, facial expressions)? How are they dressed? How do they sit and stand as they interact with one another? What mannerisms distinguish them (swinging their feet, patting their laps, pulling at their hair)? Look for the personal traits they demonstrate, and listen for their manner of speech (speed, pronunciation, grammar, vocabulary).

8. Listen for the music the children make. Be careful to note when the speech turns rhythmic and when the inflections become the sustained tones of singing. Switch on the tape recorder, but sketch as well a few graphic notes while you listen that are descriptive of the music and its performance context. For the songs with gestures, movement, and games, a video camera is handy for getting the entirety of the performance. Later, the tapes can be played repeatedly to aid the process of transcription.

9. In the initial observations, expect children to be curious and inquisitive. Be ready for questions about your work, your equipment, and the contents of your notebook. It is fair to respond to these questions briefly when it does not interfere with an observation you are making; it is also reasonable to politely state that you are not able to answer the question at the moment but that you will hope to be able to explain your work later. Children's curiosity soon fades, however, as they find other people with whom to interact and activities in which to be engaged.

Following the Visit

10. The jotted notes are dangerous if left too long to themselves, as a mnemonic word or phrase loses its grip through time's way of blurring out the details. The notes taken during observations should be written up as soon as possible, preferably the same day but not longer than two or three days after the actual time of the observations. The observer can sketch a description of the environment, the key players, local expressions, recurring incidents, and, of course, the music. Concrete details can be drafted that will show rather than simply tell about children's behaviors.

11. Listen to the audiotapes and watch the videotapes. With each repeated listening or viewing, new insights will emerge and can be added to an ever-expanding list of written observations. Five listenings (or viewings) may be too few, but ten is just about right for studying the words and scenes.

12. Transcribe the musical segments from audiotapes and the music-and-movement pieces from the videotapes. Audiotapes store in a straightforward manner the rhythms and melodies of children, may have better sound reproduction than VCRs, and can channel attention toward the musical components for study.

13. Write the report, the "tale."

Appendix 2

Questions for the Conversations

The following questions contain global concerns I had as I launched the project; they have proven useful to students pursuing information on music and its meaning in children's lives. I laid the list of questions on the desk, table, or floor in front of me (or fastened them to my clipboard) and glanced at them to remind me of the subjects to which children could give their attention during the course of the conversations. The preliminary items (*The Child and Setting*) reminded me to gauge certain personal characteristics of the children, the interview setting, teachers (or parents or siblings) with whom I might speak, the school, and the neighborhood; these descriptions later jogged my memory as I wrote my first draft of the conversation. The *General Questions* and *Musical Questions* were "prompts" for me; I often zigzagged through them in disorderly fashion, according to the flow of the conversation and the interests of each child. I improvised the "gist" of the questions to suit the mood of our exchange (and the age of the child), added questions to help them clarify their thoughts, and, in my curiosity about children's remarks, followed their thinking aloud on other subjects and in different directions. I missed questions, too, particularly when children had other thoughts to share and time was running out. Most of the time, however, the bases of my global concerns were covered, concentrated as they were in these questions.

The Child and Setting

Name of child (real, for my records only):
Pseudonym (assigned by me for the report):
Gender:
Age/Grade:
Appearance:
Interview setting:
Teacher (and others on the scene):

General Questions

1. How long have you lived in your current home?
2. How long have you attended this school?
3. What kind of work do your parents do?
4. What do you like most about school? Least?
5. What do you like to do outside of school?
6. What are you really good at?
7. What will you be when you grow up?

Musical Questions

8. Do you like music? Why?
9. How does music make you feel?
10. Is music important to you? Why?
11. Do you sing? What do you sing?
12. Will you sing a favorite song for me?
13. How many songs do you know?
14. How do you learn these songs?
15. Do any of your toys make music?
16. Do you play a musical instrument? Which one(s)?
17. Do members of your family play a musical instrument? Which one(s)?
18. Do members of your family sing? What do they sing?
19. Do you listen to music? Where? When?
20. Do you like to dance to music? What kind of music do you dance to?
21. Do you make music with your family?
22. Do you make music with your friends?
23. Do you sing or play music in school?
24. Do you sing or play music outside of school?
25. Do you go to sleep with music? What kind?
26. Do you like fast/slow music? Loud/soft music?
27. What kind of music do your parents listen to? Siblings?

28. Do you ever just think about music? What do you think?
29. Do you have any tapes/CDs/videos/recordings? What kind?
30. What are all the ways you use music in your life?
31. If you had $— to spend on music, what would you buy?
32. What do you really want to know about music?

Notes

Introduction

1. Christopher Small makes frequent use of the term "musicking" in *Music of the Common Tongue: Survival and Celebration in Afro-American Music* (London: Calder Ltd., 1987), while David J. Elliott discusses "musicing" in *Music Matters* (New York: Oxford University Press, 1995). In both cases, the reference is to the act of making music, particularly by those who engage in it as less than full-time professionals. In "Whose Music Do We Teach Anyway?" (1994), Small claims that "since I coined the verb I claim the right to define it, which I do as follows: [musicking or] to music is to take part in a musical performance, not just as performer but also as listener, or provider of material for performance—what we call composing—or in any other way, dancing, for example."

2. Marie McCarthy presents a brilliant discussion of Seeger's educational interests and advocacies in "On 'American Music for American Children': The Contribution of Charles L. Seeger" (1996).

3. By "childsong," I mean songs created by children and preserved through their transmission to other children. They are distinguished from songs composed and transmitted to children by adults. See Campbell, 1991a.

4. See "Narrative Tales" in Part I and "A Flexible System" in Part II for further details regarding my approach to gathering and interpreting these slices of life.

5. See "Narrative Tales" in Part I for a more complete indication of procedures that were undertaken to determine children's musical practices and repertoire at the periphery, or beyond the direct influence, of schools, teachers, parents, and other adults.

6. See "A Flexible System" in Part II for a discussion of global concerns that prompted these conversations. Appendix I and Appendix II contains guidelines for observ-

ing and conversing with children, with the intent of clarifying ideas that directed this project as well as suggesting further pursuits of this nature.

Part 1   In Music: Children at Musical Play

1. Realistically, it sometimes happened that I settled into an observation only to find that children's musical behaviors were not evident on that day and time. Often, if a "catalyst child" were missing from a setting, there might be much less musicking by the remaining children. Such is the unpredictable nature of these observations, yet if I stayed long enough or returned another day, children's musical behaviors would emerge.

2. My method of mostly nonparticipant observation was of the sort that Patricia A. Adler and Peter Adler describe in "Observational Techniques" (see Norman K. Denzin and Yvonna S. Lincoln, 1994). See also Atkinson and Hammersley, 1994, in the same source.

3. John van Maanen (1988) set four conventions that mark his realist tales: (1) *experiential authority*, in which as author, I am present in the text but mostly at the sidelines rather than at the forefront; (2) *typical forms*, in which much of the mundane details of the settings and activities (and children) are arranged rather systematically; (3) *native's point of view*, such that children's verbal and musical quotations are included in the text; and (4) *interpretive omnipotence*, in which any interpretations are admittedly more my own than those of the children, who present me with "data" that I then discuss from my standpoint as an educator.

4. See also *The Art of Fact* (New York: Scribner, 1997) by Kevin Kerrane and Ben Yagoda, for examples of literary journalism similar to McPhee's, where non-fiction stories shimmer like novels with the pleasures of detailed realism. From Tom Wolfe to Joan Didion, the "new journalism" style has a way of giving concepts "staying power."

5. Yet I am persuaded by Steven Feld's claim that "broad and meaningful comparisons" and the overarching statements I make in the third section "will have to be based on accurate, detailed, careful local ethnographic models," or, at least, models that are based on observations (from the first section) and interviews (in the second section). See Feld, 1984.

6. A short while after my presentation of "Jump In" at a teachers' meeting, I received a call from a producer of a nationally syndicated children's television series who had been present at the session and now sought my permission to include the song in the show. Of course, in a sense it was not my permission to give; except for the notation, the song belonged to the children. At any rate, a group of children were taught this song from the notation by the producer for the show, thus the song was passed "third-hand" to a new group of children. The semi-oral tradition continues (although the chant probably lost something in its transcription from sound to note), from the playground to teachers to TV producers and back to the children again.

7. John Blacking (1973) had observed that the Venda of South Africa made music when their stomachs were full because "they sense forces or separation [when hungry] and are driven to restore balance" through music once they are sated (p. 145).

8. These rhythmed lines have already withstood several generations of children. See Knapp and Knapp, 1976, and Withers, 1948.

Part 2   On Music: Conversations with Children

1. Cultural evolutionary theory, formulated in the nineteenth century by the likes of Charles Drawin, scientist, and Herbert Spencer, educationist, established children as weak,

unformed, and untamed "savages," and equivalent to a primitive stage in the development of the human race. Even today, the theory is in play as scholars overlook and in essence deny the complexities of children's culture, including their music and lore. See Sutton-Smith, 1984.

2. Children can be viewed as falling into numerous cultures, distinguished by such factors as age, developmental stage, gender, and ethnicity. See "Children's Big and Little Cultures" in Part III.

3. I have always, in previous experimental studies of my own and others, found myself intrigued with the "outliers"—individuals who, because of their unique and idiosyncratic perspectives, did not fit the normative scheme of child development, the parameters or the coding system of the study. In this set of interviews, several children who might be deemed "outliers," marginal, beyond any central tendency, and subject to removal in some modes of research, are retained. They offer fascinating glimpses of other musical worlds.

4. Children, particularly the very young, do "roam" a world of ideas in free-associative ways (see Imberty, 1996). While these ramblings of young children are intriguing, they are the subject of another book.

5. Indeed, questions that guided me in my conversations may also be useful in guiding other investigations of children's expressed views on music and musicking. See Appendix II.

6. For examples of texts on movement education that were once prime reading for PE teachers, see Colby, 1992, and H'Doubler, 1940.

7. The National Association for Family and Community Education, through their Family Choice TV project, provides parents with resource materials on television programs that educate children and keeps a critical eye out for those that show stereotypes, sex, and violence. Their address is P.O. Box 835, Burlington, Ky. 41005; phone (606) 568–8333.

8. Their presentation, one of 3,000 at the 102nd Annual Convention of the American Psychological Convention in Los Angeles, was funded and promoted by the National Association of Music Merchants. As an experimental study, it is quite reasonably subject to criticism for its small sample size (nineteen subjects) and minimal exposure to Mozart (sonata, K. 448, for ten minutes).

9. See Regelski, 1978, for a review of brain research and its implications for aesthetic learning and education. He cited and described the work of Roger W. Sperry and Karl H. Pribam, whose neurological research in the 1960s and early 1970s spawned the right-brain/left-brain movement among educators in the 1970s and 1980s.

10. Relevant to "small sample," this very set of conversations and cases may be construed as problematic by some. But I have attempted to clarify my position regarding my employ of phenomenological approaches to the study of idiocultures (and field-based observations of small groups of children) and have earlier noted my agreement with Feld (1984) in drawing meaningful comparisons from these accounts of particular childrens' thoughts and behaviors.

11. Robert Engle (1994) found that, because of their attempt to maintain the melodies intact, translation of Samoan song texts to English by missionaries were often replete with new meanings, some of which were not relevant to Samoan philosophies and lifestyles.

12. From my own experience as a singer and in working with other adults and children, I think that it is physiologically possible to develop multiple vocal timbres. I have

demonstrated timbres and singing styles at conferences of teachers, singers, and choral directors, and I maintain that careful listening is key to mastery. I have been much encouraged by the work of Mary Goetze, professor of music at Indiana University, and her International Vocal Ensemble of collegiate singers who have impressively rendered authentic timbral performances of songs from West and South Africa and from the Maori of New Zealand. Likewise, at the University of Washington, the World Vocal Ensemble is an experimental project wherein community musicians are invited in to model musical works and performance styles that ensemble members hope to learn.

13. The phrase "music and not-music" is borrowed from Deborah Fishkin-Kalekin (1986), who observed that kindergarten children distinguish between music and other sound phenomena, with delimitations for what constitutes music that are sometimes as restrictive as that of their teachers. The phrase surfaces as well in ethnomusicological circles as decisions are made on the parameters of a musical culture to be studied. Carol Robertson (1975) suggested that we put aside our discussions of what music is and is not and instead analyze the sound phenomena with the research tools we have developed (musical-technical, musicological, or anthropological).

Part 3   For Children: Prospects for their Musical Education

1. In *Creating Minds* (1993), Howard Gardner examined the talent and creativity of selected prodigies and geniuses (including Martha Graham, Igor Stravinsky, and Albert Einstein) and linked creativity to their intellectual strengths and weaknesses, their personalities and their family life and social environments. Gardner posited that these seemingly ordinary features of humaness can contribute to possession by these creative individuals of an extraordinary extent of kinesthetic, mathematical, or musical (or other) intelligences, all akin to talent.

2. J. Terry Gates reminded me of a relevant point made by Woody Allen in his recent film *Everyone Says I Love You.* In it, he has portrayed the impulse that quite ordinary people have to sing and dance, attesting to the fact that both young and old dream romantic dreams of transcending the everyday through some remarkable musical expression. The actors include nonprofessional singers who manage little better than a croak, which, while comic, is also tragic. Once more, I cannot help but wonder what their musical results might have been had they been nurtured from their earliest years onward.

3. More recently, David Elliott proposed a different view of music's meaning in life at large and in education (1995), arguing that music is not an aesthetic object but a human activity that involves "some kind of doing." His view is that musical meaning is enveloped in the individual's musicianship, which is strengthened through involvement in the process of performing, composing, and improvising.

4. The phrase "good for what?" sounds like something a child would whine. Yet it is also a means by which William P. Malm confronts the issue of music's functional properties, of value as determined by use. See William P. Malm's comments in the epilogue to Malm, 1996.

5. These types of learning are somewhat related to Alan P. Merriam's ways of learning by enculturation, training, and schooling (1964), although his description of training suggests that it can be more formally structured than guided learning. Anthropologist Gregory Bateson (1972) defined three broad dimensions of learning, too, which were later applied

to music contexts by Catherine J. Ellis (1986): Learning I occurs naturally and without effort; Learning II involves thought, imitation, participation, and practice toward the development of musical skills (which may result from either guided or structured instructional processes); and Learning III reaches beyond the technical skills to the personally expressive music that competent musicians can make. This third level is, in my view of learning types, less likely to be attained naturally than through the guidance or sequential instruction of expert musicians and teachers. See also Estelle Jorgensen's erudite discussion (1997) of words evocative of education, including schooling, training, education, socialization, and enculturation.

6. A significant topic in cognitive psychology related to enculturative learning is implicit learning, a result of nonconscious processes through which people come into contact with, and effectively acquire, knowledge outside of conscious awareness. See Dianne Berry and Zoltan Dienes (1996).

7. Along these lines, ethnomusicologist and master teacher William P. Malm tells the story of his friendly bantering with M.D./Ph.D. colleagues in the medical sciences at the University of Michigan regarding the contributions of their work to quality of life. As his colleagues described their aims of bringing greater longevity to people's lives ("We save lives," they said), Malm countered with one of his famous "malmisms": "Ah, but I, in my teaching them music, make their lives worth living."

8. Age twelve is frequently viewed as the outer limits of childhood, just before the onset of puberty. For purposes herein, the elementary school grades (kindergarten through sixth grade, ages five through twelve) have been the frame for the study of children.

9. All songs from the list are compiled in the collection *Get America Singing . . . Again!*, (1996).

10. Certainly, popular music, with its "square-ish" meters of 2/4 and 4/4, has done much to accelerate the fading of these lilting meters from children's nursery rhymes and singing games. Yet 6/8 meter was well evident in the musical play of the preschoolers, which may indicate that, prior to their greater exposure to popular music, young children's movement and musical play flow naturally into music that lilts, jigs, gallops, and skips.

11. See Jeff Todd Titon, "Knowing Fieldwork" (pp. 87–100), and Timothy Rice, "Toward a Mediation of Field Methods and Field Experience in Ethnomusicology" (pp. 101–120), in Barz and Cooley, 1997, for discussion of phenomenology, reflexivity, and the place of the personal self in the practice of doing and interpreting fieldwork.

12. Young Audiences "chapters" are found in over forty cities. For information on their goals and programs, contact Young Audiences Inc., 115 East 92nd Street, New York, N.Y. 10128; phone (212) 831–8110.

References

Abrahams, Roger D. 1969. *Jump-Rope Rhymes: A Dictionary.* American Folklore Society Bibliographical and Special Series, vol. 20. Austin: University of Texas Press.

Addo, Akosue Obuo. 1996. "A Multimedia Analysis of Selected Ghanian Children's Play Songs." *Council on Research in Music Education* 129, pp. 1–28.

Adler, Patricia A., and Peter Adler. 1994. "Observational Techniques." In *Handbook of Qualitative Research,* ed. Norman K. Denzin and Yvonna S. Lincoln, pp. 377–92. Thousand Oaks, Calif.: Sage Publications.

Aronoff, Frances Webber. 1979. *Music and Young Children.* New York: Turning Wheel Press.

Atkinson, Paul, and Martin Hammersley. 1994. "Ethnography and Participant Observation." In *Handbook of Qualitative Research,* ed. Norman K. Denzin and Yvonna Lincoln, pp. 249–61. Thousand Oaks, Calif.: Sage Publications.

Bakan, Michael B. 1993–94. "Lessons from a World: Balinese Applied Instruction and the Teaching of Western 'Art' Music." *College Music Symposium* 33/34, pp. 1–22.

Bandura, Albert. 1986. *Social Foundations of Thought and Action: A Social Cognitive Theory.* Englewood Cliffs, N.J.: Prentice-Hall.

Barz, Gregory F., and Timothy J. Cooley. 1997. *Shadows in the Field.* New York: Oxford University Press.

Bateson, Gregory. 1972. *Steps to an Ecology of Mind.* New York: Ballantine Books.

Becker, Howard S. 1972. "School Is A Lousy Place to Learn Anything In." In *Howard Becker on Education,* ed. Robert G. Burgess. Buckingham, U.K.: Open University Press.

———. 1986. *Doing Things Together.* Evanston, Ill: Northwestern University Press.

Becker, Judith. 1980. *Traditional Music in Modern Java.* Honolulu: University Press of Hawaii.

Beethoven, Jane, et al. 1995. *The Music Connection.* Morristown, N.J.: Silver, Burdett-Ginn.

Berendt, Joachim-Ernst. 1983. *The World Is Sound.* Rochester, Vt.: Destiny Books.

Bernstein, Leonard. 1976. *The Unanswered Question: Six Talks at Harvard.* Cambridge, Mass.: Harvard University Press.

———. Berry, Dianne, and Zoltan Dienes, 1993. *Implicit Learning: Theoretical and Empirical Issues.* Hillsdale, N.J.: Erlbaum Associates.

Blacking, John. 1967. *Venda Children's Songs.* Chicago: University of Chicago Press.

———. 1973. *How Musical Is Man?* Seattle: University of Washington Press.

———. 1992. "Theory and Method: The Biology of Music-Making." In *Ethnomusicology: An Introduction,* ed. Helen Myers. New York: W. W. Norton, pp. 301–14.

———. 1995. *Music, Culture, and Experience.* Chicago: University of Chicago Press.

Bond, Judy, et al. 1995. *Share the Music.* New York: Macmillan/McGraw-Hill.

Brailoiu, Constantin. 1954. "Le rhythme enfantin: notions liminaires." in *Colloques de Wegimonts. Cercle International d'Etudes Ethnomusicologique,* pp. 64–106. Brussels, Belgium.

Bronner, Simon. 1988. *American Children's Folklore: A Book of Rhymes, Games, Jokes, Stories, Secret Languages: Beliefs and Camp Legends.* Little Rock, Ark.: August House.

Bruner, Jerome. 1966. *Toward a Theory of Instruction.* Cambridge, Mass.: Harvard University Press.

Brunvand, Jan. 1986. *The Study of American Folklore.* New York: W. W. Norton.

Campbell, Patricia Shehan. 1991a. "The Child-song Genre: A Comparison of Songs by and for Children." *International Journal of Music Education* 17, pp. 14–23.

———. 1991b. *Lessons from the World.* New York: Schirmer Books.

———. 1991c. "Rhythmic Movement and Public School Music Education: Conservative and Progressive Views of the Formative Years." *Journal of Research in Music Education* 39:1, pp. 12–22.

———. 1995. "Of Garage Bands and Song-getting: The Musical Development of Young Rock Musicians." *Research Studies in Music Education* 4, pp. 12–20.

———. 1996. *Music in Cultural Context.* Reston, Va.: Music Educators National Conference.

Campbell, Patricia Shehan, Ellen McCullough-Brabson, and Judith Cook Tucker, 1994. *Roots and Branches.* Danbury, Conn.: World Music Press.

Campbell, Patricia Shehan, and Carol Scott-Kassner. 1995. *Music in Childhood.* New York: Schirmer Books.

Choksy, Lois. 1974. *The Kodaly Method.* Englewood Cliffs, N.J.: Prentice-Hall.

Chomsky, Noam. 1957. *Syntactic Structures.* The Hague, Netherlands: Mouton.

———. 1975. *Reflections on Language.* New York: Pantheon Books.

Clifford, James. 1988. *The Predicament of Culture: Twentieth-Century Ethnography, Literature, and Art.* Cambridge, Mass.: Harvard University Press.

Colby, Gladys. 1922. *Natural Rhythms and Dances.* New York: A. S. Barnes and Co.

Cook, Pat Moffit. 1997. *Shaman, Jhankri, and Néle.* Roslyn, NY: Ellipsis Arts.

Crafts, Susan D., Daniel Cavicchi, and Charles Keil. 1993. *My Music.* Hanover, N.H.: Wesleyan University Press.

DeGaetano, Gloria, and Kathleen Bander. 1996. *Screen Smarts*. Boston: Houghton Mifflin.

Deliege, Irene, and John Sloboda. 1996. *Musical Beginnings*. Oxford: Oxford University Press.

Denby, David. 1996. "Buried Alive." *New Yorker* 72:19 (July 15), pp. 48–54.

Denzin, Norman K. (1978). *The Research Act*. New York: McGraw-Hill.

Diamond, John. 1981. *The Life Energy in Music*. Valley Cottage, N.Y.: Archeles Press.

Dowling, W. Jay. 1984. "Development of Musical Schemata in Children's Spontaneous Singing." In *Cognitive Processes in the Perception of Art*, ed. A. R. Crozier and A. J. Chapman. North-Holland; Elsevier Science Publishers.

Dunaway, David K. 1980. "Charles Seeger and Carl Sands: The Composers' Collective Years." *Ethnomusicology* 24:2, pp. 168–86.

Dundes, Alan, ed. 1965. *The Study of Folklore*. Englewood Cliffs, N.J.: Prentice-Hall.

———. 1990. *Essays in Folklore Theory and Method*. Madras: Cre-A.

Elliott, David J. 1995. *Music Matters*. New York: Oxford University Press.

Ellis, Catherine J. 1986. *The Musician, the University, and the Community: Conflict or Concord?* Armidale, New South Wales, Australia: University of New England.

Engle, Robert. 1994. "Song Text Translation, Cultural Priority, and Implications for Vocal Music Education: An English-to-Samoan Model." Ph.D. diss., University of Washington, Seattle.

Feld, Steven. 1984. "Sound Structure as Social Structure." *Ethnomusicology* 28:3, pp. 383–409.

Finnegan, Ruth. 1989. *The Hidden Musicians: Music Making in an English Town*. Cambridge: Cambridge University Press.

Fishkin-Kalekin, Deborah. 1986. "Music and Non-Music in Kindergartens." *Journal of Research in Music Education* 34:1, pp. 54–68.

Forrai, Katalin (with Jean Sinor). 1988. *Music in Preschool*. Budapest: Corvina Press.

Frisch, Michael H. 1990, ed. *A Shared History: Essays on the Craft and Meaning of Oral and Public History*. Albany: State University of New York.

Frith, Simon. 1988. *Music for Pleasure*. Cambridge, U.K.: Polity Press.

Fulton, Eleanor, and Pat Smith. 1978. *Let's Slice the Ice*. St. Louis: Magnamusic-Baton.

Gall, Meredith D., Walter R. Borg, and Joyce P. Gall. 1996. *Educational Research: An Introduction*. 6th ed. New York: Longman.

Gardner, Howard. 1983. *Frames of Mind: The Theory of Multiple Intelligences*. New York: Basic Books.

———. 1993. *Creating Minds*. New York: Basic Books.

Gaston, E. Thayer. 1968. *Music in Therapy*. New York: The Macmillan Company.

Geertz, Clifford. 1973. *The Interpretation of Cultures: Selected Essays*, pp. 3–30. New York: Basic Books.

———. 1983. *Local Knowledge: Further Essays in Interpretive Knowledge*. New York: Basic Books.

Get America Singing . . . Again!. 1996. Milwaukee, Wis.: Hal Leonard Corporation, 1996.

Gomme, Alice Bertha, Lady, ed. 1894–98. *The Traditional Games of England, Scotland, and Ireland with Tunes, Singing-Rhymes, and Methods of Playing According to Variants Extant and Recorded in Different Parts of the Kingdom*. 2 vols. London: David Nutt. Reprint, London: Thames and Hudson, 1984.

Gordon, Edwin E. 1994. *Learning Sequences in Music.* Chicago: GIA Publications.

Green, Lucy. 1988. *Music on Deaf Ears.* Manchester, U.K.: Manchester University Press.

Han, Kuo Huang, and Lindy Li Mark. 1980. "Evolution and Revolution in Chinese Music." In *Music of Many Cultures,* ed. Elizabeth May. Berkeley: University of California Press.

Hargreaves, David. 1986. *The Development Psychology of Music.* Cambridge: Cambridge University Press.

Hart, Avery, and Paul Mantell. 1993. *Kids Make Music.* Charlotte, Vt.: Williamson Publishing.

Harwood, Eve. 1987. "Memorized Song Repertoire of Children in Grades Four and Five in Champaign, Illinois." Ph.D. diss., University of Illinois, Urbana-Champaign.

Hawes, Bess Lomax, and Bessie Jones. 1972. *Step It Down: Games, Plays, Songs, and Stories from the Afro-American Heritage.* New York: Harper and Row.

H'Doubler, Margaret. 1940. *Dance: A Creative Experience.* New York: F. S. Crofts and Company.

Hegyi, Erzebet. 1975–79. *Solfege according to the Kodaly Concept.* 2 vols. London: Boosey and Hawkes.

Heidegger, Martin. 1978. *Being and Time.* Oxford: Blackwell Press.

Hood, Mantle. 1960. "The Challenge of Bi-Musicality." *Ethnomusicology* 4:2, pp. 55–59.

Hopkin, John Barton. 1984. "Jamaican Children's Songs." *Ethnomusicology* 28:1, pp. 1–36.

Howarth, William L. 1976. Introduction to *The John McPhee Reader.* New York: Farrar, Straus, and Giroux.

Imberty, Michael. 1996. "Linguistic and Musical Development in Preschool and School-Age Children." In *Musical Beginnings,* ed. Irene Deliege and John Sloboda. Oxford: Oxford University Press.

Jorgensen, Estelle. 1997. *In Search of Music Education.* Urbana: University of Illinois Press.

Kartomi, Margaret. 1991. "Musical Improvisations by Children at Play." *The World of Music* 33:3, pp. 53–65.

Keil, Charles. October 1994. Remarks at the annual meeting of the Society for Ethnomusicology, Milwaukee, Wis.

Keil, Charles, and Steven Feld. 1994. *Music Grooves.* Chicago: University of Chicago Press.

Kemp, Anthony E. 1996. *The Musical Temperament.* Oxford, U.K.: Oxford University Press.

Kenney, Maureen. 1974. *Circle Round the Zero.* St. Louis: Magnamusic Baton.

Kerrane, Kevin, and Ben Yagoda, 1997. *The Art of Fact.* New York: Scribner's.

Kingsbury, Henry. 1988. *Music, Talent, and Performance: A Conservatory Cultural System.* Philadelphia: Temple University Press.

Kline, Stephen. 1995. *Out of the Garden.* New York: Routledge, Chapman and Hall.

Knapp, Mary, and Herbert Knapp. 1976. *One Potato, Two Potato: The Folklore of American Children.* Toronto: George J. McLeod Limited.

Kodaly, Zoltan. 1974. *Selected Writings of Zoltan Kodaly.* London: Boosey and Hawkes.

LeBlanc, Albert. 1988. "The Culture as Educator: Elements in the Development of Individual Music Preference." In *Music Education in the United States,* ed. J. T. Gates, pp. 33–43. Tuscaloosa: University of Alabama Press.

Lehrdahl, Fred, and Raymond Jackendoff. 1983. *A Generative Theory of Tonal Music.* Cambridge, Mass.: MIT Press.

Livingston, Tamara E., et al. 1993. *Community of Music: An Ethnographic Seminar in Urbana-Champaign.* Champaign, Ill.: Elephant and Cat.

Lomax, John Avery. 1910. *Cowboy Songs and Other Frontier Ballads.* New York: Macmillan.

Lomax, John A., and Alan Lomax. 1934. *American Ballads and Folk Songs.* New York: Macmillan.

Loza, Steven. 1996. "Steven Loza on Latino Music." In *Music in Cultural Context,* ed. Patricia Shehan Campbell. Reston, Va.: Music Educators National Conference.

McCarthy, Marie. 1996. ""On 'American Music for American Children': The Contribution of Charles L. Seeger." *Journal of Research in Music Education* 43:4, pp. 270–87.

Machover, Wilma, and Marienne Uszler. 1996. *Sound Choices.* New York: Oxford University Press.

Malinowski, Bronislaw. 1922. *Argonauts of the Western Pacific.* London: Routledge.

Malm, William P. 1996. *Music of the Pacific, the Near East, and Asia.* 3d ed. Englewood Cliffs, N.J.: Prentice-Hall.

Marsh, Kathryn. July 1994. "Processes of Variation in Australian Children's Playground Singing Games: The Playground versus the Classroom." Paper presented at the meeting of the International Society for Music Education, Tampa, Fla.

———. 1995. "Children's Singing Games: Composition in the Playground?" *Research Studies in Music Education* 4; pp. 2–11.

Mead, Virginia H. 1994. *Dalcroze Eurhythmics in Today's Classroom.* New York: Schott.

Merriam, Alan P. 1964. *The Anthropology of Music.* Evanston, Ill.: Northwestern University Press.

Merrill-Mirsky, Carol. 1988. "Eeny Meeny Pepsa Deeny: Ethnicity and Gender in Children's Musical Play." Ph.D. diss., University of California, Los Angeles.

Meyer, Leonard B. 1956. *Emotion and Meaning in Music.* Chicago: University of Chicago Press.

Moog, Helmut. 1976. *The Musical Experience of the Preschool Child.* Trans. C. Clarke. London: Schott.

Moorhead, Gladys E., and Donald Pond. 1978. *Music of Young Children.* Santa Barbara, Calif.: Pillsbury Foundation.

Myers, I. B., and M. H. McCaulley. 1985. *Manual: A Guide to the Development and Use of the Myers-Briggs Type Indicator.* 2nd ed. Palo Alto, CA: Consulting Psychologists Press.

National Standards for Arts Education. 1994. Reston, Va.: Music Educators National Conference.

Nattiez, Jean-Jaques. 1990. *Music and Discourse.* Trans. Carolyn Abbate. Princeton: Princeton University Press.

Nettl, Bruno. 1978. *Eight Urban Musical Cultures: Tradition and Change.* Urbana: University of Illinois Press.

———. 1983. *The Study of Ethnomusicology: Twenty-Nine Issues and Concepts.* Urbana: University of Illinois Press.

———. 1990. *Folk and Traditional Music of the Western Continents.* 3d ed. Englewood Cliffs, N.J.: Prentice-Hall.

————. 1992. "Recent Directions in Ethnomusicology." In *Ethnomusicology: An Introduction*, ed. Helen Myers. New York: W. W. Norton.

————. 1995. *Heartland Excursions: Ethnomusicological Reflections on Schools of Music*. Urbana: University of Illinois Press.

Neuman, Daniel M. 1980. *The Life of Music in North India*. Detroit: Wayne State University Press.

Newell, William Wells. 1883. *Games and Songs of American Children*. New York: Harper and Brothers. Expanded edition, 1903. Reprint, New York: Dover, 1963.

Opie, Iona, and Peter Opie. 1985. *The Singing Game*. Oxford: Oxford University Press.

Osborn, F. E. Ann. 1988. "A Computer-Aided Methodology for the Analysis and Classification of British-Canadian Children's Traditional Singing Games." *Computers and the Humanities* 22; pp. 183–92.

Papousek, Hanus. 1996. "Musicality in Infancy Research: Biological and Cultural Origins of Early Musicality." In *Musical Beginnings*, ed. Irene Deliege and John Sloboda. Oxford: Oxford University Press.

Paynter, John. 1972. *Hear and Now*. London: University Edition.

Phillips, Kenneth. 1992. *Teaching Kids to Sing*. New York: Schirmer Books.

Piaget, Jean. 1951. *Play, Dreams, and Imitation in Childhood*. London: Routledge and Kegan Paul.

Pond, Donald. 1981. "A Composer's Study of Young Children's Innate Musicality." *Council for Research in Music Education* 68, pp. 1–12.

Prim, Fernanda Magno. 1995–96. "Tradition and Chance in Children's Games: Its Implication for Music Education." *Council for Research in Music Education* 127; pp. 145–54.

Rauscher, F. W., G. L. Shaw, L. J. Levine, K. N. Ky, and E. L. Wright. 1994. "Music and Spatial Task Performance: A Causal Relationship." Paper presented at the American Psychological Association annual convention, Los Angeles, Calif., August.

Regelski, Thomas A. 1978. *Arts Education and Brain Research*. Reston, Va.: Music Educators National Conference.

Reimer, Bennett. 1970. *A Philosophy of Music Education*. Englewood Cliffs, N.J.: Prentice-Hall.

Rice, Timothy. 1994. *May It Fill Your Soul*. Chicago: University of Chicago Press.

Riddell, Cecilia. 1990. "Traditional Singing Games of Elementary School Children in Los Angeles," Ph.D. diss., University of California, Los Angeles.

Robertson, Carol. 1975. *Tayil: Musical Communication among the Mapuche of Argentina*. Ph.D. diss., Indiana University.

Sachs, Curt. 1943. *The Rise of Music in the Ancient World*. New York: W. W. Norton

Sam, Sam-Ang, and Patricia Shehan Campbell. 1992. *Silent Temples, Songful Hearts: Traditional Music of Cambodia*. Danbury, Conn.: World Music Press.

Sartre, Jean-Paul. 1981. *The Family Idiot: Gustave Flaubert*. Chicago: University of Chicago Press.

Schafer, R. Murray. 1965. *The Composer in the Classroom*. Scarborough, Ont.: Berandol Music.

————. 1967. *Ear Cleaning*. Don Mills, Ont.: BMI Canada.

————. 1976. *Creative Music Education*. New York: Schirmer Books.

Schmidt-Wrenger, Barbara. 1985. "Tshiyanda Na Ulili—Boundaries of Independence, Life,

Music, and Education in Tshokwe Society, Angola, Zaire." In *Becoming Human through Music*. ed. David P. McAllester. Reston, Va.: Music Educators National Conference.

Schnebly-Black, Julia, and Stephen F. Moore, 1997. *The Rhythm Inside*. Portland, OR: Rudra Press.

Schwartzman, Helen B. 1978. Transformations: The Anthropology of Children's Play. New York: Plenum Press.

Scott-Kassner, Carol. 1992. "Research on Music in Early Childhood" In *Handbook of Research on Music Teaching and Learning*, ed. Richard Colwell. New York: Schirmer Books.

Seeger, Anthony. 1996. "Anthony Seeger on Music of Amazonian Indians." In *Music in Cultural Context*, ed. Patricia Shehan Campbell. Reston, Va.: Music Educators National Conference.

Seeger, Ruth Crawford. 1948. *American Folk Songs for Children*. New York: Doubleday.

Slobin, Mark. 1993. *Subcultural Sounds: Micromusics of the West*. Hanover, N.H.: University Press of New England for Wesleyan University Press.

Sloboda, John. 1985. *The Musical Mind*. Oxford: Clarendon Press.

Small, Christopher. 1977. *Music-Society-Education*. London: John Calder.

———. 1987. *Music of the Common Tongue: Survival and Celebration in Afro-American Music*. London: Calder Ltd., Press.

———. 1994. "Whose Music Do We Teach Anyway?" In *Muse Letter* no. 2, ed. Charles Keil. Buffalo, New York: Stiges.

Standley, Jayne M. 1991. *Music Techniques in Therapy, Counseling, and Special Education*. St. Louis: MMB Music.

Stewart, David, and Algis Mickunas. 1990. *Exploring Phenomenology*. 2d ed. Athens: Ohio University Press.

Sutton-Smith, Brian. 1976. *A Children's Game Anthology: Studies in Folklore and Anthropology*. New York: Arno Press.

———. 1984. The origins of fictions and the fictions of origin. *American Ethnological Society Proceedings*, pp. 117–32.

———. 1985. *Toys as Culture*. Palm Beach Gardens, Fla.: Gardner press.

———. 1995. *Children's Folklore: A Source Book*. New York: Garland Publications.

Swanwick, Keith. 1988. *Music, Mind and Education*. London: Routledge.

———. March 1996. "Alternative Paradigms in Current Music Education Research." Paper presented at the meeting of the Society for Research in the Psychology of Music and Music Education, Cambridge, U.K.

Szonyi, Erzebet. 1972–79. *Musical Reading and Writing*. Pupil's book, vols. 1–8. London: Boosey and Hawkes.

Upitis, Rene. 1992. *Can I Play You My Song?* Portsmouth, N.H.: Heinemann.

Van Maanen, John. 1988. *Tales of the Field: On Writing Ethnography*. Chicago: University of Chicago Press.

———. 1990. *Researching Lived Experience*. New York: SUNY Press.

Vygotsky, Lev S. 1978. *Mind in Society*. Cambridge, Mass.: Harvard University Press.

Wade, Bonnie C. 1979. *Music in India: The Classical Traditions*. Englewood Cliffs, N.J.: Prentice-Hall.

Waterman, Christopher. 1991. *Juju: A Social History*. Chicago: University of Chicago Press.

Whiting, Beatrice Blyth, and Carolyn Pope Edwards. 1988. *Children of Different Worlds.* Cambridge, Mass.: Harvard University Press.

Wiseman, Ann. 1979. *Making Musical Things.* New York: Charles Scribner's Sons.

Withers, Carl. 1948. *A Rocket in My Pocket.* New York: Henry Holt.

Zemp, Hugo. 1979. "Aspects of 'Are'are Musical Theory." *Ethnomusicology* 23:1, pp. 5–48.

Zonis, Ella. 1973., *Classical Persian Music.* Cambridge, Mass.: Harvard University Press.